1994

JAPAN'S
EMERGING
GLOBAL ROLE

JAPAN'S
EMERGING
GLOBAL ROLE

AN INSTITUTE FOR THE STUDY OF DIPLOMACY BOOK

edited by
DANNY UNGER
PAUL BLACKBURN

LYNNE RIENNER PUBLISHERS • BOULDER & LONDON

Published in the United States of America in 1993 by
Lynne Rienner Publishers, Inc.
1800 30th Street, Boulder, Colorado 80301

and in the United Kingdom by
Lynne Rienner Publishers, Inc.
3 Henrietta Street, Covent Garden, London WC2E 8LU

Library of Congress Cataloging-in-Publication Data
Japan's emerging global role/editors, Danny Unger, Paul Blackburn.
    Includes bibliographical references and index.
    ISBN 1-55587-356-1 (alk. paper)
         1-55587-387-1 (pbk. : alk. paper)
    1. Japan—Foreign economic relations. 2. Japan—Foreign
relations—1945– . I. Unger, Danny, 1955– . II. Blackburn, Paul,
1937– .
HF1601.J37   1993
337.52—dc20   92-39194
                                                            CIP

British Cataloguing in Publication Data
A Cataloguing in Publication record for this book
is available from the British Library.

Printed and bound in the United States of America

The paper used in this publication meets the requirements
of the American National Standard for Permanence of
Paper for Printed Library Materials Z39.48-1984.

Contents

158,821

v

Preface

Through the 1980s, Japan's emergence as an economic power grew increasingly visible. Its diplomatic profile, however, changed less dramatically. In fact, Japan has been undertaking important new initiatives in its political and security policies; but these do not seem to add up to a coherent international posture. It remains clear to observers both inside Japan and abroad that the country has not yet adequately identified its global interests and the means by which it proposes to pursue them. Meanwhile, pressures continue to mount for Japan to acknowledge forthrightly its stakes in the international political economy and to act to serve those. With economic and technological strength becoming increasingly important bases of international power, Japan clearly has some of the capabilities needed to shape the international system to suit its interests.

Certainly Japan finds it increasingly difficult to watch the unfolding of global economic and political struggles from the sidelines. Although it played a large role in funding the Gulf War, its voice was not heard in decisionmaking circles. And it resented "taxation without representation." The United States complained of Japan's "checkbook diplomacy." That crisis triggered an important debate inside Japan concerning the nature of its interests and the means appropriate to pursue them. One result was the dispatch, in September 1992, of Japanese military forces to Cambodia to assist the operations of the United Nations Transitional Authority in Cambodia. This was the first time since 1945 that Japan sent its forces abroad.

Japan's search for a new global role may disrupt its relations with other nations, including the United States. The collapse of the Soviet Union has weakened many of the premises underlying the traditional U.S.-Japan relationship. It is crucial for both countries, as well as the Asia Pacific region as a whole, that the interests and perspectives that these two countries share are made to serve as the foundations of a new relationship reflecting the changed underlying global realities.

A goal of this book is to contribute to efforts to understand the constraints and opportunities that establish the frameworks within which Japan will be identifying and pursuing its global interests. The study developed from a conference, "Japan's Future Global Role," held at Georgetown University on March 11–14, 1992. Cosponsored by the Japan Economic Institute (JEI) of America and the Institute for the Study of Diplomacy (ISD) at Georgetown University's School of Foreign Service, that conference brought together some thirty Japan experts and international relations specialists. JEI president Arthur Alexander, ISD diplomatic associate Paul Blackburn, and Georgetown professor Danny Unger organized the conference. Papers were presented by Kent Calder, Robert Gilpin, Keikichi Honda, Norman Levin, Edward Lincoln, David Mowery, Masashi Nishihara, Yoshio Okawara, Kenneth Pyle, Masaru Tamamoto, and Danny Unger. All of the contributors to this book attended the conference and gained a great deal from the other participants.

There are always difficulties in moving even the finest collection of papers, by authors on different continents, from draft form to publication within a year. The contributors to this book, however, have made the task as easy as humanly possible. As a result, we have been able to produce a book that addresses recent Japanese developments, as well as evolving trends.

The Institute for the Study of Diplomacy and the editors are grateful to the Japan Foundation Center for Global Partnership, whose financial support made this publication possible.

Danny Unger
Paul Blackburn

Part 1

Framework of Constraints and Opportunities

1

The Problem of Global Leadership: Waiting for Japan

Daniel Unger

As the saying goes, "The more things change, the more they stay the same." And so, many argue, it goes with Japan. An unbroken line of descent links Emperor Akihito, Japan's current monarch, with a dynasty that has reigned, and occasionally ruled, over Japan stretching back for millennia. The Liberal Democratic Party (LDP) has ruled over Japan continuously for close to two generations. Throughout the postwar era, Japan has seemed content to accept as given the frameworks within which it has operated.

And yet Japan itself has played a crucial role in changing the underlying structures of the global political economy. Japan has produced wealth for its people at an unprecedented pace, produced friction in the world trading system, challenged existing paradigms dominating global management and manufacturing systems, stimulated debate about the mutability of capitalism, and paved the way for many Asian countries and would-be emulators to follow in its wake. Japan has both changed and remained the same, but its influence has worked largely to transform the global context that sets the parameters within which Japanese leaders define their country's national interests.

In any study of new and emerging patterns of behavior, one has to decide whether to assign relative emphasis to themes of continuity or change. Generations of historians have secured their careers debating the extent to which various revolutions in human organization represent radical new departures or simply modifications of underlying and largely static structures of behavior. Despite the pervasiveness of these debates throughout the social sciences, it is tempting to assert that in no study of a contemporary nation do scholars devote so much attention to these themes as they do in the case of Japan.

A perusal of literature on modern Japan will unearth countless references to discussions of the theme of change versus continuity. The "transwar thesis" that has shaped much recent scholarship on Japan's political

3

economy argues for the importance of fundamental continuities between Japan's postwar development and its prewar antecedents. The thesis rejects the view that Japan emerged from military defeat and occupation as an essentially new political community with few principles of organization and animation emanating from its first century of development.

Both foreign and Japanese discussions of the last thirty years of Japan's foreign policy are full of predictions of change in Japan's international behavior. Analysts and policymakers repeatedly predict the emergence of a Japanese global role "commensurate with" Japan's alleged capacities. Kenneth Pyle's contribution in this volume suggests that younger Japanese politicians from the LDP may push Japan in the direction of a more activist, engaged supporter of the international system. Pyle's analysis echoes that of Haruhiro Fukui, who wrote more than twenty-five years earlier that "today's Young Turks [in the Foreign Ministry] may be begging to fight against postwar pacifism and 'economic diplomacy' in the name of an independent foreign policy."[1]

The persistence of these assertions of imminent change in Japan's foreign policies reflects change and continuity in Japan. Probably no previous society experienced such sustained rapid and wrenching changes as did Japan during its era of high economic growth beginning in the 1950s and continuing into the early 1970s. Structural economic changes that other societies effected over generations were accomplished in one generation in Japan as a previously rural society became an urban one. From a relatively insignificant base, Japan produced the capitalist world's second-largest economy. Japan's stake in, and its potential to contribute to (or to undermine), the international system increased dramatically. And yet neither Japan's friends nor foes discerned much change in the broad principles guiding Japan's foreign policy. This disjuncture between enormous latent power and only modest and intermittent efforts to exercise influence explains the enduring expectations of big changes in Japan's global role.

This book explains and describes the ways in which Japan is changing and suggests directions in which it is likely to move in the future. To do so requires that we understand the dynamics of Japan as well as its environment—the global political economy. To aid the reader in judging debates about emerging trends in Japan's foreign policy, the following section provides a quick overview of modern Japan's foreign policy.

The Roots of Contemporary Japan's Foreign Policy

Following centuries of self-imposed isolation from global politics, in the middle of the nineteenth century a group of new Japanese leaders launched Japan on a modernization drive aimed at strengthening the country and preserving its political independence. The Meiji Restoration opened Japan to broader international trends, including new technologies as well as unfamiliar principles of economic and political organization. Even outsiders easily discerned the rapidity of change in Japan: in *From Egypt to Japan,* published in 1877, English essayist Henry M. Field commented on the "sudden revolution" in Japan that

> in a few years, has changed a whole nation, so that from being the most isolated, the most exclusive, and the most rigidly conservative, even in Asia, it has become the most active and enterprising . . . [the change] has, as it were, unmoored Japan from the coast of Asia, and towed it across the Pacific, to place it alongside of the New World.[2]

U.S. naval strategist Alfred Thayer Mahan recognized in these developments the rise of a new power capable of challenging the previously dominant Western nations.[3]

Bereft of raw materials, in search of secure foreign markets, and crowded on the home islands, Japan began in the late nineteenth century to expand its influence across Asia. Ultimately this process took on a decisively military cast that brought Japan into conflict with the United States, another rising power expanding across the Pacific. Japan's unconditional surrender concluded World War II and left Japan under the authority of U.S. military occupation. Impoverished and demoralized, the Japanese set about the task of rebuilding their nation.

Following the end of the Supreme Command of the Allied Powers occupation of Japan in 1952, Prime Minister Shigeru Yoshida committed Japan to a course that emphasized political, security, and economic dependence on the United States while Japan worked to rebuild its economy. Free to ignore broader international political and security issues, Japan's foreign policy took on a peculiarly mercantilist cast. Initiatives were limited to the goal of promoting its own prosperity.[4] In the 1950s, the future Japanese prime minister, Yasuhiro Nakasone, described Japan's dependence on the United States as unhealthy and argued for an independent self-defense capacity. In the 1970s, political scientist Hans H. Baerwald observed that "many Japanese are convinced that their country does not have any foreign policy."[5]

Over time, the Japanese people increasingly grew attached to their pacifist foreign policy and to Article IX of the U.S.-authored constitution, which barred Japan from maintaining armed forces. As political scientist Donald Hellman observed, Article IX "moved Japan from the European diplomatic tradition of power politics into the peculiarly idealist American tradition."[6] In ways not foreseen by Henry Field in the previous century, the United States "unmoored Japan . . . and towed it across the Pacific . . . alongside of the New World."[7] By allowing Japan the luxury of ignoring security issues, the United States nurtured in Japan an idealism that the United States itself had once fostered but now was forced to reject.

Following World War II, Japan gradually reintegrated itself into the international political economy. Japan relied heavily on the United States as a source of both resources and markets, but it also began to use war reparations payments as tools to reestablish trade links with Southeast Asian economies. These ties were particularly important to Japan as its dependence on the United States bound Japan to U.S. containment policies and therefore precluded Japan from rebuilding fully its trading relations with China.[8] The United States helped Japan to refashion its trade networks and championed Japan's admission into the United Nations in 1956 as well as in international economic organizations such as the General Agreement on Tariffs and Trade (GATT), the World Bank, and the International Monetary Fund (IMF).

Japan's postwar mercantilist policy stemmed from the opportunities afforded by the U.S.-Japan Mutual Security Treaty (MST) of 1960 (which modified an earlier treaty signed in 1951 and implemented in 1952) as well as Japan's extreme dependence on external sources of raw materials. Following the foreign policies of a trading state,[9] Japanese leaders separated political and economic issues and pursued resources and markets wherever they might be found.

In one sense, it is possible to view Japan's search for a set of foreign policies that will gain Japan security and prosperity as the history of Japan's foreign-exchange balances. Until the 1970s, Japan was constantly struggling to earn foreign exchange sufficient to meet its burgeoning import needs. Political scientist Chalmers Johnson notes that the "preoccupation with balance-of-payments problems runs through Japan's modern history like a litany."[10] More recently, of course, Japan's problems have stemmed from its balance-of-payments surpluses, as Japan's trading partners ceaselessly complain about their trade deficits with Japan.

The first shocks to Japan's postwar development strategy came in the early 1970s. U.S. President Richard Nixon unilaterally suspended U.S. willingness to convert U.S. dollars into gold at $35 an ounce, thereby spelling the end of the dollar-backed international monetary system. Also under the Nixon administration in the early 1970s, the United States placed a surcharge on imports, embargoed the export of soy beans, moved to establish diplomatic relations with the People's Republic of China, and began to disengage from its commitment to the security of the government of South Vietnam. Meanwhile, rapid oil price increases helped to trigger global stagflation, precipitating the first postwar sputter in the Japanese economic machine.

Despite the force of these accumulated shocks, Japan's economy proved astonishingly resilient, and Japan soon resumed rates of economic growth faster than did the other industrialized democracies (although much slower than during the high-growth era). Japan was also able to move rapidly to make a crucial adjustment in its diplomacy, shifting recognition from Taiwan to the People's Republic of China in 1972. As the United States began to reduce its military presence in Southeast Asia, Japanese leaders prepared to launch new diplomatic initiatives aimed at making Japan a bridge between capitalist Southeast Asia—the Association of Southeast Asian Nations (ASEAN)—and the communist countries of Indochina. F. C. Langdon's study of Japanese foreign policy in the early 1970s saw "Japan on the threshhold of a new era in Asian international relations."[11]

Ultimately, however, Japan's foreign policy was marked more by continuity than by change. The explosion of regional tensions accompanying Vietnam's invasion of Cambodia in 1978 and China's invasion of Vietnam the following year forced Japan to align itself firmly with ASEAN, China, and the United States against Vietnam and the Soviet Union. Rather than being marked by increasing independence in a fundamentally new regional context, Japanese foreign policy instead drew closer to the United States. The Soviet Union's growing military deployments in the Pacific, sharper superpower confrontation following the Soviet invasion of Afghanistan, and the influence of Prime Minister Nakasone (1983–1987) all contributed to this shift.

In large part as a response to U.S. pressures, Japan began to increase its military spending. In 1988, Japan breached for the first time the LDP's commitment to limit defense spending to 1 percent of gross national product (GNP). More significant, during the 1980s Japan took on new security commitments (in 1981 agreeing to patrol its sea-lanes to a distance of 1,000 nautical miles from the home islands) and worked with the United States to enhance the complementarity of the countries' military forces.

Throughout the 1980s, Japan also rapidly increased its official development assistance (ODA). By the end of the decade Japan had matched U.S. spending on ODA. Working in consultation with the United States, Japan increased its aid to countries of particular strategic significance such as Egypt, Indonesia, Pakistan, the Philippines, Thailand, and Turkey.

Meanwhile, national security officials in Japan and the United States cooperated effectively across an ever-widening range of issues. Two related developments, however, have undermined these achievements. First, intensification of U.S.-Japan economic disputes and the politicization of these issues have made bilateral cooperation more difficult to achieve. Second, the collapse of the Soviet Union has scuttled the assumptions that guided policymakers in Japan and the United States over the past forty years. To a disturbing degree, Japanese and U.S. leaders now find themselves strangers in a strange land.

In the first major international security crisis following the collapse of the Soviet Union, U.S. President George Bush led the United States in moving rapidly to block Iraq from consolidating its control over Kuwait. Having initially acted alone to defend Saudi Arabia, the United States turned quickly to its allies and the United Nations to gain political and material support for the goal of forcing Iraq to withdraw from Kuwait. The Japanese ultimately provided a major share of the financing (some $13 billion) for the successful multilateral effort to compel Iraq's withdrawal.

The Gulf conflict precipitated a new crisis in Japanese thinking about security issues. The United States and other nations were critical of Japanese policies, despite Japan's major financial contribution. Many Japanese also were frustrated that the mechanisms of security policymaking in Japan resulted in Japan's failing to gain international recognition for its contribution to the multilateral effort in the Gulf. The debates sparked by this episode resulted, in June 1992, in the Japanese Diet's adoption of legislation enabling Japan to dispatch overseas Japan's Self-Defense Forces (SDF) as part of United Nations peacekeeping operations, albeit only under sharply circumscribed conditions. By September of that year, Japan decided to dispatch forces to Cambodia as part of the UN-sponsored transitional authority aimed at bringing an end to Cambodia's endemic conflict.

Compounding the anxiety felt in Japan as a result of U.S.-Japan economic tensions, debates surrounding the Gulf conflict, and the unfamiliar post–Cold War world, the liberal international economic order established by the United States after World War II appears fragile. Protectionism, often aimed at Japan, has increased in North America and the European Community (EC). The EC's apparent commitment to the Single Market Act stimulates outsiders' concerns about the potential for European economic insularity. Together with Canadian, Mexican, and U.S. efforts to conclude a North American Free Trade Agreement and the continued stalemate besetting the Uruguay Round of trade talks, Japan is concerned about being isolated economically from its principal trading partners.

With the contours of its international environment increasingly unfamiliar, how can outsiders expect Japan to act to define and secure its interests? Will Japan raise its profile in an effort to exert greater leadership? Will Japan work to sustain an inclusive, multilateral economic order or will it settle for leadership of an East Asia–centered economic region? The framework introduced below, reflecting some of the questions that have guided the chapters in this volume, suggests some of the ways to think about these issues. It distinguishes broadly between perspectives that locate the principal opportunities and obstacles facing future Japanese policymakers at the national and international levels. If the task facing Japanese leaders is that of creating "compatibility between domestic and international policy objectives,"[12] will domestic or foreign factors play the key roles in determining the ways in which policymakers attempt to achieve such compatibility?

Thinking About Japan's Foreign Policy

At the international level, the framework describes three approaches: realist, liberal institutionalist,[13] and liberal economic. At the national level, the framework offers two categories of explanation of Japanese foreign policy: those that concentrate on explaining, often through reference to historical or cultural factors, particular Japanese preferences; and those, drawing more on assumptions of microeconomics (utility-maximizing behavior), that would explain Japanese policies in terms of incentive structures embedded in Japanese institutions.

Systemic Approaches to the Study of Japanese Global Interests

Systemic approaches to understanding Japan's global interests by and large ignore the particularities of Japanese history and institutions. Rather than emphasize distinctive Japanese preferences, these approaches focus on the constraints and opportunities that the international system poses for Japan's leadership. In Chapter 2, Robert Gilpin offers the reader a review of debates concerning trends in the international political economy. According to this type of analysis, the actual structure of the international political economy will establish incentives encouraging some kinds of Japanese foreign policies while discouraging others. Systemic approaches, including those supplied by "realists," seek to explain regularities in the behavior of nation-states despite dissimilar national attributes.[14]

Nonrealist approaches to the study of Japanese foreign policy also may tend to emphasize conditions external to Japan in making predictions about future Japanese foreign policies. For example, liberal economic and liberal institutionalist perspectives (unlike those of realists) suggest that technological and institutional innovations are producing qualitative changes in the very nature of the international system. In general, these perspectives locate the origins of those changes outside Japan.[15]

Realist Views

Realist perspectives expect changing Japanese conceptions of Japan's national interests to flow from alterations in the international structure of power and Japan's place in that structure. If Japan is experiencing a rise in relative power, realists anticipate that at some point Japan will see (1) a closer fit between its own interests and those of the international system; or (2) the necessity to try to alter the international hierarchy of prestige to better reflect the underlying structure of power.[16] The "Japan 2000" draft report, commissioned by the U.S. Central Intelligence Agency (CIA), for example, suggests the latter perspective: Japan is aiming at "unequivocal economic dominance," but is "unimpeded by any sense of responsibility for world leadership or global welfare."[17]

Is Japan engaged in a struggle for the position as "top dog"? Does it seek to go further and work to tailor institutions to suit its particular national strengths and interests? Systemic approaches generally do not offer means of analyzing such issues. Some insight into these questions, however, may be gained by looking at the transition earlier this century from a British to a U.S.-dominated global economy.

Early this century, as U.S. producers of manufactures became more dependent on export markets, a proliferation of study groups looked at how other countries penetrated foreign markets. These groups recognized that

> as they made the national interest the interest of each component group at home, they had to make American interest the world's interest. If they could do that, they could give potentially competing nations a stake in stabilizing and securing a system which was in the first instance beneficial to the United States.[18]

When the entente powers signaled at the Paris Economic Conference in 1916 a move away from free toward managed trade, U.S. government and business leaders searched for appropriate countermeasures. Among their goals, they sought to have New York replace London as the global financial center.

Today, Japanese leaders try to make the national interest the world's interest. Japanese officials seek to increase their country's status within international organizations such as the IMF, the World Bank, and the United Nations. Former prime minister Nakasone, recognizing the lack of enthusiastic U.S. support for securing Japan a permanent seat on the UN Security Council, calls for a stronger role for the Group of Seven (G-7)—the annual meetings of the heads of state of the world's largest capitalist economies: Canada, France, Germany, Italy, Japan, the United Kingdom, and the United States. (The group addresses issues of concern, primarily economic, requiring international cooperation.) He calls on the group to lead in seeking "peace by consortium."[19] Giving Japan a stronger role in the G-7 could be a means of institutionalizing a stronger Japanese international role.

It is frustrating to many in the United States that Japan seems intent only on gaining status commensurate with its capabilities—permanent membership in the UN Security Council—without indicating the ends to which Japan would use any enhanced influence. U.S. leaders complain that Japan attempts to sustain an apolitical posture and insist that real leadership depends on the articulation and defense of particular principles. It finds confusing the apparent Japanese predeliction to be a leader without a cause. This U.S. view, however, may simply assume that Japan and the United States fully share global goals. To the extent that international politics are characterized by zero-sum as well as variable-sum games (in which one player's gain need not produce another's loss and all players may be able to gain), it is logical for Japanese leaders to desire greater influence, even if in pursuit of unspecified goals.

The hegemonic stability theory also draws on realist assumptions. It bases explanation of periods of relative international economic openness (the late nineteenth century, the post–World War II era) on the underlying structure of world power. In this conception, the dominant "game" is variable sum and the principal problem is to overcome the obstacles inherent in international "anarchy" to international cooperation. This approach suggests that, with its rising economic power, Japan is likely to be increasingly committed to liberalism and able and willing to pay more of the costs of supplying the associated public goods. Supporting that assumption, a Ministry of International Trade and Industry (MITI) report issued in 1987[20] features a section, "Expectations of Japan and lessons from history," which warns of the dangers of Japan following the path taken in the 1930s when

> the United States, oblivious of its responsibility as the world's largest creditor country, pursued a protectionist trade policy by imposing high tariffs on imports, and . . . thus undermined the ability of debtor countries to earn dollars to service their debts to the United States.[21]

The report suggests that Japanese officials are intent on having Japan follow the more enlightened policy of Great Britain in its heyday. Britain "abided by the principle of free trade," and the capital it exported to European countries and the United States was

> employed to finance the construction of infrastructure, was instrumental in integrating the recipient economies and developing regional economies, while the technology transferred to them in the form of industrial facilities accelerated the industrial revolution in these countries.[22]

The commitment that a nation gives to international economic openness vary, however, with the gains it can realize from free trade.[23] This variation implies the need to look not only at the international structure of power, but also at the particular economic characteristics of the dominant state(s). For example, economist Kozo Yamamura suggests that, however slowly reflected in LDP policy changes, the needs of large Japanese firms and financial institutions for closer links to overseas customers and suppliers are driving Japan in the direction of a commitment to free trade.[24] This line of analysis falls under the heading of national level approaches.

Liberal Institutionalist Views

Liberal institutionalist views describe a world in which the inherent properties of international anarchy that frustrate the achievement of international cooperation are partially overcome through institutions that lower transaction and information costs, create a repetitive bargaining context, alter actors' estimates of their own utility functions, and induce convergence of expectations.[25] Although these analyses generally are grounded in realist assumptions, often liberal institutionalist views also are informed by functionalist assumptions. Such a perspective is suggested by the title of this book: *Japan's Emerging Global Role.* "Role" implies a broader context supported by the relevant actors. Emphasis is on the goal of cooperation and shared values, and the significance of relative gains is often downplayed.[26] These assumptions are directly contrary to the realist view that the anarchical international system is not characterized by any division of labor.[27]

Japanese analyses reflecting liberal institutionalist perspectives envision the future of Japan as a technological or cultural superpower.[28] Such a future depends on acceptance of some of the assumptions explicit in the model of complex interdependence by political scientists Robert Keohane and Joseph Nye,[29] in particular the reduced utility of force and the enhanced status of welfare concerns in nation-states' hierarchy of preferences. Japan might be able to help create such a world by enhancing U.S. dependence on Japan and thereby constraining the former's freedom of maneuver, thus facilitating Japan's participation in the management of an increasingly interdependent world.[30]

Liberal Economic Views

The liberal economic perspective makes little reference to interstate conflict. Insular or protectionist state policies are seen as atavistic holdovers that are crumbling in the face of growing international flows of goods, services, and information. With the spread of wealth, liberal economists anticipate increasing appreciation of the pervasiveness of nonmarket failures and the corresponding need to restrict interference with markets. The operation of universal market principles also means that Japan's remarkable rate of growth in the last century is destined to decline and conform more closely to industrialized country norms. In particular, the rapid growth rates of the late 1980s should be viewed as aberrant.[31] This view does not see Japan significantly altering the existing international structure of power. Nor does it believe that the Japanese institutions of capitalism represent significant innovations requiring major responses on the part of other powers.

Where liberal institutionalists emphasize institutional changes fostering cooperation, liberal economists are more prone to focus on the role of

technological change in driving economic processes. The former emphasize the political acts necessary to create new institutions; the latter tend to
regard them simply as by-products of more fundamental underlying
sources. Liberal economists see an expanding network of market relations
undermining the bases of national sovereignty and, through increasing interdependence, compelling increasing cooperation.

National Level Approaches to Understanding
Japanese Perceptions of Japan's Global Interests

National level analyses concentrate on Japan-specific factors in attempting
to predict future Japanese policy preferences. Rather than explaining how
structural factors override particular differences among nations, national
level analyses accord those differences overwhelming importance. It is
useful to look first at those that allegedly shape Japanese preferences and,
subsequently, at those that, according to some, influence the selection of
particular strategies to realize given preferences.

Factors Shaping Preferences

Japan scholars emphasize a wide range of historical, geographic, and cultural variables in suggesting reasons for the emergence of particular
Japanese preferences. These factors include Japan's geographic isolation
and resource poverty, its racial identity as an Asian nation, its hierarchical social structures, and the relative absence in Japan of universal beliefs.
These, in turn, are used to explain Japanese preferences for mercantilist
economic strategies, emphasis on integration of a Japan-led East Asian
economy, difficulty in cooperating internationally on a basis of sovereign
equality, and profound problems in operating in any cultural milieu shaped
by adherence to universalistic norms.

At the most general level, some scholars claim that Japanese leaders
have an "emotional commitment to Asia"[32]; that the hierarchical Japanese
weltanschauung leads Japanese leaders to be more comfortable dealing
with foreigners in roles of superiors or inferiors, rather than as equals; or
that Japanese "take the phenomenal world as absolute"[33] and do not em-
brace universal principles. Some scholars link this last attribute to Japanese groupism, which is seen as a source of Japan's economic success. The
lack of universal principles, however, means that group-based norms cannot be extended beyond Japan and will produce continuing frictions between Japan and other countries.[34] This view, then, does not locate the
source of tensions between Japan and other states in Japan's rapid growth
and the ensuing international structural disequilibria and national economic dislocations. Rather, the Japan-is-different view links those tensions
explicitly to sociological traits of the Japanese. Tensions between Japan

and the United States, for example, are simply one (albeit the most important) manifestation of a broader phenomenon. This view also sees the absence of universal ideals as an obstacle to the emergence of Japanese international leadership, to the extent that such leadership is based on more than coercive capacities.[35] Put bluntly, "A country wishing to challenge American power must first persuade the rest of the world that it has a more compelling global vision and the courage to implement it. Japan has neither."[36]

The CIA-commissioned draft report, "Japan 2000," suggested that Japan is pursuing economic domination that it will use to implement a new system of values free of absolutes or moral imperatives, based on Japan's "ageless, amoral, manipulative and controlling culture."[37] What is described as the lack of universal ideals, however, can also be linked to one of Japan's generally recognized strengths: its nonideological search for solutions to problems. The Japanese "appreciation of the fallibility of critical rationalism" underlies Japanese leaders' "strategic pragmatism" and the capacity to successfully combine the seemingly antithetical policy prescriptions of John Maynard Keynes and Arthur Laffer.[38]

A final example of arguments based on alleged Japanese characteristics stresses particular Japanese traditions in the exercise of power. This view links the Japanese acceptance of distinctions between surface and underlying realities to a tradition of disguised exercise of power. If the Meiji oligarchs were content to exercise power in the nineteenth century through the emperor, and Japanese bureaucrats have been willing to exercise power through the LDP,[39] perhaps contemporary Japan can be expected to be ready to exercise power discreetly behind the scenes, possibly even propping up continuing U.S. global dominance. Acceptance of this argument suggests the need to look closely at what Japan is actually doing and not to expect Japan to advertise its efforts to serve its interests when those efforts risk alienating powerful actors.[40] The drawbacks of such an approach were apparent to Nakasone (as noted earlier), as well as to Edwin O. Reischauer, the former U.S. ambassador to Japan:

> There is something unhealthy about a country as economically powerful and technologically advanced as Japan attempting to remain politically out of sight. This falsifies the real situation, creating confusion and suspicion among others and breeding resentments within Japan as well.[41]

Pursuing Preferences

Many Japan scholars believe that institutional factors influence the ways Japanese leaders pursue their interests. These scholars differ widely in their views of the ways in which power is exercised in Japan. Chalmers Johnson and Leon Hollerman, for example, see contemporary Japan led by an elite coalition of big business, LDP leaders, and bureaucrats, with the last as the dominant partners in the coalition.[42] Bureaucratic dominance makes possible careful crafting and implementation of strategic policies. If these have been largely economic in nature, that simply reflects bureaucrats' views of Japanese interests. Another view, articulated most clearly in the work of Karel van Wolferen, sees a similar elite coalition, but one without overall leadership.[43]

Johnson and others see in Japan the design of a different kind of capitalism built on significant institutional innovations. These observers anticipate ongoing struggle among competing models of capitalism.[44] For Van Wolferen, the headless Japanese state is presumed to be on a collision course with the United States. Divergence from that path is beyond the capabilities of existing Japanese political institutions unless assisted by intervention from abroad.

There is widespread agreement among scholars using institutional perspectives that the position of prime minister in Japan is a weak one. For structural reasons, national executives in all countries are more prone to be sensitive to their states' national interests, whereas legislators are more prone to respond to subnational groups' interests. The weakness of Japanese prime ministers,[45] therefore, poses a challenge to any effective Japanese international leadership. In Japan, the voice for the overall interest is weak. Japan's strategic pragmatism, under which emerging problems shape national direction,[46] may operate effectively only within a broader framework established by other powers. Japan may not be capable of acting alone to shape that framework.

The effective administration of Japan's foreign policy by the Ministry of Foreign Affairs is threatened by challenges to the ministry's prerogatives. This problem grows more severe as particular Japanese constituencies find they have a growing stake in the international system and are, therefore, less willing to leave management of those interests in the hands of the Ministry of Foreign Affairs. The challenge comes from other ministries, the LDP, and even business organizations. The desire to play a more direct role in conducting foreign policy is legitimated by expressions of concern over the dangers of Japan's reactive foreign policy: "Waiting for demands from the Americans and then responding to them . . . is the basic theme running through Japan's post-war foreign relations."[47] Japan's institutional framework hampers the design and implementation of comprehensive Japanese national strategies.

Institutional design, suggests this view, must play a role in facilitating a more activist Japanese international posture. Even more important, however, will be the mobilization of an effective domestic base of support for Japanese foreign policies. The active role of business in formulating and implementing Japanese ODA policies helps to explain the relatively high level of domestic political support for Japan's rapidly expanding program. The domestic coalition underpinning continuous LDP rule may be inadequate to sustain a Japanese global policy of activist leadership. As one observer asks, "Can a globally responsible foreign policy be pursued by the leaders of a country without a sympathetic and supportive population?"[48]

Overview of the Book

The chapters in this volume facilitate an understanding of Japan's emerging global role by highlighting the structure of constraints and opportunities within which Japanese policymakers will be defining and seeking to serve their interests. In the next chapter, Robert Gilpin launches the analysis at the broadest level, reviewing trends in the international political economy that will be structuring Japanese leaders' policy choices. He notes that the unprecedented postwar achievement of cooperative relations among the world's major capitalist economies is under challenge. Although economic concerns are clearly high on the agendas of most states, it remains unclear whether they will prove to be a source of cooperation or conflict. Neither do we yet know, Gilpin notes, whether the post–Cold War era should be seen as a unipolar world under U.S. domination or as a multipolar arena increasingly conducive to conflict.

Departing from structural analysis, Masaru Tamamoto, in Chapter 3, concentrates on the Japanese political culture that has taken root in the postwar period, but which has antecedents in Japan's emphasis on mercantile policies in the late nineteenth century. Tamamoto sees Japanese foreign policy continuing to rely on U.S. initiatives for its animating impetus. Where Gilpin sees a more powerful Japan challenging U.S. global leadership, Tamamoto insists that Japan wants only to be liked—it has no desire to surpass the United States as a dominant world power. Continuing strong U.S.-Japan ties, in Tamamoto's view, are critical to Japan's search for an international role that supports an open international political economy.

Yoshio Okawara details the steps Japan is taking to achieve such a goal in Chapter 3. Okawara argues that the Gulf crisis catalyzed an important debate in Japan about its global interests and responsibilities. The result, he maintains, has been Japan's rejection of its traditional unilateral pacifism in favor of global partnership—cooperation with other rich, industrialized states in addressing a broad range of global concerns. Even Japan's private sector, writes Okawara, is moving away from unbridled competition in favor of a sort of peaceful coexistence with foreign firms. Full realization of Japan's potentially critical global roles, however, requires institutionalization of Japan's new status. If Japan's importance cannot be reflected by its inclusion among the permanent members of the UN Security Council, Japan must push to broaden the roles of the Group of Seven, the only multilateral group aimed at policy coordination of which Japan is now a member.

Also pointing to the centrality of the U.S.-Japan relationship, Norman Levin notes in Chapter 5 that the Mutual Security Treaty provides a broad overall framework within which mutually supportive relations can be nested. He argues that the Tokyo Declaration put forth by Kiichi Miyazawa and Bush builds on the MST and recognizes that, even after the Cold War, Japan and the United States remain closely linked and retain shared interests. In short, they still need each other.

In Chapter 6, Masashi Nishihara sees the need for cooperative U.S.-Japan relations to underpin stability in the Pacific region. With the former Soviet Union, and Russia in particular, preoccupied with its own political and economic concerns, China, Japan, and the United States are now the key players in a region shaped by integrative economic developments and divisive territorial conflicts. Like Tamamoto, Nishihara indicates that Japan's definition of its security role in Northeast Asia is likely to come in large part as a response to U.S. initiatives, or the lack thereof. Together, these authors' contributions demonstrate the necessity of returning to the U.S.-Japan relationship when trying to understand the forces shaping Japan's foreign policies.

A new generation of Japanese, including some of the leadership of the LDP, stands ready to support an activist Japanese foreign policy, writes Kenneth Pyle in Chapter 7. Washington should exploit existing opportunities to take the initiative in defining a new relationship with Tokyo that can serve as the keystone of a broader regional order. Failure to do so, Pyle believes, raises the danger of Japan's abandoning its efforts to integrate itself fully into the existing global order in favor of an emphasis on its potential leadership role in Asia.

Turning from external constraints to domestic ones, Kent Calder describes in Chapter 8 those facets of the Japanese political system that tend to militate against Japan assuming an activist international policy. Japan's electoral system, the key role played by complex personal networks among the policymaking elite, and the structure of Japan's bureaucracy all frustrate the emergence of a more internationalist Japan. It should not be assumed, however, that these factors will remain fixtures constraining Japanese foreign policies. Calder suggests that with the weakening of the key pillars underlying the LDP's postwar dominance of Japanese politics, Japan appears ripe for important changes.

In Chapter 9, Edward Lincoln notes that with Japan's increased stake in the international system, particularly as a result of its increased foreign direct investment, Japan now has a domestic constituency in support of a more activist foreign policy. Japan must deflect, however, foreign annoyance with continuing imbalances in Japan's trade and in the ease with which foreign direct investment moves out of rather than into Japan.

So long as others believe that Japan maintains such asymmetries in its foreign economic policies, whatever the truth of the matter, Lincoln concludes that those foreigners will not be receptive to an enlarged global role for Japan.

By studying Japan's modus operandi in East Asia, suggests Daniel Unger in Chapter 10, it is possible to gain clues concerning Japan's future behavior as a global leader. Nowhere else beyond its borders has Japan so successfully married the overseas activities of the state and private firms. The results, largely successful from the perspectives of Japan and many other countries in the region, suggest the increasing plausibility of a regional economy able to hold its own should it have to compete, as a region, with the European Community and North America.

Analyzing Japan's contributions to the global development and diffusion of learning, in Chapter 11 David Mowery finds that Japan is a major source of research and development (R&D) in science and technology. Outside access to Japanese research is made difficult, however, by the largely private nature of the institutions that dominate Japan's R&D effort. Mowery suggests that there is considerable potential for expansion of U.S.-Japan cooperation in R&D activities.

In the concluding chapter, Daniel Unger argues that collapsing Japanese asset prices (notably in land and securities) beginning in the late 1980s heralded the end of the economic boom that followed Japan's recovery from the yen's appreciation in the mid-1980s. Nonetheless, the foundations of Japan's economy remain sound and the bases of potential Japanese global leadership are not under challenge. Japan, Unger concludes, will try to find an appropriate institutional setting for the exercise of its increased power, either in the United Nations or in such fora as the Group of Seven.

Notes

1. Haruhiro Fukui, "Policy-making in the Japanese Foreign Ministry," in Robert A. Scalapino, ed., *The Foreign Policy of Modern Japan* (Berkeley: University of California Press, 1977), p. 35.

2. Quoted from Akira Iriye, *Pacific Estrangement: Japanese and American Expansionism, 1897–1911* (Cambridge, Mass.: Harvard University Press, 1972), p. 14.

3. *Ibid.*, p. 31.

4. F. C. Langdon, *Japan's Foreign Policy* (Vancouver: University of British Columbia Press, 1973), p. 3.

5. Hans H. Baerwald, "The Diet and Foreign Policy," in Scalapino, *Foreign Policy of Modern Japan*, p. 37.

6. Donald Hellman, "Japanese Security and Postwar Japanese Foreign Policy," in Scalapino, *Foreign Policy of Modern Japan*, p. 322.

7. *Ibid.*, p. 37.

8. In fact, Japan's ability to continue its economic links with China made it China's major trading partner by the mid-1960s. Political scientist Chalmers Johnson characterizes this achievement as "one of the most skillfully executed foreign policies pursued by Japan in the postwar era—a clever, covert adaptation by Japan to the Cold War and a good example of Japan's essentially neomercantilist foreign policy." Quoted by William Nester, "The Third World in Japanese Foreign Policy," in Kathleen Newland, ed., *The International Relations of Japan* (New York: St. Martin's Press, 1990), p. 74.

9. See Richard N. Rosecrance, *The Rise of the Trading State: Commerce and Conquest in the Modern World* (New York: Basic Books, 1986).

10. Chalmers Johnson, "MITI and Japanese International Economic Policy," in Scalapino, *Foreign Policy of Modern Japan*, p. 260.

11. Langdon, *Japan's Foreign Policy*, p. xii.

12. Peter J. Katzenstein, "Domestic and International Forces and Strategies of Foreign Economic Policy," *International Organization* 31, no. 4 (Autumn 1977): 587–604.

13. This term is borrowed from Joseph M. Grieco, "Anarchy and the Limits of Cooperation: A Realist Critique of the Newest Liberal Institutionalism," *International Organization* 42, no. 3 (Summer 1988): 485–507.

14. See Kenneth Waltz, *Theory of International Politics* (Reading, Mass: Addison-Wesley, 1979).

15. Robert Keohane and Stephen Krasner, for example, argue that although international regimes mediate between international structure and outcomes, a particular international (hegemonic) structure of power may be necessary for the establishment of those regimes. Their emphasis is on international structure rather than on the particularities of any single state. Groatian, or social institutionalist, perspectives are unambiguously systemic.

16. Robert Gilpin, *War and Change in World Politics* (Cambridge: Cambridge University Press, 1981).

17. *The Economist*, June 15, 1991, p. 29.

18. Carl P. Parrini, *Heir to Empire: U.S. Economic Diplomacy 1916–1923* (Pittsburgh: University of Pittsburgh Press, 1969).

19. *Washington Post*, September 7, 1991.

20. *The Present State and Problems of Japan's Economic Cooperation: 1987* (summary). Translated and distributed by Foreign Press Center, Japan, June 1988.

21. *Ibid.*, p. 21.

22. *Ibid.*, p. 19.

23. Mark R. Brawley, "Institutional Innovation and Hegemonic Ascendance: Dutch Hegemony and the Creation of the Bank of Amsterdam," paper presented at the American Political Science Association conference, Atlanta, 1989.

24. Kozo Yamamura, "The Deliberate Emergence of a Free-trader," conference paper, Woodrow Wilson Center, Smithsonian Institution, 1992.

25. See Kenneth Oye, ed., *Cooperation Under Anarchy* (Princeton, N.J.: Princeton University Press, 1986).

26. For a critique, see Grieco, "Anarchy and the Limits of Cooperation."

27. See Waltz, *Theory of International Politics*.

28. Masataka Kosaka, *Japan's Choices: New Globalism and Cultural Orientations in an Industrial State* (New York: Pinter Publishers, 1989).

29. Robert D. Keohane and Joseph S. Nye, *Power and Interdependence* (New York: Harper Collins, 1989).

30. See Henrik Schmiegelow and Michele Schmiegelow, "How Japan Affects the International System," *International Organization* 44, no. 4 (Autumn 1990): 553–588.

31. See, for example, Bill Emmott, *The Sun Also Sets* (New York: Simon and Schuster, 1989).

32. Seizaburo Sato, quoted in Robert E. Bedeski, "Japan: The Diplomacy of a Developmental State," *Journal of Asian and African Studies* 25, no. 1–2 (1990): 60.

33. Hajime Nakamura, quoted in Kanji Haitani, "The Paradox of Japan's Groupism," *Asian Survey* 30 (March 1990): 241.

34. *Ibid.*

35. G. John Ikenberry and Charles A. Kupchan suggest that both material incentives and substantive beliefs are critical to the exercise of hegemonic power. Beliefs are spread through the socialization of leaders in secondary nations. See G. John Ikenberry and Charles A. Kupchan, "Socialization and Hegemonic Power," *International Organization* 44, no. 3 (Summer 1990): 283–315; see also Andrew Fenton Cooper, Richard A. Higgott, and Kim Richard Nossal, "Bound to Follow? Leadership and Followership in the Gulf Conflict," *Political Science Quarterly* 106, no. 3 (1991): 391–410.

36. Nobuo Noda, *Los Angeles Times*, September 30, 1991, p. B5.

37. *Far Eastern Economic Review*, June 27, 1991, p. 15.

38. Schmiegelow and Schmiegelow, "How Japan Affects the International System"; see also Chalmers Johnson's discussion of Japan's ability to "square the circle," in Chalmers Johnson, *MITI and the Japanese Miracle* (Stanford, Calif.: Stanford University Press, 1982).

39. Johnson, *MITI.*

40. For example, when former Thai Prime Minister Choonhavan Chatichai went to Tokyo in April 1990, newspaper reports suggested that he urged former Prime Minister Toshiki Kaifu to host a meeting between Prince Sihanouk and Hun Sen. Subsequent reports indicated that Japanese diplomats had urged this suggestion on Chatichai before he left Bangkok. Nayan Chanda, *Christian Science Monitor*, June 13, 1990, p. 18.

41. Quoted in Marvin S. Soroos, "Global Interdependence and the Responsibilities of States: Learning from the Japanese Experience," *Journal of Peace Research* 25, no. 1 (1988): 17–29.

42. See Johnson, *MITI*; Leon Hollerman, "The Headquarters Nation," *The National Interest* (Fall 1991): 16–25.

43. Van Wolferen's analysis draws also on historical and cultural factors.

44. Ken'ichi Imai and Yoshi Tsurumi also endorse this conclusion. See *Far Eastern Economic Review*, December 27, 1990, p. 44.

45. See Johnson, *MITI*; see also Kent E. Calder, "Japanese Foreign Economic Policy: Explaining the Reactive State," *World Politics* 40, no. 4 (July 1988): 517–541.

46. Schmiegelow and Schmiegelow, "How Japan Affects the International System."

47. Atsuyuki Saasa, quoted in *Far Eastern Economic Review*, July 18, 1991, p. 18.

48. Soroos, "Global Interdependence," p. 26.

2

The Debate About the New World Economic Order

Robert Gilpin

The end of the Cold War has stimulated debate on whether a new world order is emerging. Since the 1989 collapse of the Soviet empire in Eastern Europe, the subsequent fragmentation of the Soviet Union itself, and the decisive U.S.-led victory in the Gulf War, speculations on the transformation of the international system and the nature of the post–Cold War era have reached flood tide. With the defeat of the communist threat, some—including U.S. President George Bush—view the United States as the only true superpower. They believe that U.S. values have triumphed, and the world is at long last on the verge of an unprecedented era of prosperity, democracy, and peace.[1] Others, however, believe that the bipolar stability of the postwar world is being supplanted by a multipolar world characterized by new forms of intense ethnic, political, and economic conflict.[2] Members of this latter group believe that the world may one day look back with envy and nostalgia to the simpler and more certain bipolar Cold War world and what historian John Lewis Gaddis has called its "long peace."[3]

At the beginning of the Cold War itself, there was a comparable situation of intellectual confusion. In the United States, this was an era characterized by intense political and intellectual debate. In the political arena, the issues were concerned with the nature of the Soviet challenge and how the United States should respond to that challenge. In the intellectual sphere, traditional U.S. "idealists," who favored a reliance on international law and the United Nations, debated the "political realists," who stressed the role of military power and the primacy of national interests in international affairs.

Ever since George Washington's farewell address, the basic premise of U.S. foreign policy had been that the United States should have friendly commercial relations with all nations, but should not join any "entangling alliances." This premise was rejected when the realist view predominated and the policy of containment of the Soviet Union was established.

21

Following the victory of the realists, the North Atlantic Treaty Organization (NATO) was created, and then followed the Mutual Security Treaty with Japan. For the first time since the Revolutionary War, the United States set aside its idealism and joined two "entangling alliances" across the Atlantic and Pacific oceans. Japan, however, moved in the opposite direction, embracing pacifist idealism, secure with the benefit of U.S. military power.

The resulting military and political structures across the Atlantic and Pacific became the bases for a historically unprecedented era of global prosperity and economic cooperation among the three major capitalist societies: Japan, Western Europe, and the United States. In the interest of alliance unity, the United States and its allies subordinated economic differences in order to achieve political cooperation. For the first time in the history of the world, the three dominant capitalist economies were allies cooperating with one another.

Today, with the ending of the Cold War, the major capitalist economies once again face political and intellectual issues whose resolution will have a profound effect, perhaps even a decisive one, on the nature of international relations in the closing decade of the twentieth century and into the twenty-first century. Will these nations continue to cooperate or, with the loss of the common foe, will they turn on one another? The universal recognition that the world is once again at a crucial turning point has given rise to another great debate over the implications of contemporary developments. At both policy and intellectual levels can be found confusion and controversy. It is generally agreed that we no longer live in a bipolar world, but do we now live in a unipolar, nonpolar, tripolar, trilateral, multipolar, or, as one commentator has described it, a "unimultipolar world"?[4] And, whatever the precise architecture of the new world order, what is its significance for world politics and foreign policy?

The many questions at issue in the sometimes heated and frequently confused exchanges over the nature of the new world order and the transformed international system encompass a vast array of economic, political, and other topics. This chapter will consider only the most important matters in the area of international economics. There is, in fact, widespread agreement that economic matters will be at the heart of the new world order. Intense controversy is waged, however, about the role of economic factors and the nature of the world economy. There is disagreement about the importance of economic factors in international affairs, about the relative importance of global and regional structures of the international political economy, and also about the possible implications, especially for Japan, of the transformation of the global political economy. Inevitably, the particular features of this argument vary in different countries. Although the discussion is still in its beginning stages, the debate in the United States, which this chapter addresses, is important because of the major international influence of that country. Furthermore, in the past, Japanese leaders have taken their cues from the United States when crafting their own political and economic strategies. Japan's continuing ability to follow the U.S. lead—indeed, its interest in doing so—will depend in large part on the outcome of the debate in the United States.

The Role of Economic Factors

At the core of the debate about the nature of the new world economic order is the issue of the role of economic factors and, especially, whether economic activities will be a source of international cooperation or international conflict. There is an overall consensus that economics will play an increasingly important role, but fundamental differences exist about whether economic affairs will encourage continued political cooperation among the three dominant economic powers or will become a source of political conflict. Although it is somewhat of an oversimplification, two schools of thought on this issue can be discerned in the writings of U.S. commentators. Both positions agree that economics has become of greater importance in the interrelationship of economic activities and national security. They also agree that, whereas military security issues predominated in the Cold War era, economic issues, whether cooperative or conflictive, will henceforth become more important. The two positions, however, diverge when they address the ways in which the increased importance of economic affairs will affect world politics.[5]

The first position suggests that, with the collapse of communism and the victory of market ideology, humanity is moving into a politically borderless and highly interdependent world economy that will foster international cooperation and discourage war. In the words of one enthusiast for this interpretation, we are entering a new "golden age" of world capitalism in which unfettered markets will unite the world and promote world peace and unprecedented prosperity.[6] In this triumphal return to the "free market" and "laissez-faire" ideals of the nineteenth century, global corporations will take the lead in organizing international production and promoting the maximization of global wealth.

A corollary of this position is that the U.S. economic and political systems have become the models for the world. In economic terms, this position foresees the discrediting of state intervention in the economy. Of equal importance, the United States—as the only true superpower—is "bound to lead," to use the expression of Joseph Nye, in the post–Cold War era.[7] Furthermore, proponents of the position believe that established international norms and institutions, such as the International Monetary Fund and the United Nations, will ensure continued cooperation between the United States and its allies.[8]

A significant implication of this position is that traditional national security concerns will be of decreasing importance and the world will finally achieve the democratic and universal world order embodied in the United Nations and in the open world economy envisioned by Franklin D. Roosevelt toward the end of World War II. Rejecting the views of realist writers, with their emphasis on military power and national interests, advocates of this position believe that new forms of power such as exemplary ideals and democratic values will ensure world peace. Such traditional goals of "realpolitik" as territorial control and national prestige are meaningless in an era of nuclear weapons. Moreover, the nations of the world have become too interdependent economically, and the benefits of economic cooperation too great and obvious, for any rational nation to revert to the ways of the past. In the optimistic scenario of this position, economic interdependence will cause nations to substitute *international* security for more parochial and archaic conceptions of *national* security. Indeed, as Kenneth Pyle suggests in Chapter 7, it seems likely that Japan will broaden its definitions of its own national security to include issues of a global nature.

The opposed and less optimistic thesis suggests that in the post–Cold War era, international economic competition will be more important than military competition in determining national security and national welfare. With the defeat of the Soviet security threat, many adherents of this position believe that the East-West conflict will be followed by a West-West conflict. In particular, many in the United States believe that Japan has become a strategic threat to their country.[9] They deny that U.S. economic and political ideals are sweeping the world. Free trade does not mean U.S. preeminence, and free elections do not mean the election of democrats. The Cold War, the adherents frequently quip, is over, but Germany and Japan won.

A corollary of this position is that the economic preeminence of the United States has slipped dangerously while the economic strength of both Japan and united Germany has grown considerably. At the least, some argue, unless far-reaching domestic reforms are taken, the U.S. position in the world will continue to decline economically and politically. Some, however, go further and argue that the economic expansion of Japan must be contained. As stated in the *New York Times*, the Bush-Miyazawa January 1992 summit was the first post–Cold War world summit of the two economic superpowers.[10] The clash between the two is over computer chips and automobile imports rather than over troop levels and intercontinental missiles. Instead of a U.S.-led world, the ideological competition between capitalism and communism has been supplanted by a competition between various forms of capitalism and especially between the U.S. and Japanese forms of capitalist systems. Whereas the former emphasizes the importance of the market freed from state intervention, the latter is based on a greater partnership between private enterprise and the state.

Adherents of this position believe, to paraphrase the German strategist Karl von Clausewitz, that in the post–Cold War world, economic competition will become the pursuit of foreign policy and national security by other means. Whereas some fear that the world economy will deteriorate to the intense economic and regional conflicts of the 1930s, a less extreme position would agree with former West German Chancellor Helmut Schmidt that the nations of the world are becoming involved in what he called "the struggle for the world product."[11] Many believe that this global struggle will be among competing regional centers of economic power. Although not always stated explicitly, the fear among many in the United States is that failure in this new competition could jeopardize U.S. security interests. The possibility of regionally based competition leads to a second major issue regarding the nature of the new world economic order.

A Globalized or Regionalized System

The second fundamental issue debated by U.S. observers concerns the nature and structure of the world economy. The transformation of the international economy is proceeding at a remarkable pace and in contradictory ways. At the same time that an overall process of economic integration and globalization is taking place, powerful centrifugal forces are also reshaping the world political and economic systems. Although all the consequences of these counteracting political and economic vectors cannot be foreseen at this time, it is obvious that the postwar international economy is undergoing a historic transformation. Gaddis has characterized the situation in his assertion that the new world is being shaped by conflicting forces of social integration and disintegration.[12]

The integration of national economies into a global and transnational economy is occurring at an astonishing rate in the areas of trade, finance, and production. Today, a world market of goods and services is replacing a world economy composed of relatively isolated national markets. Domestic financial markets have been integrated into a truly global system. The multinational corporation is becoming the principal mechanism for the allocation of investment capital and determination of the location of production throughout much of the world. Western Europe has reinitiated the process of economic unification, and the postwar division between Eastern and Western Europe has virtually disappeared. The North Atlantic–centered world economy is rapidly being displaced by a global economy in which dynamic non-European economies in East Asia and elsewhere have also become independent and self-generating sources of economic growth and technological innovation.

While this process of globalization and transnational integration is taking place, economic protectionism and economic alliances among states and corporations are also rapidly expanding. These economic alliances are being used to influence and, in some cases, to determine market relations and economic outcomes. As tariffs have come down, quantitative restrictions on imports have gone up. For example, in 1980, just 5 percent of U.S. imports was affected by quantitative restrictions; by 1986, 18 percent was so affected. Western Europe and many developing countries have also increased their use of nontariff restrictions on their imports.[13] Important sectors of the Japanese economy are similarly protected, and no doubt that will continue. On the whole, perhaps as much as 40 percent of world trade is "managed trade" of some kind, rather than simply subject to market forces. Such bilateral and regional arrangements as the North American Free Trade Agreement (NAFTA) and the accelerated movement toward European integration are spreading. As *The Economist* has observed, "the world economy shows signs of moving towards a trading system partitioned into three blocks: the Americas, the European Community and the Asia-Pacific region centered on Japan."[14] In brief, the regionalization of the world economy appears to be accompanying the contradictory trend toward economic globalization.

It is imperative that the meaning of the term "regionalism" be precisely understood. For many writers, "economic regionalism" conjures up an image of the 1930s when the world collapsed in the face of exclusive and antagonistic economic and political blocs. Some writers who reject the idea of a regionalization of the world as either undesirable or impossible may have in mind a return to the economic conflicts of the interwar years. Few of those observers who foresee a greater regionalization of the world economy, however, believe that a return to the 1930s is inevitable or even likely. Instead, they regard regionalism as an alternative to the postwar movement toward economic multilateralism and trade liberalization. For this reason, with the possible exception of Western Europe, "trading regions" rather than "economic blocs" might be a more appropriate term to describe the new entities that are emerging. Today, the term "regionalization" is applied to three quite different processes taking place in East Asia, North America, and Western Europe.

North American Regionalism

Despite the increasing pressures for economic protectionism, U.S. foreign policy in the 1990s remains strongly committed to trade liberalization and the movement toward a multilateral world economy. For both economic and political reasons, the United States wants an open world economy. The interests of U.S. industry, agriculture, and services lie with a liberal trading regime. For political and security reasons also, the United States favors a multilateral world economy. As distinguished journalist and political analyst Walter Lippmann noted three decades ago, the United States would have difficulty maintaining its world position without the capacity to earn foreign exchange and influence world economic activities.[15] For the United States, economic regionalism and a fragmented world economy would mean a greatly diminished economic and political presence in the world.

This continuing U.S. commitment to a liberal and multilateral world economy underlies the U.S. initiative that led to launching the Uruguay Round of GATT negotiations in 1986. In these negotiations the United States has tried to remove those economic barriers and practices that it believes to be detrimental to U.S. interests. Among other demands, the United States has wanted to free agricultural trade, open foreign economies in the service sectors, and protect intellectual property rights. Whereas the Japanese generally supported this U.S. initiative, West European concurrence resulted primarily from a desire to head off the growth of protectionist sentiment in the U.S. Congress. The U.S. disappointment with the slow progress of the Uruguay Round has intensified protectionist pressures and encouraged the U.S. tendency to pursue bilateral and regional arrangements.

The United States–Canada free trade agreement and the effort to establish the North American Free Trade Agreement are the most important results of this shift in U.S. foreign economic policy. The United States pursued this bilateral agreement, at least in part, as a means of improving the North American bargaining position in the Uruguay Round. It also has been considered to be an alternative in the event that GATT negotiations fail. Increasingly, however, the attractiveness of a huge North American market has become more significant in U.S. thinking. The U.S. Congress, however, remains unconvinced of the merits of Mexico's inclusion, given its oil wealth and cheap labor among other concerns. Meanwhile, the Caribbean economies have grown closer to their northern neighbor and, in June 1990, President Bush launched his Enterprise for the Americas Initiative, aimed at integrating the economies of Latin and North America.

For some observers, these efforts by the United States to create some sort of regional economic arrangement reflect the relative economic decline of that nation and its growing disenchantment with its European and Japanese economic partners. As U.S. international competitiveness eroded, the idea of a protected continental market has grown more attractive. More people in the United States now believe that U.S. trading partners have not been playing fair. Many point out that whereas Japanese goods and firms have almost unrestricted access to the U.S. market, it is exceedingly difficult for U.S. goods and firms to penetrate the Japanese economy. Today, the question of whether there will be sufficient economic and political benefits to balance the painful and obvious costs to particular groups of keeping the U.S. market open to the outside world is of increasing importance. Or, to put it another way, is the Lippmann argument that the United

States needs an open world economy for political and strategic purposes still valid? With the end of the Cold War, the domestic political influence of that idea has lessened considerably.

Although sentiment for a regional economic or trading bloc has grown in North America, what is actually being proposed, and the difficulties of achieving it, must be appreciated. Efforts are being made to create a free trade area, but the goals of its proponents fall short of the goals of the European common market originally created by the Treaty of Rome and do not approach the political goals of the 1992 initiative. Whereas a free trade area involves only the elimination of internal tariffs among the members, a common market entails a common external tariff toward outside parties. Yet even the more modest objective of eliminating internal tariffs is resisted by powerful interests in Canada, Mexico, and the United States. No one other than the most paranoid nationalist seriously contemplates the possibility of regional political unity. Nonetheless, many commentators believe that the abandonment of unquestioned multilateralism and the movement toward a regional trading arrangement signify an important shift in the international political economy. Clearly, the actual direction of the global political economy will greatly influence Japanese leaders' perceptions of their vital interests.

West European Regionalism

There is broad agreement that the enactment in 1986 of the Single Europe Act, with its program for the Completion of the Internal Market by 1992, is an economic and political initiative of historic significance. The complete integration of the several European national markets into a single market of more than 300 million people obviously will be difficult to achieve and require many additional years to complete. Even in 1992, it is still too soon to be certain of the final shape of the internal European market or what its policies toward the rest of the world will be. But, even after the setback of the Danish referendum in 1992, it is clear that the European Community has moved to a radical new attitude toward itself and the rest of the world. Increased unity would enhance the bargaining leverage of Western Europe vis-à-vis the United States and, especially, Japan. All the available evidence suggests that West Europeans are seeking to improve their negotiating position in the world economy and will continue to do so. Like the United States, the West European countries will attempt to achieve greater reciprocity with other economies as well as use their increased economic strength for political and diplomatic purposes.

The reinvigoration of the West European effort to achieve economic and political unity is a response to both long-term forces and short-term developments. Since the initial launching of the EC in the 1950s, West

Europeans have been committed, at least verbally, to the ideal of greater unity. During the 1960s and the 1970s, this goal became subordinated to the more immediate concerns of the West Europeans, their several rivalries, and the stagnation of the world economy caused by the oil crisis of 1973. The economic primacy of the United States, the political rigidity of the Soviets, and simple inertia countered the forces that had begun to push Europeans toward greater unity. The Single Europe Act and the EC decision to "complete the internal market" signaled a profound shift in West European economic and political objectives.

The major purpose of West Europeans in enacting the Single Europe Act was psychological: it was intended to overcome the "Europessimism" and "Eurosclerosis" of the 1970s and 1980s. The competitive environment of a huge internal market, it was argued, would have a stimulating effect on European corporations and enable them to achieve the economies of scale and global competitiveness of U.S. and Japanese firms. In addition, greater economic and political unity would increase the bargaining power of West Europeans in international economic negotiations. In a significant departure from the earlier Rome Treaty, the Single Europe Act for the first time made political unity a specific goal of the community (Article 30). This Single Europe Act was designated to create a European entity that one day would take its place as an economic as well as a political equal with the other great powers.

In the early 1990s, the unification of Western Europe is proceeding in important ways and is transforming world economic and political affairs. Japanese and U.S. firms are investing huge sums to establish a strong position in the unified European internal market. After considerable vacillation, the U.S. government has decided to work with rather than oppose a strengthened community. Although the United States still desires to maintain a presence in Western Europe through a reduced commitment to NATO, the United States has in effect decided not to challenge West European preeminence in such European developments as the reforms in Eastern Europe and leadership in the newly created European Bank for Reconstruction and Development. As witnessed in the Uruguay Round of GATT negotiations, the community is often able to speak with one voice.

Despite these important developments, the Maastricht conference of December 1991, and its subsequent rejection by many West Europeans, made it clear that fundamental issues are yet to be resolved. How these issues are ultimately resolved will have a profound influence on the nature and structure of the EC. The first and most significant question to be decided is the degree to which the new European economic and political entity will be integrated. Will it be the Brussels model of a tightly unified EC promoted by community bureaucrats or the loosely constructed Bruges model of former British Prime Minister Margaret Thatcher? Another important question involves the geographical scope of the EC. Will West European leaders opt for a deepening of the community of the twelve members or a broadening of the EC to encompass the whole of the European Economic Area? Yet another question is how open to the outside world the internal market will be. Will it be a fortress Europe or a Europe open to the world?

The nature of the entity being created on the European continent defies classification in terms of the traditional categories employed by historians and political scientists. Western Europe, which gave birth to the modern nation-state, appears to be fashioning once again a novel political form that cannot be easily comprehended by the Brussels versus Bruges formulation. As it is now conceived, the renovated European Community will be much less than the Brussels model of a united political entity, but much more than the Bruges model of essentially an economic and political alliance of sovereign and independent states. Although the decision to "complete the internal market" entails the transfer of considerable responsibility to a central bank, a European parliament, and the Brussels bureaucracy, no European state has yet agreed to surrender the fundamental attributes of national sovereignty: the right to maintain independent military forces, the right to coin money, and the right to taxation. As long as these powers continue to be national monopolies, a significant upper limit is placed on regional economic integration and the political unity of the continent.

The debate about "deepening versus broadening" also oversimplifies the issue of the political and geographical dimensions of the EC. Certainly the inclusion of additional members would increase the difficulties of the current twelve members of the community in working out among themselves the exceptional problems that they confront. The decision to forgo the ambitious goal of harmonizing national practices in favor of mutual recognition attests to the difficulty of the task. Despite these difficulties, the EC will undoubtedly incorporate a few additional members, such as Austria and Norway. Moreover, it is difficult not to believe that the logic of the situation will lead eventually to a large European Economic Area. Through a series of bilateral and multilateral agreements, the countries of Eastern Europe and the European Free Trade Association (EFTA) will certainly establish links of varying strength with the EC. The result could be a set of concentric circles with the community at the center. Under the leadership of Brussels, this large European entity would exercise a powerful influence on the international economic system.

The resolution of the issue of a closed or an open EC will vitally affect possible regionalization of the world economy. As the theory of customs unions teaches, regional economic integration can have a positive or a negative impact on the outside world, depending upon its trade-creating or trade-diverting effects—does it tend to stimulate new trade links or simply divert existing, more difficult patterns? With the exceptions of Great Britain and, to some extent, Germany, most West European nations have never been very sympathetic to free trade and open markets. The members of the EC and domestic interest groups are deeply divided over trade matters, and the internal debate will take many years to resolve. It should be remembered that the West Europeans are creating a unified *internal* market primarily for their own benefit. Many Europeans would no doubt agree with the statement of a Brussels official that "the EC sees no reason why the benefits of its internal liberalizations should be extended unilaterally to others."[16]

Although West Europeans do have a strong interest in a relatively open international economy, they do not want to throw open their economies to foreign (especially Japanese) competition. This is particularly true in such sectors as automobiles, electronics, and agriculture, where politically important European producers would be harmed by lowered trade barriers. Whether for outright protectionist or bargaining purposes, West Europeans can be expected to maintain firm control over the access of outside competitors to the enlarged internal market through the use of antidumping and local-content rules, quantitative restrictions and "transition periods," and demands for greater reciprocity from other countries. The EC's position on agricultural trade in the Uruguay Round has been the major factor in the continuing failure of those negotiations. Ultimate failure would likely lead to increased protectionism and more bilateral arrangements throughout the world.

East Asian Regionalism

In the opinion of most observers, Western Europe and North America are both clearly moving toward greater regionalization; the situation in the Pacific Basin region is more ambiguous. Although the Pacific Basin is the most rapidly growing economic region in the world, almost without exception its economies are dependent on *world* markets rather than *regional* markets. A more regionalized global economy would be damaging to these exporting economies. Moreover, again differing from the other trading regions, the Pacific Basin and East Asian region is extremely diverse in terms of culture, economic interests, and levels of economic development. As was demonstrated by the positions taken in the recently concluded GATT negotiations, Asian countries can be divided into several rather loose groupings. Japan, as the only highly advanced economy in the region, stands by itself as both a regional and global economic power. The Newly Industrializing Countries (NICs) of East Asia and some members of ASEAN seek to protect their export industries. Australia and New Zealand share interests as major commodity exporters. Although these differences complement one another, they are also a source of economic tension.

Moreover, in the 1990s there is no obvious leadership for a regional bloc in the Pacific. No Germany or United States is ready and willing to take the lead. The most obvious leader, Japan, is reluctant to assume this leadership role. It prefers dealing with other regional economies on a bilateral basis and is fully aware that some other nations in the region would fear and resist its efforts to establish regional hegemony. The political and economic role of China is unsettled, to say the least. One also has to ask where and how Russia, a Pacific power with a desire to play a major role in Pacific affairs, will fit. What leadership does exist, therefore, is largely split between Japan and the United States. Neither of these dominant Pacific economic powers, however, has an interest in an exclusive intra-Pacific economic bloc.

Despite the resistance to a regional bloc, a number of initiatives have been taken in the direction of creating Pacific Basin institutions and formulating common policies. Although a subregional organization, ASEAN has achieved some success in coordinating economic and foreign policies. In 1989, the intergovernmental Asia Pacific Economic Cooperation (APEC) conference was established to facilitate greater regional economic cooperation. The Pacific Basin Economic Council (PBEC), the Pacific Economic Cooperation Conference (PECC), and other private or semiprivate organizations also play a role in expediting intraregional communications. Although such regional efforts have certainly intensified in recent years, these cooperative efforts have not proceeded very far.

Yet, the Pacific Basin and East Asia are unaffected by the trend toward a greater regionalization of the world economy. Intra–Pacific Basin trade has grown much more rapidly in recent years than trade with the outside world. In what Japanese like to call the "flying geese pattern," economic growth is spreading downward along the East Asian seaboard from Japan and the NICs to the ASEAN countries. It is noteworthy that both Taiwan and South Korea, which were once merely the recipients of foreign investment, have now become major foreign investors in their own right, and their imports have become a major stimulus to the growth of other economies in the region.

The most important force in the regionalization of the Pacific Basin is the activity of Japanese corporations. Principally through the mechanisms of international trade and foreign investment and with the encouragement of their government, these firms are integrating the Pacific Basin into an increasingly interdependent system of trade, production, and finance. By one estimate, more than 4,500 Japanese firms, alone or in joint ventures, employ nearly one million workers throughout the region. In 1990, Japan invested about twice the U.S. investment in the region. Whereas Japanese trade with the region was only $61.8 billion in 1982, it reached $126.4 billion in 1989. Japanese foreign aid to the region has grown to $4.4 billion in 1989 and has become a major instrument in Japan's effort to reshape domestic and international developments in the region.[17]

Despite these developments, few observers believe that Japan is seeking to create a closed and exclusive economic bloc. Although the Pacific Basin is of increasing economic importance for Japan, the region continues to be a complement to Japan's primary interest in the global economy. Japan resists the idea of a yen or exclusive trading bloc, even though it is increasingly exercising an influence in the region commensurate with its growing economic power. Japan is redirecting more of its multilateral economic aid to the Asian Development Bank, in part because it does not have a sufficiently important voice in global economic institutions. The long-range purpose of Japanese bilateral foreign aid in the region is to promote the commercial interests of Japanese firms and to encourage Asian countries to adopt the Japanese economic model. A regional bloc, however, is regarded by the Japanese mainly as an alternative in the event that the global system breaks down. Nevertheless, a unified economic bloc in the Pacific Basin and East Asia will continue to emerge step by step in response to growing regionalism in Western Europe and North America.

Contrasting Interpretations of Economic Regionalism

The movements toward regional integration differ greatly from one another; they range from the politically motivated and institutionalized movement toward integration in Western Europe to the primarily economic and less institutionalized nature of East Asian integration. The West European movement toward regional integration is proceeding faster than the others, is creating potentially the largest market, and is most likely to create an at least partially closed market. Indeed, the crucial importance of European integration has led some observers to posit a world economy composed of "the European Community and all the rest."[18] The outcome of the debate about the significance of economic regionalism will undoubtedly be decided by Europeans.

The predominant U.S. interpretation of these contradictory developments, especially among professional economists, emphasizes the process of global integration. This position holds that a linear and essentially irreversible movement toward global interdependence is driving the economies of the world to ever higher levels of economic integration. The overall process of economic integration and globalization is sometimes limited by irrational forces and those threatened interests that respond to the forces of economic integration with appeals to economic nationalism and demands for economic protectionism. In time, however, this position argues, the inherent logic of economic efficiency will prevail and nations will move in the direction of increased globalization. As economist C. Fred Bergsten has put it, although "virtually all countries on occasion attempt to resist these external pressures, efforts to resist the forces of market globalization can succeed only partially and for limited periods of time."[19]

A second interpretation, put forth in particular by some so-called re-visionist authors and other critics of Japanese economic policies, is that, with the end of the Cold War, the international economy is rapidly frag-menting into antagonistic regional economic blocs centered on the three dominant economic powers. Some adherents of this position believe that the East-West military conflict is being replaced by a world in which eco-nomic conflict becomes the functional equivalent of military conflict. Pro-ponents emphasize the fact that as formal tariffs have come down, infor-mal barriers have become more important. To support their position, these individuals call attention to the increase in the 1980s in the share of U.S. imports covered by quantitative restrictions from 5 to 18 percent. Western Europe has been particularly active in forging nontariff barriers, especially against Japanese goods. Although Japanese formal tariffs have come down, many informal barriers have continued. Bilateral trading arrange-ments are rapidly spreading. The rules of the GATT may cover a small fraction of global economic activities. As a consequence of these and other developments, this position argues, it is highly probable that economic competition among the three economic regions will degenerate into polit-ical conflict.

A third interpretation is that what is taking place today in the interna-tional political economy is a dialectical process. Both the economic glob-alization emphasized by the first position and the economic regionalism emphasized by the second are taking place simultaneously. The two de-velopments are in fact complementary and responsive to one another. They reflect a world in which states want the *absolute* benefits of a global econ-omy at the same time that they are seeking to increase their own *relative* gains through economic protectionism, the formation of regional arrange-ments, and managed trade. We are not witnessing a linear process in which the forces of economic integration will eventually triumph decisively over the forces of economic nationalism and political boundaries will cease to have economic significance. But it is also not inevitable that the regional blocs will lead to a total breakdown and fragmentation of the world econ-omy and thence to political conflict. The ultimate balance between global and regional emphases, however, has yet to be decided.

Although potential regional blocs are motivated in part by economic considerations, they are primarily motivated by the political ambitions of regional powers and the effort of each bloc to improve its bargaining po-sition. They reflect a world in which political and economic leaders be-lieve that economic competition has or at least could become the conduct of foreign policy by other means. It would be highly ironic, but certainly possible, that the end of the Cold War between capitalism and communism may be followed by a clash among the three major capitalist powers them-selves. Whether such a competition would be one against all or two against one has yet to be determined.

If this interpretation is correct, it should be appreciated that a North American bloc and a Pacific Basin bloc, at least by themselves, would not be nearly as powerful as the EC. The North American region is led by the world's largest debtor, and the United States has become highly dependent upon Western Europe, with which it has an overall trade surplus. The Pacific region is insufficiently unified, both economically and politically, to have much bargaining leverage vis-à-vis the Europeans. Only if the United States and Japan were to set aside the differences between them and challenge the EC with a united front and coordinated strategy could they possibly have the leverage to prevail over the community.

Conclusion

A unipolar political world in which Japan continues to be an ally of the United States and where there is an open, interdependent global economy would have vastly different implications for Japanese society than a tripolar regionalized world in which economic competition becomes the conduct of war by other means. The ways in which Japan uses its power will significantly affect the resolution of these issues. Although it will be extraordinarily difficult for Japan to assume a greater global leadership role, it has the power and perhaps even the obligation to make its positive impact on the course of history as these issues are resolved. Failure to assume greater leadership in the effort to maintain an open world economy threatens the triumph of a regionalized world economy. Japan, then, is a major actor at the same time that it is acted upon. It is no longer possible for Japan to view the debate reviewed here as a concerned, albeit nonengaged, spectator. Japan's policies, like those of the other powers, will crucially shape the political economic framework within which future Japanese leaders will identify and pursue Japan's national interests.

Notes

This chapter was written with the support of Princeton University's Center of International Studies.

1. Francis Fukuyama, "The End of History," *The National Interest* 16 (Summer 1989): 3–18; Charles Krauthammer, "The Unipolar Moment," in "America and the World 1990/91," *Foreign Affairs* 70, special issue (1991): 23–33.

2. Graham E. Fuller, *The Democracy Trap: Perils of the Post Cold War World* (New York: Dutton, 1991); John J. Mearsheimer, "Back to the Future: Instability in Europe After the Cold War," *International Security* 15, no. 1 (Summer 1990): 5–56.

3. John Lewis Gaddis, *The Long Peace: Inquiries into the History of the Cold War* (New York: Oxford University Press, 1987).

4. Samuel P. Huntington, "America's Changing Strategic Interests," *Survival* 33, no. 1 (January/February 1991): 6.

5. Kenneth A. Oye, "Beyond Postwar Order and New World Order: American Foreign Policy in Transition," in Kenneth A. Oye, Robert J. Lieber, and Donald Rothchild, eds., *Eagle in a New World: American Grand Strategy in the Post–Cold War Era* (New York: Harper Collins, 1992), pp. 3–33.

6. David Hale, "The World Economy After the Russian Revolution or Why the 1990s Could Be the Second Great Age of Global Capitalism Since the 19th Century," Kemper Securities Group, Inc., Special Report, October 25, 1991.

7. Joseph S. Nye, Jr., *Bound to Lead: The Changing Nature of American Power* (New York: Basic Books, 1990).

8. Robert O. Keohane, *After Hegemony: Cooperation and Discord in the Political Economy* (Princeton, N.J.: Princeton University Press, 1984); Raymond Vernon and Ethan B. Kapstein, "National Needs, Global Resources," *Daedalus, Journal of the American Academy of Arts and Sciences* 120, no. 4 (Fall 1991): 1–22.

9. Huntington, "America's Changing Strategic Interests," p. 8.

10. *New York Times*, January 10, 1992, p. A11.

11. Helmut Schmidt, "Struggle for the World Product," *Foreign Affairs* 52 (April 1974): 437.

12. John Lewis Gaddis, "Toward the Post–Cold War World," *Foreign Affairs* 70, no. 2 (Spring 1991): 102–122.

13. C. Fred Bergsten, *America in the World Economy: A Strategy for the 1990s* (Washington, D.C.: Institute for International Economics, 1988), p. 72.

14. *The Economist*, "Survey of World Trade," September 22, 1990, p. 6.

15. Walter Lippmann, *Western Unity and the Common Market* (Boston: Little, Brown and Company, 1962), p. 38.

16. *The Economist*, "Survey of World Trade," p. 40.

17. These figures come from "The Rising Tide: Japan in Asia," *The Japan Economic Journal*, special supplement (Winter 1990): 4.

18. Lawrence Krause, "Trade Policy in the 1990s: Good-Bye Bipolarity, Hello Regions," *The World Today* 46, no. 3 (May 1990): 83–84.

19. Bergsten, *America in the World Economy*, p. 60.

3

The Japan That Wants to Be Liked: Society and International Participation

Masaru Tamamoto

After the ignominious failure in 1945 of its bid for expanded military and political power, Japan turned inward and toiled to rebuild the war-devastated lives of its people. Following defeat, and having lost their faith in the state's wisdom, the people no longer gave their allegiance to the national state. Their locus of primary allegiance and public identification became the corporation, the place of their work. There developed in Japan a culture of "corporate warriors" (*kigyo senshi*) with an ambivalent sense of the nation.[1] As Yasuhiro Nakasone, who would serve as prime minister in the 1980s, once complained, "As far as the Japanese are concerned, there is no state, it has such a scant existence."[2]

Throughout the postwar decades, each individual effort contributed to the successes of corporations, which in turn resulted in Japan's spectacular national economic performance. Now Japanese are ready to enjoy the benefits of nearly a half-century of hard work and to be recognized for their accomplishments. And they seek this recognition from the international world. In looking to the international world for recognition, there has been in Japan a corresponding resurgence of national pride. This process of reconstituting national identity, especially evident since the mid-1980s, has helped forge a public consensus in favor of increasing Japan's international contributions. Japanese tend to see international relations in personal terms. Hence, in return for their international contributions, Japanese want to be recognized and liked. Behind Japan's willingness to assume an enhanced role in international affairs is the society's desire to "feel good."

Herein lies one difficulty in reading Japan. Emotions such as the need to be liked are not normally part of the lexicon of students of international politics. After all, most analysts of international politics understand the world as a self-help system in which states seek to maximize their gains through cold calculations of national interests. The director of the U.S. State Department's Center for the Study of Foreign Affairs echoes a widespread U.S. tone when he writes that, in a world without Soviet military threat, Japan is feeling the stirring of liberation from its forced submission to U.S. domination, and Japan's choice is to go its own way and assert its independence.[3]

In fact, however, this is a misreading of Japan today. Despite differences between official U.S. and Japanese positions on certain issues, it is largely U.S. perceptions of propriety that the Japanese policy elite and public seek to satisfy in the search for international recognition. Although individual Japanese corporations may engage in world class competition, Japan does not want world political competition or leadership. Japan now has the capacity to shape international politics and a newfound willingness to take on responsibilities. Japan does not, however, have the will to become a rule-maker in the international system. Rather, Japan will continue to be content to work within existing institutions and practices, accepting those as given.

Despite ongoing passivity, Japan is undergoing a transformation in its international posture. Having achieved the twin postwar goals of acquiring wealth and guarding its international peace, Japanese are looking for a new set of goals. Thus, in conjunction with the process of reconstituting national identity and the search for international recognition, Japanese are talking of the nation's "third opening" to the world. More than an attempt to adopt a more active foreign policy, the notion of a third opening is about the reorientation of postwar Japan's societal attitudes toward international participation. The degree to which Japan's international behavior may be altered, however, is circumscribed by its national personality.

Nations have personalities. They shape the long-run pattern of the international behavior of nations. And, in the short run, they delineate the limits and possibilities of foreign policies. Thus, an effort to understand Japan's role in the post–Cold War world makes necessary an explication of the Japanese national personality.

When one looks for internal explanations for international behavior (so-called second-level analysis),[4] a customary focus of analysis concerns the effects of domestic political structure on decisionmaking.[5] In tackling the question of Japan's national personality, this chapter addresses the broader issue of cultural traits. As with other nations, Japan is bound by a national personality that, despite a degree of mutability, tends to endure through radical changes in political structure. Such consistency is evident in societal attitudes toward international participation under the prewar imperial state (1868–1945) and the postwar democratic state (since 1945).

Japan and the United States

Japanese tend to look to the outside world for a model and leader. For most of its history, Japan looked toward China. Between the mid-nineteenth century and 1945, France, Britain, Germany, and the United States also played such roles. In the postwar era, Japan has focused on the United States, and the most important determinant of Japanese international behavior has been its perception of that country. The degree to which the United States influences not only Japanese foreign policy but also the current process of reconstituting national identity should not be underestimated.

Japan remains possessed by the United States. The United States with which Japan feels most comfortable continues to be a powerful, confident, and responsible United States. In its current search for international recognition or a more prominent global role, Japan remains dependent on U.S. ratification.

Public opinion polls offer a glimpse of Japanese views of the United States. In a poll conducted in November 1991, 77 percent of the Japanese responded that U.S.-Japan relations are important; 59 percent responded that they have favorable feelings toward the United States, whereas 32 percent do not.[6] It should be noted that not having favorable feelings does not imply dislike. In a poll taken in January 1992—at the height of U.S. negativity toward Japan (economist John Kenneth Galbraith deemed President Bush's trip to Japan "possibly the most disastrous journey since the Fourth Crusade")[7]—when specifically asked to name a country the Japanese dislike, only 6.7 percent named the United States.[8] The United States is the country Japanese like by far the most and dislike the least. This attitude has been true throughout the postwar years, with the exception of the Vietnam War period when Switzerland, a nation with a peaceful image, ranked slightly higher.[9]

This psychological dependence on the United States is in part a result of World War II. The disaster of defeat impressed upon the Japanese the inherent ugliness of international politics. Thus, Tokyo sought to retreat from international politics and found the United States willing to act as a shield. Throughout the Cold War, the United States had been for Japan the protector and guide in international politics. As a result, Japan is dependent on the United States for its very sense of self. Now, with the end of the Cold War, Japanese society has made Washington into its motive force, or source of exuberance.

For many in the United States who see Japan as a potential competitor for world leadership, the notion of their country being Japan's source of exuberance is problematic, if not simply odd. To begin with, they are not in the habit of regarding nations as if they were personalities. Moreover, sources of exuberance, like the related notion of identity, are supposed to be found within oneself and not dependent on an outside source. But this supposition ignores the essentially passive nature of Japanese culture, which suppresses individualism and subjectivity. And, in that society, which is commonly described as group oriented and consensus seeking, the sources of identity, including exuberance, are found in the group and outside of the individual.

Language, which both expresses and molds cultural norms, underlines the passivity of Japanese culture. In a Japanese sentence, the subject generally remains undeclared, thus obscured, and verbs are formulated so that the subject is acted upon rather than acting upon an object. Even such individualistic acts as to eat, to love, and to think are not plainly stated; the "I think" as in "therefore I am" becomes "it can be thought that."[10] It is this passivity, reflecting the lack of subjective identity, that makes Japanese society seek U.S. recognition. In this context, U.S. recognition serves as a source of exuberance, as if the United States constitutes the group for the selfless Japanese subject.

Japan today is disoriented, for the United States is disoriented. The United States won the Cold War and the battle with Saddam Hussein, but the jubilation did not last long. U.S. victories failed to address the country's social and economic ills. Rather than concentrate on its own problems, the United States preferred to blame others. Thus, according to an often repeated phrase that captured the mood of President Bush's 1992 trip to Japan, the recession was a Japanese export. That notion, in turn, set the initial tone of U.S.-Japan relations for the post–Cold War era. In a U.S. public opinion poll conducted following the Bush trip, 65 percent responded that anti-Japanese feelings are on the rise and 63 percent responded that they make a conscious effort to avoid buying Japanese products.[11] Yet, in another U.S. poll reflecting a more balanced view, 75 percent responded that a major reason for the trade imbalance with Japan is poor management by U.S. business leaders.[12]

The U.S. public is extremely uncertain about the future. In stark contrast to the heady optimism that characterized the Reagan years, the population now seems fixated with pessimism, and that attitude translates into ambivalence with shades of hostility toward Japan. Years from now, the Japan-bashing of the late 1980s and 1990s will be seen for what it really is: the U.S. domestic debate on the making of a post–Cold War society. For the time being, the U.S. public will continue to vent its anxiety toward Japan with heated rhetoric. And that makes the Japanese, who continue to see their nation's place in the world through its relationship with the United States, nervous. In a November 1991 opinion poll, 52 percent of the Japanese respondents thought that the post–Cold War world was heading toward instability.[13]

The meeting between an anxiety-ridden United States and an affection-seeking Japan is not benign. Serious damage can be done to what is simultaneously the most important bilateral relationship of the United States and the one it understands least. Although the fundamentals of the relationship between the two pillars of liberal international order are sound, emotions can wreak havoc. In both countries, constructive leadership is lacking; consequently, the people are increasingly unsure of what to think of the relationship. According to Koichiro Matsuura, deputy minister of foreign affairs, although the two peoples continue to stress the importance of their bilateral ties, each side increasingly feels that the other is unreliable. And, Matsu'ura emphasizes, the deterioration of confidence in the other, more marked in the United States than in Japan, is cause for concern.[14]

The U.S.-Japan relationship, firmly anchored since 1945, is in danger of going adrift. During the Cold War, U.S. interests in Japan were rooted in geostrategic calculation. Although geostrategy certainly was critically important, Japan's psychological attachment to the United States also played a crucial role. That bond has now outlived the Cold War. The leadership of both countries must now forge a new rationale accompanied by a new set of rules capable of underpinning a healthy relationship. But the United States is suspicious of Japan's intentions. The truth, however, is that Japanese behavior is largely dependent on U.S. behavior. U.S. policy, then, is crucially important because more than formulation of a new set of Japanese foreign policies is at stake. Japan is again engaged in the fundamental redefinition of its national identity. How the United States behaves will influence the transformation of Japan's national personality.

Japan's Third Opening to the World

The Japanese have fulfilled their twin postwar goals of catching up economically with the advanced industrial countries and avoiding entanglement in war. Japan commands the world's second-largest GNP, and Japan's per capita GNP in nominal terms exceeds that of the United States. (In terms of real per capita income or purchasing power parities [PPP], Japan's PPP in 1990 was 79.4 percent, using that of the United States as 100.) The dissolution of the Soviet Union greatly reduced the possibility of Japan being dragged into a major war.

With these achievements, there arose in Japan discussion of the nation's third opening to the world (*dai san no kaikoku*). This search for a new role is an admission of the inadequacy of postwar Japan's willfully limited participation in international political affairs. It is also a recognition that the post–Cold War world is likely to suit Japan's commercial and pacifistic orientations. Japanese are resolved to bear greater world political responsibilities. The talk of a third opening signals the beginning of the formulation of a new set of national goals and the transformation of society to meet the norms of the world. Japan has opted to make the end of the twentieth century another historical turning point, although, to be sure, the third opening is much less dramatic and disruptive than the previous two.

Japan's first opening was announced with the Meiji Restoration of 1868, which put an end to feudalism and more than two centuries of deliberate national seclusion. The restoration launched Japan on the quest for modernity. The Meiji emperor's charter oath, celebrating the birth of a new Japan, read, "Evil customs of the past shall be broken off and everything shall be based upon the just laws of Nature; knowledge shall be sought throughout the world."[15]

Eight decades later, in 1945, Imperial Japan's unconditional surrender in World War II marked the second opening. Masao Maruyama, a leading liberal political thinker, captured the intellectual climate of the time when he declared that the defeat—the end of the valley of darkness of militarism, war, and rebellion against the world—again permits Japan to seek reason and rationality from the world.[16] Philosopher Tetsuro Watusuji blamed the mistake of militarism on Japan's retarded condition of modernity caused by the spirit and fact of isolationism of the feudal era, a handicap from which Japan had not recovered fully.[17] Conservative political leaders, including Shigeru Yoshida, who served as prime minister for most of the U.S. military occupation years (1945–1952), would evoke the Meiji charter oath to capture the spirit of another new beginning.

The two openings shared the urge to transform Japan according to dominant global norms, the West of Pax Britannica in 1868 and of Pax Americana in 1945. The outside world provided the primary impetus for these changes, thrusting them upon passive Japan by threatening imperialism in 1868 and actual military occupation in 1945. The intended third opening shares a similar urge and cause. The transformation, induced to a large extent by U.S. demands for burden sharing, shall be based upon the norms of the world, and Japan again looks toward the United States.

The Structural Impediments Initiative (SII) talks conducted between the United States and Japan during the 1980s symbolized the beginning of the third opening. The SII talks aimed to revamp Japan's domestic economic organization and procedures to make the Japanese economy accessible to foreign goods and capital. Although entrenched interests and habits were at stake, the Japanese were willing to mend their ways. They understood the changes to be requisite to their nation's full participation in international affairs. And, despite the sacrifice of certain vested interests, there were benefits. The gains accrued by Japanese consumers from the streamlining of the distribution system, for example, were evident. Washington sought to redress the bilateral trade imbalance through the SII talks; for Tokyo, at issue was the transformation of what critics in the United States called the "Japan system" in order to make itself more compatible with U.S. normative views. More than a trade negotiation, SII for the Japanese was part of the larger process of internationalizing their society.

Japan's opening began to falter in the early 1990s when the United States asked two things of Japan—one of which Japan was unable to do even if willing, and the other the one thing Japan was unwilling to do. The Bush administration asked Japan to contribute militarily in the war against

Saddam Hussein. Given the depth of its postwar pacifism, this was a request that Japan was unwilling to grant. In Japan's "peace" constitution, which was authored by the U.S. military during the occupation and which literally prohibits Japan from acquiring any instruments of war, is enshrined the society's aversion toward war. Japan's pacifistic idea is one of its few sources of innovation and leadership and served as a base upon which Japan stood ready to remake itself into a responsible world power.[18] When, during the Gulf War, Washington deemed that military participation in world affairs should be a vital component of Japan's internationalization, many among the Japanese public found the price too high. They initially thwarted the government's effort to pass a bill in parliament that would allow the Self-Defense Forces—whose constitutional status continues to be debated—to be sent to the Gulf. As a result of the Japanese refusal to dispatch troops to the Gulf, the $13 billion Japanese financial contribution notwithstanding, there grew in the United States a view of Japan as a selfish and untrustworthy ally. In Japan, there was growing frustration; the first major test of its willingness to become a responsible world power was an impossible one to confront.

Before the uneasy feelings on both sides of the Pacific could subside, President Bush arrived in Japan in January 1992 with an entourage of U.S. executives of automobile manufacturing companies. To the Japanese, the presidential message seemed to suggest that Japan must restore full employment in the United States, another impossible test. And the U.S. public seemed to attribute Japan's economic successes to sly and unfair tactics rather than to what the Japanese saw as the reason for their successes— nearly half a century of hard work.

At the root of the economic friction between the United States and Japan are two different patterns of capitalism in the process of accommodating each other. Yet the discussion so far on both sides of the Pacific assumes that there is only one form of capitalism. Thus both Japan and the United States ask whether the Japanese economy is compatible with capitalism. This question leads only to confusion and U.S. accusations of Japanese unfair practices. U.S.-Japan economic relations and the public opinions surrounding them will continue to produce friction until the diversity in capitalism and the legitimacy of the Japanese variant are recognized.[19]

The Gulf War and Bush's visit began to dampen Japan's enthusiasm for greater international participation. Behind the post–Cold War national consensus to assume greater world political responsibilities lies Japan's desire to be recognized for its postwar achievements as measured by the standards of the Western liberal international economic order. Yet, to the Japanese, the United States seems bent on repudiating Japan's achievements instead of according them prestige. Many Japanese also want the United States to approve of Japan's postwar pacifism. The passage through parliament of the peacekeeping operations bill in the summer of 1992, which readies Japan for the next U.S. request for a military contribution, is a testament to the importance Japan attaches to its relationship with the United States.

Natsume Soseki, a leading novelist of Meiji Japan (1868–1912), captured the current Japanese predicament some eighty years ago when he wrote of the frustration, ambivalence, and emptiness that must accompany the Japanese attempt to open itself, to pursue progress (*kaika*). Because the standards for opening come from the West and not from within, Soseki argued, each time a new standard is imposed, the Japanese, who do not even fully comprehend the old standard, are made to feel left out. He likened the process of Japan's opening to being served an exotic yet delicious-looking meal only to have it taken away before anything can be tasted.[20] For Japan, the world continues to be seen as something out there and apart. Today, Japan increasingly sees it as a source of frustration as well.

Between Uniqueness and Cosmopolitanism

The feeling that the world is something out there and apart is an enduring cultural theme that sways Japan between claims of uniqueness and longing for cosmopolitanism. In 1910, Count Shigenobu Okuma, one of the architects and prime ministers of Meiji Japan, authored a book titled *Fifty Years of New Japan*. It was written "to preserve an authoritative account of the development of the Empire of Japan during the fifty years that have elapsed since the ratification of its first treaties with the outside world."[21] Okuma portrayed the spirit and direction of the modernizing nation when he wrote:

> It is a most distinguished honour for me that His Britannic Majesty, King Edward the Seventh, Emperor of India, and our Great Ally, whose influence with Japan has been most widespread and salutary, should have granted me permission to dedicate this humble compilation to His Majesty's illustrious name.[22]

Okuma celebrated Japan's achievements in Westernization and sought to advertise them to the world. In a world where military prowess determined the rank and even the fate of nations, he claimed that the new Japan, which defeated Russia in war (1905), possessed a powerful army and navy, "but it was after Western models that we laid their foundations."[23] Okuma concluded the work by stating that the achievements of Japan

> are nothing but the results of adopting the superior features of Western institutions. That Japan has been enabled to do so is a boon conferred on her by foreign intercourse, and it may be said that the nation has

succeeded in this grand metamorphosis through the promptings and the influence of foreign civilization.[24]

Okuma's Japan stood ready to enjoy the benefits of a half-century of hard work at Westernization and to be recognized for its achievements by the West. It was a Japan ready to assume greater international responsibilities and to have its efforts recognized. It was a Japan wanting to be liked.

The Japanese response to the West paralleled that of other latecomers into this civilization. The inclination to covet full membership in the Western comity of nations has been the dominant motif of Japanese international relations since the mid-nineteenth century. Yet, at the same time, this covetousness has been cause for strains in cultural identity. Whereas Okuma glorified Japan's Westernization, for example, many Japanese anguished over the source of national self-respect. In a sensitive study of the intellectual climate of the time, Kenneth Pyle wrote:

> In making self-confidence dependent on Japan's achieving the civilizing values and institutions of the West, [Japanese] left unanswered the questions that most needed answering if Japanese were to believe in themselves. If . . . Japanese were equal in ability to Westerners, why had they not independently produced a society and culture equal to those of Western countries? Was there nothing of intrinsic value in the Japanese past?[25]

Japanese of the modern era have not been able to produce satisfactory answers to these questions. And there can never be satisfactory answers, given the way the questions are posed.

Such questions tend to sway the intellectual imagination and public mood during moments of societal and political uncertainty together with what the Japanese perceive as a rejection of their country by the West. These questions acquired increasing relevance, for example, after the West's refusal to include the Japanese demand for a racial equality clause in the League of Nations charter. Japan was invited to the Versailles conference as a great power, but not accorded full honor. In such moments, the Japanese tend to take refuge in claims of cultural uniqueness, sometimes coupled with a proclamation of superiority, as they did during World War II.

During that revolt against the West, the notion of Japanese culture "transcending modernity" (*kindai no chokoku*) captured the political imagination, and Western civilization became an object of denunciation. By transcending modernity, Japanese culture was meant to fuse the best of Eastern and Western civilizations and create a civilization greater than either.[26] The vainglorious attempt to invent a new source of national self-respect, and thus to free the nation from the nagging questions about the worth of native values, came to a fantastic end with the atomic bombings of Hiroshima and Nagasaki. Claims to uniqueness and spiritual superiority proved no match to the material prowess of Western civilization.

World War II was for Japan a heightened moment of deep cultural and spiritual crisis about its place in the world and history. The need to identify a source of national self-respect has lingered into the postwar era. After the war, Japan once again fashioned its national identity with the West as its standard. Today, Japan again seeks recognition for its achievements in Westernization and search for a source of national self-respect. And it looks toward the United States. Whether Japan can finally assume a cosmopolitan identity and shed the distinction of being a non-Western outsider is dependent largely on U.S. recognition of and willingness to accommodate Japan's historical and cultural yearning to transcend cultural difference into cosmopolitanism. An alternative remains the unproductive retreat into uniqueness.

The evolution of the postwar quest for cosmopolitanism can be summarized thus. Since 1945, Japan has gone through four distinct phases of cultural identity. The period 1945–1955, most of which coincided with the U.S. military occupation (1945–1952), was marked by an utter loss of faith in native cultural values and a powerful desire to identify with U.S. values. General Douglas MacArthur's observation at that time that Japan is like a twelve-year-old child seems an apt description of Japan's cultural confusion.

In 1955, the Japanese economy recovered to its prewar level, and the government's economic planning agency declared the postwar era over. From 1955 until the early 1970s, the Japanese gradually recovered faith in themselves. The mood was best described by social critic Shuichi Kato, who spoke of Japan as a "mutt" culture, a mixture of Japanese and Western values.[27] Kato sought to assure the Japanese of the value of the native traditions.

By the 1970s, social order clearly had been restored and economic prosperity reached an unimagined level. Japan's GNP surpassed that of Britain and West Germany. The pessimism privately expressed in the late 1950s by Shigeto Tsuru, a leading economist, that Japan would never be able to export enough to achieve full employment was completely dispelled. It was in the 1970s that the talk of Japanese uniqueness gained currency. Such talk underlined the argument that, according to Western economic standards, Japan's economic success was proof of superior native Japanese qualities. Many observers in the West saw this as Japan's continuing sense of separateness and even arrogance. The claim to uniqueness can be properly understood, however, as a reaction to the self-effacement, cultural confusion, and lack of confidence of the early postwar years.

During the late 1970s and 1980s, Western observers rescued Japanese from the possibility of cultural isolationism. In the United States, for example, an effort grew to learn and adopt Japanese management techniques.

Harvard sociologist Ezra Vogel's book, *Japan as Number One: Lessons for the United States*, translated into Japanese, became a best-seller.[28] Japanese read into the book and other Western efforts to learn from Japan the cosmopolitan implication and possibilities of universal application of Japanese cultural values. Predictably, it took a Westerner to make this argument compelling to the Japanese. The national slogan in vogue during the 1980s, "internationalization of Japan," captured the mood of a nation with a balanced sense of confidence, no longer swaying to the extremes of confusion and uniqueness.

Today this fourth phase of postwar Japanese cultural identity is under attack. "Japan bashers" and "revisionists," such as Karel van Wolferen (*The Enigma of Japanese Power*), claim that Japanese culture is fundamentally incompatible with the rules of the West.[29] Such a claim prods Japan to retreat once again into a sense of separateness from the world. If that should happen, Japan's willingness to shoulder greater world responsibilities would dissipate, with critical implications for the making of a post–Cold War world.

Competition and Leadership

Another cultural trait that shapes Japan's international behavior is its sense of leadership. Many Japanese see Malaysia's recent attempt to build an Asian economic zone to counter the European Community and the North American Free Trade Agreement as reckless. At the same time, they take note with a tinge of admiration the bravado that the economically inferior country shows toward the United States. Japan needs U.S. acknowledgment even for its bravado. Maverick politician Shintaro Ishihara's 1989 book, *The Japan That Can Say No*, became a best-seller in Japan because the United States found in the book proof of its suspicion of Japan's true intentions and made much ado about it. The Japanese bought the book to find out what the fuss was all about. The much touted Japanese defiance of the United States, which set the mood for the U.S. reading of Japan for the post–Cold War era, was made in part in the United States. To be sure, there always has been anti-Americanism in Japan, but it has been confined to the narrow margins of the political left and right.

The Japanese often speak of misunderstandings as causes of U.S.-Japan tensions. "If only the Americans understood what we are about" is a common Japanese sentiment. Indeed, behind the current travail in the relationship lies a critical U.S. misunderstanding of the Japanese conceptions of competition and leadership.

Whereas the U.S. public sees the "rising sun" challenging their supremacy, the Japanese want to run away from the contest for leadership. They understand such a contest to be self-defeating. Individual corporations thrive on both domestic and international competition; this is the nature of the market. But competition at that level does not describe Japan's perception of national competition.

Recently, Japanese automobile manufacturers have started to wonder in private whether the Ministry of International Trade and Industry is a U.S. government agency. The ministry has issued a series of administrative directives "requesting" Japanese automobile manufacturers to curtail exports to the United States to a level below that stipulated by the voluntary export restraint agreement and to raise prices. Moreover, Japanese automobile manufacturers agreed among themselves to lengthen the product cycle from four to five years to ease the "excessive" competition they pose to U.S. automobile manufacturers. Japanese have begun to employ collusive tactics, which the United States has been criticizing as predatory, to serve U.S. needs.

Practically speaking, Japan's continuing prosperity depends in large part on access to the U.S. market; thus Japan's goal is to further the already historically unprecedented degree of economic interdependence. In an interdependent world, it makes little sense to talk of competition among nations in a zero-sum manner; the idea behind interdependence is mutual gain. Thus, Japan is wary of the Malaysian proposal to create an Asian economic bloc for fear that it may jeopardize relations with the United States. The Japanese economy is simply too large to be sustained only by the Asian economy. When Ishihara proudly asserts that the "Japan that can say no" belongs in Asia, that can only be idle, if not dangerous, talk.[30]

For the majority of Japanese, the talk of Japan leading Asia is an acute reminder that its leadership was bankrupted in World War II. Memory of the one attempt in its modern history at world leadership sustains the conviction that Japan ought to remain passive. The war years exposed Japan's lack of ideas, which are necessary ingredients for leadership. Wartime Japan's pan-Asianism, which had been so inclusive and sought to accommodate the ideas of left and right, of Islam, Christianity, and Buddhism, had no substance. It was nothing but a cover for naked aggression. As Yoshimi Takeuchi, a leading scholar on Japanese political thought, put it, Japan's pan-Asianism absorbed all ideologies and stifled them; it was a pretense of an ideology.[31] Since the war, the marked routinization and depoliticization of society have made Japan even less fertile for ideological development. In a wealthy, stable, and faddish society, countercultures are commercialized and reduced to objects of consumption. Even the annual labor disputes (*shunto*) are choreographed into ritualized spring performances.

The intellectual justification for Japanese passivity is reinforced by cultural assumptions about the nature of leadership. Japanese do not contest leadership; one grows into the task over a long time. Leadership is a vocation that demands long training. The selection of prime ministers illustrates these notions. To become a prime minister requires decades of slow promotion through the ranks of the ruling party. Similarly, the Japanese assume that to lead internationally is a vocation for countries and takes perhaps centuries. If Japan is to lead, the present is the initiation of a very long apprenticeship.

The U.S. conception of leadership is different. Leadership is to be contested—democracy bestows upon everybody the right to compete for leadership. And because leadership is to be contested, the United States searches for challengers, especially during moments of weakness. And today, during a cyclical downturn of its economy in need of structural adjustments, the United States regards Japan as a challenge. Surely, the argument goes, Japan will translate its economic prowess into world political leadership and challenge the United States.

Indeed, there is willingness in Japan to assume greater world political responsibilities, but this is different from a bid for world leadership.[32] Japan is willfully a junior partner of the United States; it seeks to fulfill the functions of a middle power, not a great power.

Japanese society's conception of leadership and the memory of World War II constrain Japan's leadership and innovation. The extraordinary growth in Japan's international participation of recent years is mostly of routine nature. Japan has done little about issues calling for leadership and innovation. This pattern is disappointing to foreigners as well as a source of concern and criticism. Yet, Japan does not think that the United States will welcome its leadership and innovation. By definition, in a world led by the United States, Japanese innovation and leadership will be in areas in which the United States is uninterested or is in disagreement. Japan fears that any attempt at innovation and leadership will incur U.S. wrath and may cause irreparable damage to their most important relationship. The Japanese suspect that most of the U.S. public is happy with Japan's lack of innovation and leadership. Although there are many domestic obstacles, the biggest constraint to Japan's leadership and innovation is U.S. intolerance—perceived and real.

Japan as a Child

The Japanese tend to think of international relations in terms of personal relationships. They project their sense of debt, dependence, and other traits that are central in the functioning of their culture to their interaction with other nations. Japan's postwar diplomacy has been marked by apologies; its diplomatic language is filled with words such as earnest effort, goodwill, and understanding, often to the bafflement of U.S. diplomats who cannot tell whether Japan's promise to make an earnest effort is a yes or a no. But that is how the Japanese deal with each other, and how the country deals with the world. International relations thus conceived, the Japanese for most of the postwar decades have been prone to see their country as a child in relation to the United States as a parent.

Now, it is as if the child confronts a hysterical parent, and that threatens the child's sense of security and induces psychological instability. "American workers are lazy," the Japanese speaker of the lower house of parliament lashes out. The child truly does not want to further anger the parent; he wants the parent to calm down and normalcy to be restored in the relationship. The Japanese Foreign Ministry apologizes for any misunderstanding and emphasizes the speaker meant no insult. Yet the parent, aware of the physical strength of the grown child, finds the child's insecurity threatening. This is how one Japanese intellectual described the negativity that currently characterizes U.S. and Japanese attitudes toward each other. Even this analogy underscores the trickiness of the current predicament, for the implications drawn from the analogy in the two cultures are likely to be quite different. In the United States, the child is expected to surpass the parent, whereas in Japan a child is expected to continue to revere the parent.

There are many reports today in the U.S. press of the growing sense of superiority among the Japanese public. Yet, what dominates the Japanese mood is disillusionment with the United States. The pedestal on which Japan had placed the United States for so long is crumbling; it is supposed to be a model and object of admiration. When, as noted earlier, 77 percent of the Japanese in a public opinion poll say that the United States is important to Japan, this response from a people who think of the world in terms of hierarchy is an attribution of superior status to the United States. For those who place high value on order, the breakdown of the hierarchy is an unnerving prospect.

The primary cause of this disillusionment is U.S. diplomatic style, notably President Bush's January 1992 trip to Japan. And if style is the problem, the remedy may not be so difficult. Many Japanese found the Bush trip unbecoming and distasteful. Japanese experienced for the first time a U.S. president being less than lofty—U.S. presidents have grand designs; they do not merely peddle wares. And, when Bush pressured Japanese automobile companies to agree to sell U.S. cars in Japan instead of promoting the sale of those cars by U.S. companies, many Japanese were struck by its impropriety, by its "un-American-ness."

Most of the U.S. public remain unaware of the degree to which Japan holds their country in esteem. Prior to the Bush visit, Prime Minister Kiichi Miyazawa emphasized in his speeches that now is the time to help the United States, the country to which postwar Japan owes much. The public could well understand how a debt needed to be repaid.

The men of Miyazawa's generation currently lead Japan. Their views of the United States were profoundly affected by Japan's unconditional surrender in 1945. As young men, they experienced the humiliation of defeat and were awed by the superiority and attractiveness of U.S. society and its values—the fundamental sources of U.S. power. To further confuse their emotions, the U.S. victory had destroyed their own government, which had promised to make all Japanese martyrs to the imperial cause; the United States delivered them from seemingly certain death.

Miyazawa's generation could not completely rid its sense of awe of the victor. The Japanese of the next generation inherited that sense of awe. Although they did not fully share the older generation's depth of humiliation, nevertheless the United States served for them as a guide to the possibilities of material wealth and democratic freedom. But what of the younger generation? What do those in their twenties feel today—those who know only peace and prosperity and for whom World War II is arcane history? Do their attitudes toward the United States differ from those of Miyazawa's generation?

The answer is no. Indeed, younger Japanese are more likely than their elders to indicate positive feelings toward the United States.[33] Yet, as a casual visitor to Japan can observe readily, the younger generations do not share the older generations' awe. Youths who are fond of U.S. culture and values increasingly expect to be treated more equally by the United States than do their elders. The younger generations assume their country's right to cosmopolitanism. In time, the Japan led by today's youths is likely to look at the world less as "something out there" and feel itself more a natural part of the world.

What Is to Be Done?

Mankind has just survived the Cold War, in which Washington and Moscow had set the rules and norms of international relations. Concepts such as balance of power and mutually assured destruction had given meaning and substance to that era of international relations. And behind these seemingly sophisticated concepts lay base emotions for which children are castigated—"my stick is bigger than yours" and "you hit me first." Meanwhile, the rest of the world scrambled to guard national interests through alliance and nonalignment politics. Future historians will debate the excesses of Cold War international politics, whether clear thinking and human will could have averted a half-century of anxiety and brinkmanship tempting the fate of humanity.

The relationship between the United States and the Soviet Union constituted the rules and norms of Cold War international relations. The rules and norms of post–Cold War international relations are likely to be constituted by the relationship between the United States and Japan. The U.S.-Soviet "condominium" is about to be replaced by a U.S.-Japanese one.

Current trends point toward the primacy of economics in the emerging world order. The United States and Japan—the two largest economies of the world, which together account for 40 percent of the world's GNP—are natural leaders of the liberal international economic order. And they share goals and values. The historically unprecedented degree of economic interdependence between the two can be made the hallmark of a new world order. How successfully and with what speed the United States and Japan can establish a condominium will greatly influence the prospect, for example, of whether the European tendency toward autarky will be strengthened or weakened to create a more open and vibrant world economic order.

In the post–Cold War era, there is the opportunity to realize as the world's norm the shared founding spirit of the United States and postwar Japan, which, as George Washington articulated it in his farewell address, is to build a nation of commerce while avoiding the dark side of international politics. Whereas the United States during the nineteenth century and Japan during the Cold War could only strive to guard their notion of commercial and peaceful existence by avoiding involvement in international politics, now the two countries in cooperation—and only in cooperation, for it is the example of their relationship that matters—have the opportunity to remake the world according to their respective founding spirits.

What is to be done? There is clearly a lack of leadership on both sides of the Pacific to set a constructive mood for the relationship. A concerted effort in both countries is needed to improve the attitudes of the public. Because the fundamentals of the relationship are sound and mutually beneficial, altering public attitudes certainly is feasible. A solution may be as simple as the leaderships in both countries—especially those in politics and the media, who shape to a large extent what the public thinks—emphasizing what is admirable about the other country.

Democracy is a value the United States and Japan share. It is a value the two countries can spread in the making of a post–Cold War world. Democracy respects public opinion. It will be a shame if unwary public opinion in the United States and Japan denies mankind the possibility of constructing a more peaceful, prosperous, humanistic, and democratic world.

Notes

The author wishes to thank Philip Brenner, Tom Farer, Hwei-ling Huo, Nicholas Onuf, Kenji Takita, Jiro Tamamoto, and Nathaniel Thayer for discussing with him the psychology of U.S.-Japan relations.
  1. The Japanese public's ambivalence toward national identity and pride can be seen, for example, in the continuing controversy over whether the national flag ought to be displayed in public school graduation ceremonies. For a postwar trend

in public opinion toward national symbols such as the flag, anthem, and emperor, see NHK hoso yoron chosa-jyo, *Sengo yoron-shi* (History of postwar public opinion) (Tokyo: Nihon hoso shuppan kyokai, 1982), pp. 204–213.

2. Yasuhiro Nakasone, *Atarashii hoshu no ronri* (A new conservative theory) (Tokyo: Kodansha, 1978), p. 33.

3. Michael Vlahos, "Culture and Foreign Policy," *Foreign Policy* 82 (Spring 1991): 61, 65.

4. This chapter emphasizes the interpretation of Japanese international behavior as an expression of the nation's internal qualities. For a contrasting explanation that stresses the character of the international environment/structure, see Michael Mandelbaum, *The Fate of Nations* (Cambridge: Cambridge University Press, 1988), pp. 329–396.

5. Kent Calder addresses in Chapter 8 the constraints imposed by Japan's domestic political structure on pursuing a more active foreign policy.

6. *Asahi Shinbun*, November 18, 1991.

7. Quoted in Chalmers Johnson, "Japan in Search of a 'Normal' Role," mimeograph, p. 4.

8. "Jiji yoron chosa tokuho" (Jiji public opinion special release), February 1, 1992.

9. *Sengo yoron-shi*, pp. 182–185.

10. For a discussion of passivity in Japanese culture, see Hiroyuki Araki, *Nihon-jin no shinjyo ronri* (Theory of the sentiment of the Japanese) (Tokyo: Kodansha, 1976).

11. *Washington Post*, February 14, 1992.

12. *Time*, January 20, 1992.

13. *Asahi Shinbun*, November 18, 1991.

14. Koichiro Matsuura, "Tokyo sengen no rekishi-teki igi" (The historical significance of the Tokyo Declaration), *Gaiko foram*, no. 42 (March 1992): 78.

15. An English version of the 1868 charter oath is found in Ryusaku Shinoda et al., eds., *Sources of Japanese Tradition* (New York: Columbia University Press, 1958), p. 644.

16. The English translation of Maruyama's writings on the theme can be found in Masao Maruyama, *Thought and Behaviour in Modern Japanese Politics* (London: Oxford University Press, 1969).

17. For an effort to locate the cause of the disaster of militarism in Japan's failure to rid itself of feudal and isolationist tendencies, see Tetsuro Watsuji, *Sakoku* (Closing of the country) (Tokyo: Iwanami shoten, 1950).

18. For an explication of the Japanese predicament during the Gulf War, see Masaru Tamamoto, "Trial of an Ideal," *World Policy Journal* (Winter 1990–1991): 89–106.

19. For a critique of the inability of U.S. economic theory to explain Japan and the Japanese-type economies, see Chalmers Johnson, "Studies of Japanese Political Economy: A Crisis in Theory," in The Japan Foundation, *Japanese Studies in the United States*, part 1 (Ann Arbor, Mich.: Association for Asian Studies, 1988), pp. 95–113. For a discussion of the emerging literature that recognizes the variations within capitalism, see James Fallows, "What Can Save the Economy?" *New York Review of Books*, April 23, 1992, pp. 12–17.

20. For an analysis of Soseki's thoughts and the present, see Tamotsu Aoki, *Nihon bunka-ron no henyo* (Transformation of the theory of Japanese culture) (Tokyo: Chuo koron-sha, 1990), pp. 7–16.

21. Shigenobu Okuma, *Fifty Years of New Japan,* vol. 1 (London: Smith, Elder & Co., 1910), p. vii. The original Japanese version was published in Tokyo under the title *Kaikoku gojunen-shi.*

22. Ibid.

23. Okuma, *Fifty Years of New Japan*, vol. 2, p. 555.

24. Ibid.

25. Kenneth Pyle, *The New Generation in Meiji Japan* (Stanford, Calif.: Stanford University Press, 1969), pp. 146–147.

26. For a thoughtful historical analysis of Japan and modernity, see Yoshimi Takeuchi, *Kindai no chokoku* (Transcending modernity) (Tokyo: Tsukuma shobo, 1983). For a systematic inquiry of the issue in the contemporary framework, see Tokyo daigaku shakai kagaku kenkyu-jyo, *Gendai nihon shakai* (Contemporary Japanese Society), vols. 1–8 (Tokyo: Tokyo daigaku shuppan-kai, 1991).

27. Shuichi Kato, "Nihon bunka no zatshu-sei" (The mixed nature of Japanese culture), *Shiso* (June 1955).

28. Ezra Vogel, *Japan As Number One: Lessons for the United States* (Cambridge, Mass.: Harvard University Press, 1979).

29. Karel van Wolferen, *The Enigma of Japanese Power* (New York: Vintage Books, 1990).

30. For a discussion of Japan's place in Asia, see Masaru Tamamoto, "A New Order in Asia?: Japan's Uncertain Role," *World Policy Journal* (Fall 1991): 579–590.

31. Yoshimi Takeuchi, *Ajia-shugi* (Asianism) (Tokyo: Tsukuma shobo, 1963), pp. 7–41.

32. For an explication of Japan's limited will to power, see Masaru Tamamoto, "Japan's Search for a World Role," *World Policy Journal* (Summer 1990): 493–520.

33. *Jiji yoron chosa tokuho*, February 1, 1992.

4

Japan's Global Responsibilities

Yoshio Okawara

Japan's international contribution is a fashionable and much debated topic today among academic circles as well as in government, political parties, and business communities. Increasingly, greater numbers of Japanese recognize that Japan must play a more active role in the international community.

This issue, of course, is not new. In 1988, the administration of former Prime Minister Noboru Takeshita announced the "International Cooperation Initiative," listing three foreign policy areas that Japan would emphasize as important parts of its global responsibility: cooperation for world peace, quantitative and qualitative improvement of Official Development Assistance, and the promotion of international cultural exchanges. This initiative reflected growing awareness within the government that Japan should assume a greater responsibility in the international community. Both Japanese and foreigners welcomed this initiative. Because sensitive issues of peace and security had not been broached, the issue was not controversial.

The Gulf Crisis as a Turning Point

It was the Gulf crisis that sparked heated domestic debates about Japan's role in the international community, particularly regarding world peace and security. The Iraqi invasion of Kuwait was a great shock to many Japanese. The Japanese people disagreed among themselves concerning the seriousness of the issue. Setting aside the Japanese hostage issue, the crisis had only a limited impact on the daily lives of most Japanese. For this reason many people were inclined to act as if the crisis were someone else's concern. Public opinion was divided, and the proponents of "one-nation (unilateral) pacifism" hindered the Japanese government from fully participating in international crisis management.

Given these circumstances, Japan had great difficulty in working out a
policy package to contribute to international efforts to cope with the crisis.
The government lacked both a grand strategy and experience in such crisis
management. The Japanese people were not psychologically ready to make
sacrifices. Because Japan had enjoyed peace for the past forty-five years
under the U.S. security umbrella, the Japanese had come to take peace for
granted. The international community, however, did not allow Japan to
remain an outsider in the Gulf conflict.

In fact, Japan had a great deal at stake in the conflict. International
law and order are fundamental underpinnings of Japan's own peace and
security. Furthermore, Japan depends heavily on oil imports from the Gulf.
Indeed, Japan's vital interests were very much at stake.

Many observers, particularly in the United States, criticized the slow
Japanese decisionmaking, the lack of a physical presence in the Gulf, and the
indecisive attitude regarding Japan's role in restoring peace to the region.
Some even voiced doubts as to Japan's credibility as a U.S. ally. The
Japanese tended to feel ambivalent in response to international criticism. On
the one hand, some felt unhappy that although Japan was helping to pay bills,
it was not participating in important policy decisions made by the United
States. On the other hand, intellectuals in particular were disappointed by the
Japanese government's indecisive response to the crisis and were prompted
seriously to reconsider Japan's role in assuring world peace and stability.
This latter group felt annoyed that even though Japan made a substantial financial contribution, it made almost no visible contribution in terms of personnel. They also were disturbed by the government's lack of clear vision
and strategy regarding Japan's global responsibility. Hence, heated debates
began on what and how much Japan should do for world peace and security.

The debates continue, and the scope of discussions has expanded. The
Japanese now debate not only Japan's peace and security role, but Japan's
global strategy, or lack thereof, as well. The Japanese government prepared a Peace Keeping Operations (PKO) bill that the Diet finally adopted
in June 1992. Former LDP Secretary-General Ichiro Ozawa established a
special study group within the LDP to review Japan's role in the international community and to work out a new vision. Business groups such as
Keizai Doyukai also took up this issue. The *Yomiuri Shimbun* organized
a panel of intellectuals to discuss Japan's international contribution from a
constitutional point of view.

Changes in the International Environment
and Japan's Status

Drastic changes in the international arena necessitate a review of Japan's
global role. The East-West confrontation is over, and the economic power
balance among the major industrial democracies has changed significantly.

Today, the potential military threat from the former Soviet Union has declined substantially. Instead, uncertainties in the Third World and within the former Eastern bloc have become major sources of concern. Faced with global structural changes, each nation is obliged to reassess its own external policy orientation.

The traditional emphasis on military elements in foreign policy has gradually shifted to a new emphasis on economic factors. The relative economic power of the United States has declined, whereas that of Japan and Germany has grown over the past two decades. The United States cannot afford to manage by itself all the global issues handled after World War II. Many issues that confront the world cannot be solved by just one country. This change in the economic power balance has forced allied countries to review burden-sharing in various fields from a new perspective.

The response of the international community to the Gulf crisis has clearly demonstrated how crucial international coordination is today. Coping with regional conflict, preventing nuclear proliferation, managing the world economy, and addressing environmental issues all require concerted action by the international community. Japan is expected to play an active role, and it is in Japan's own interest to participate in creating rules and new systems rather than being forced to accept rules created by others. Hence, the world watches to see what course Japan will take in foreign policy in the coming years and what Japan will do for the international common good.

Japan's Role in the World

There is a rough consensus among the Japanese today, based upon the experience of the Gulf crisis, that Japan should assume a larger responsibility and play a more active role in the world. Various opinion polls clearly show this general trend. However, no one has yet devised a grand design for Japan's global strategy. Elements of such a vision, nevertheless, are evident in former prime minister Toshiki Kaifu's keynote speech to the National Diet in March 1990:

> The new international order that we seek must be one that strives: first, to ensure peace and security; second, to respect freedom and democracy; third, to guarantee world prosperity through open market economics; fourth, to preserve an environment in which all people can lead rewarding lives; and fifth, to create stable international relations founded upon dialogue and cooperation.

Yet, Japanese leaders have not created a consensus on what Japan should do in concrete terms to achieve these goals, particularly those pertaining to peace and security. This remains a sensitive issue, tethered to postwar pacifist sentiment.

Some Japanese argue that Japan should concentrate on economic efforts because Japan is a peace-oriented economic power. This is a typical unilateral pacifist argument, one that a priori excludes any security role outside Japanese territory. Proponents of this argument, however, are increasingly being isolated. Foreigners expect Japan, as an economic power, to participate in decisionmaking and policy implementation concerning global economic, political, and security issues. A great power cannot shirk responsibilities purely for internal reasons.

Japan must therefore find means of working within its constitutional and political constraints. Given Japan's unfortunate war history, various self-imposed restrictions continue to be necessary. As a result, Japan has an unbalanced power structure—it is a large economic power with a limited self-defense capability and many constraints on its security role. Therefore, Japan's contribution to international security inevitably needs to take a different form from that of other industrial democracies.

Japan must take a hard look at the tremendous suffering it caused to neighboring countries during World War II so that these mistakes will be avoided by future generations. This assumption of responsibility is also indispensable if Japan is to play a more active role in establishing peace and security in the Asia Pacific region. Although memories of Japanese aggression will linger, Japan should continue to foster the development of constructive relations with its neighbors.

Japanese initiatives are likely to concentrate on three major areas. First, Japan should assume responsibilities for world peace and stability. Second, Japan should continue to play a key role to ensure the sound development of the world economy. Third, Japan should join forces with other countries in addressing transnational issues. The 1991 Diplomatic Blue Book published by the Foreign Ministry elaborates these tasks. The Tokyo Declaration and Plan of Action announced after Prime Minister Kiichi Miyazawa's meeting with President George Bush in Tokyo in January 1992 also specifies tasks Japan will address, individually as well as jointly with the United States.

Japan's Role for World Peace and Stability

Despite the collapse of Cold War tensions, regional conflicts based on religious confrontations, ethnic tensions, and border disputes persist. Japan can be expected to help manage these conflicts in a variety of ways. First, Japan can pursue diplomatic efforts—bilateral or multilateral—to prevent armed conflict, ease tensions, and secure peaceful settlement of armed conflicts. Japan, for example, has been playing a key role in facilitating the peace process in Cambodia. Japan also will continue to exert leverage on North Korea to open its society to the outside through ongoing negotiations for normalization of the Japan–North Korea relationship. And Japan can participate in the Middle East peace process, helping to improve economic and social conditions in the region.

A second means of facilitating peace is through Japanese contributions to UN peacekeeping operations. Japan's contribution thus far has been mostly in helping finance the operations, but increasingly Japan will participate in truce observation teams and peacekeeping forces. Passage of the PKO bill may help Japan remain a respected member of the international community. Japanese forces joined in peacekeeping operations in Cambodia.

Arms control is a third area in which Japanese initiative can be expected. One of the most serious issues that confronts the world today is nuclear proliferation and transfers of weapons to conflict-prone areas. New uncertainties abound relating to control over the former Soviet Union's huge nuclear arsenal and the risk of a brain drain of former Soviet nuclear weapons scientists and engineers. Japan is in a position to cooperate with other countries to address these issues. Indeed, Japan can take the initiative in an international effort to dispose of Soviet nuclear warheads by offering both money and ideas. Former Prime Minister Yasuhiro Nakasone recommended such a policy early in 1992.[1]

Suspicion of North Korean nuclear weapons development is another source of international concern directly related to Japan's own security. Japan has worked together with China, South Korea, the United States, and others to press North Korea to accept nuclear inspection. The conclusion of an International Atomic Energy Agency (IAEA) safeguards agreement by North Korea in January 1992 was a welcome step. Japan should now seek full implementation of nuclear inspections in North Korea through both the IAEA and North-South mutual inspection schemes.

In the area of conventional arms transfers, Japan has a strict policy prohibiting weapon exports. Japan also has taken the diplomatic initiative in advocating a scheme for reporting weapon transfers to the United Nations. In the process of pushing this initiative toward eventual adoption in 1991, the Japanese government had to clear a number of hurdles raised by traditional arms-exporting nations, including China, which feared a serious impact on their export businesses. And, of course, nations facing legitimate security threats are concerned about maintaining weapons necessary to secure their defense.

Japan's friends are often critical of Japan's failure to take global political initiatives. Japan sometimes has found, nonetheless, that on occasions when it does attempt to lead, it encounters sharp objections from the major powers. During a recent annual meeting of the Asian Development Bank in Hong Kong, the Japanese government urged an increase in the bank's capital. This effort, however, was blocked by the U.S. government.

The fourth task for Japan is to promote the principles of democracy throughout the world in conjunction with the other industrial democracies. The spread of liberal democratic values will decrease the likelihood of armed conflict as countries make efforts to settle disputes by peaceful means rather than by force. In recent years, Japan has helped developing countries undergoing democratic transitions, such as the Philippines, to stabilize their domestic economic and social conditions. In April 1991, the Japanese government introduced democratization as one of the four elements to be considered in extending ODA to developing countries.

Japan's Role in the Sound Development
of the World Economy

The world economy is currently beset by bleak and sluggish conditions. Nations now face uncertainties surrounding the liberal multilateral trading system, the widening economic gap between North and South, growing economic frictions between developed and up-and-coming economies such as the newly industrializing countries, difficulties in implementing economic reforms in the former command economy countries, and a worldwide shortage of capital. These issues all impinge upon the sound development of the world economy. It is no exaggeration to say that Japan, as an economic power highly dependent upon the rest of the world for its prosperity, has special responsibilities in these areas that dictate three roles in particular.

The first role is to strengthen the nondiscriminatory, multilateral trading system. Relatively free trade is not only indispensable for the development of the world economy but also vital to Japan's own economic prosperity. Japan has an especially strong interest in successfully concluding the Uruguay Round of trade negotiations, and it is unfortunate that the Japanese government has been intransigent on the rice issue. In any country, opposing entrenched special interests is difficult. Yet it is incumbent on Japan to evaluate its long-term interests versus its short-term pain. Japan's agriculture system should be restructured to improve competitiveness so that it may stand on its own.

The second role for Japan is to join hands with other nations in assisting reform efforts in the former socialist countries. No one wants to suffer the consequences should these reforms fail. Successful transformation of former command economies into market economies and their incorporation into the global economy would have historical significance and produce a more stable and prosperous world. Japan has been extending support for economic reform in Eastern Europe through the Group of 24 framework. Japan contributed about 10 percent of the European Bank for Reconstruction and Development's funds and offered an economic package totaling $1.95 billion to Poland and Hungary when Kaifu visited these two countries in 1990. Substantial parts of this pledged amount have been disbursed to these countries as planned. One problem that remains unsettled is the $500 million loan offer to Poland by the Export-Import Bank of Japan that forms a part of the package. The Japanese government has been urging the Polish government that the improvement of economic conditions in Poland, including its agreement with the IMF for its economic reform program, is essential for expediting the actual disbursement of this credit from Japan.

Japanese support to the former Soviet Union is linked inextricably to the territorial dispute over the four northern islands. Yet Japan shares a common interest with the other industrial democracies in having a stable, pluralistic, peaceful, market-oriented Russia. Japan has been providing food and medical supplies as humanitarian assistance to help meet the population's basic needs. Japan has also been extending technical assistance to provide basic know-how to help in the transition to a market economy. In October 1991, the Japanese government offered the former Soviet Union a $2.5 billion economic package and followed this with a $50 million grant for food and medical supplies. Japan will continue to play an active role, striking a balance between participating in international cooperative efforts and pursuing bilateral negotiations with Russia to conclude a peace treaty.

The third role for Japan is to extend economic assistance to developing countries. The economic and social development of developing countries is vital to the peace and prosperity of the entire world. Japan has been active in this area, recognizing the interdependence of nations in the global economy. ODA has been an important policy instrument for this purpose. Japan is one of the top donors of ODA today. Between 1988 and 1990, Japan extended approximately $9 billion in ODA annually, and its ODA is set to increase further. In addition, Japan will improve the quality of its ODA, emphasizing grants and technical assistance over soft loans, and strengthening its administration by training more aid experts to ensure the effective use of Japanese assistance.

The Japanese private sector also has been active in direct investment and technology transfers to developing countries, particularly in East Asia. Japanese government policy encouraging creation of a favorable environment for investment in recipient countries helps to attract Japanese firms. Finally, throughout the past decade Japan has gradually opened up its market to absorb foreign exports, including those from Asian NICs, the ASEAN countries, and other developing countries. Serving as a market, a role the United States long has played, stimulates growth in developing countries. Increasingly, Japan will be playing this kind of a role. In all these ways, Japan has been the driving force for fast economic growth in East Asia. In the post–Cold War world, Japan must shoulder an even larger burden.

Japan's Role in Addressing Transnational Issues

Today, a growing number of issues cannot be solved by countries single-handedly. Global environmental issues, refugees, drugs, AIDS, and terrorism are problems that demand collective action. Such issues may be regarded as nonconventional sources of threat to mankind. With growing awareness of the serious nature of these issues, the world has been moving toward cooperative efforts to address them. Japan's emphasis on environmental issues in extending ODA to developing countries is a part of such efforts. Japan's financial contributions to international organizations for helping refugees and combating drug trafficking are others. Japan will further strengthen its efforts in these areas.

Institutional Frameworks

What kind of institutional frameworks should be used to address issues of global concern? This is an important question, and one that Japan must consider in fulfilling its global responsibility. The strengthening of the United Nations is an option that has been reevaluated in the wake of the Gulf crisis. The declaration of the 1991 Group of Seven meeting in London noted the enhanced role of the United Nations. The 1991 summit meeting of the UN Security Council also emphasized the importance of strengthening the UN security role.

Japan's policy stance is to make effective use of the United Nations as the world's most authoritative institution. No organization can compete with the United Nations in terms of universality. At present, it provides the best forum in which to address issues and to allow international community members to share a common recognition and build consensus through discussions and exchanges of information. It should be strengthened and utilized. The United Nations is too large a body for policy formulation and implementation, however, particularly regarding urgent issues that require immediate action.

To a certain extent, the UN Security Council can play such policy roles, but a variety of factors limit UN peace enforcement activities. First, a veto by a dissenting permanent member could paralyze the entire effort. China, for example, does not always share the same values as the industrial democracies. Second, individual states determine whether or not to participate in joint military operations. Third, Japan and Germany are not permanent members despite their large financial contributions. As Japan's involvement in world affairs increases, institutional reform of the UN Security Council should be seriously considered so that the permanent membership reflects the reality of the international power balance.

On balance, although the United Nations is an important body for building international consensus, it would be risky to expect too much of it. Hence the vital importance of policy coordination among the Group of Seven countries is clear. These are the core industrial democracies: Canada, France, Germany, Great Britain, Italy, Japan, and the United

States. These countries share common beliefs in freedom and democracy as well as in market economics. They share a strong sense of responsibility to the world, even though their policies are not always the same. In addition, these countries have the political, economic, and military means to implement policies. These countries have played a crucial role in world peace and prosperity and they will continue to do so. Because the diverse interests of nation-states constrain the United Nations, particularly in the security area, the Group of Seven must play a leading role while effectively using the authority of the United Nations for policy consultation and close coordination.

Japan has been advocating strengthening of the group's political functions, calling for more frequent, timely meetings of Group of Seven directors-general to discuss political affairs. Although the French have opposed such steps, the Group of Seven summit already has evolved from an economic summit into a de facto comprehensive policy coordination body. Japan will continue to play an active role within the Group of Seven framework. Among the seven, Japan is the only country that is not involved in any institutional policy-coordinating mechanism on political issues. Japan is not a member of the permanent five on the UN Security Council, the North Atlantic Treaty Organization, nor the Council for Security and Cooperation in Europe. Thus, the Group of Seven seems to be the only possible framework for effective policy consultation and coordination.

Thus far, Group of Seven ministerial meetings have been limited largely to financial issues. Recently, however, the group convened trade ministers and organized a meeting of environmental ministers. The group has discussed a meeting of labor ministers. With the globalization of production, the need for Group of Seven policy coordination is growing. Japan may decide to propose the creation of a permanent secretariat for the group to carry on liaison work among its members.

In addition to using and adapting existing institutions, Japan is likely to consider new organizations or frameworks for policy coordination to handle emerging issues, particularly international economic issues. For example, is a new trade organ such as a Multilateral Trade Organization needed to transform the General Agreement on Tariffs and Trade? Should a new framework replace the International Monetary Fund regime? Japan is likely to continue to consider such alternatives.

Domestic Constraints to Overcome

Money and Labor

Despite the international community's growing expectations, Japan has been slow to assume larger global responsibilities, due mainly to a number of constraints under which the Japanese government operates. Public opinion has been changing gradually since the Gulf crisis, but not drastically enough to enable the government to push through its foreign policy agenda, particularly in the peace and security field. A strong pacifist sentiment still remains, and Japanese are reluctant to accept tax increases to finance Japan's international contributions. The strong sense of crisis that emerged during and immediately after the Gulf War has tapered off. Awareness among the political parties of the need for a more active Japanese role in the world is growing, but views are divided, even among the members of the Liberal Democratic Party, on what Japan's peace and security role should entail.

Legislation and Financial Means

First, a deficiency in existing legislation must be corrected. After long and detailed deliberations on the PKO bill with particularly severe scrutiny of its constitutionality, the National Diet approved it, establishing the framework that enables Japan to participate in the peacekeeping operations of the United Nations. A unit of some 600 men of ground Self-Defense Forces has been sent to Cambodia to be engaged in the UN peacekeeping operations, undertaking cease-fire monitoring and civil engineering activities. It should be noted in this connection that Japan's constitution prohibits "the threat or use of force as means of settling international disputes."

Second, budgetary appropriations should be made available so that Japan can fully contribute to international causes in a timely manner. LDP Diet members recently proposed an international contribution tax to raise a certain amount of revenue tax, pool it in a fund, and use it, for example, in support of multinational forces deployed in the Gulf, Japan's future participation in peacekeeping duties, or as a contribution to a possible environmental protection fund. To date, nothing has come of this initiative. In any case, government and party leaders need to ensure that expenditures for international contributions be given high priority and that the process of interagency coordination and Diet deliberation be expedient so that timely disbursement of funds is possible.

Yardstick for International Contribution

These tasks are not easy to achieve in the short term. Without the strong support of the people, the government alone cannot effect such policies. Garnering public support for an international role in which Japan bears greater burdens for the common world good is vital. To attain this, strong, enlightened political leadership is necessary to educate the public and mobilize support. The Third Commission on Administrative Reform's

Subcommittee on Japan in the World emphasized this point in its interim report, issued in June 1991.[2]

The U.S.-Japan Commission on the 21st Century proposes that Japan pursue a policy target of earmarking 3 percent of its GNP for international contributions, including defense spending, ODA, contributions to international organizations, research and development funds for environmental protection, and the like. Such a yardstick may be useful to the government as leverage in mobilizing domestic support.

Japan should work out a medium-term target for each policy objective or policy instrument, as it has done with its ODA program. The Japanese government introduced various target figures for ODA, such as the medium-term target to extend $50 billion over five years from 1988 to 1992. It is time for Japan to pursue a policy of increasing ODA from the current 0.31 percent to 0.7 percent of its GNP, as advocated by the Organization for Economic Cooperation and Development (OECD).

Can Japan Display World Leadership?

What world role can Japan exercise in the future? Will the twenty-first century be an age of the Asia Pacific, with Japan at its center? Some in the United States and Europe suspect that Japan aspires to lead the world. These people either overestimate Japan's power or are simply enjoying a joke. Others argue that Japan cannot be a world leader because it will not be able to meet the necessary qualifications. In other words, Japan is an economic power and may become a political power in the future, but it cannot be a military power or a leader in the sense of creating universally accepted values. This assessment of the nature of Japan's power is probably closest to the mark.

Japanese leadership will involve collaboration with the United States and Europe to address world issues. The idea of a Japan-U.S. "global partnership" clearly indicates the global position Japan seeks—a partner, leading in cooperation with others. The role the United States has played in the postwar world is unique; no country can assume this role in place of the United States. The issue now in question is how to share responsibilities among the industrial democracies in an era of *pax consortis* led by the United States.

Japan is a democracy; it has taxpayers. If larger burdens guarantee a larger voice, this will serve to increase public support for a more active international role by Japan. This is one reason to support granting Japan permanent membership to the UN Security Council. Such a step would demonstrate to all Japanese that the sharing of burdens and power are two sides of the same coin of responsibility-sharing. Although this may be a chicken-and-egg issue, the important relationship between greater burden-sharing and a greater voice should not be underestimated. When the United States stresses greater responsibility-sharing by allied countries, it should be ready to incorporate them more intimately in the decision-making process.

Japan is an economic power with limited self-defense capabilities. Although most Japanese believe that Japan must play a more active role in the international arena, no consensus has been achieved on what Japan should actually do or what burdens it should bear. Japanese leaders should not rely on *gaiatsu* (foreign pressure) to handle sensitive domestic issues or wait to obtain a consensus before deciding an issue, but should take initiatives even at their own political risk before decisions are forced upon Japan by other countries.

The peaceful environment Japan has enjoyed for the past forty-five years, together with bitter war memories, have created among the Japanese a taste for peace, the so-called one-nation pacifism or unilateral pacifism. Using the momentum created by the Gulf crisis, the Japanese must turn this passive pacifism into active pacifism, enabling Japan to act more forcefully to defend, restore, and create peace as a member of the United Nations.

In view of the global scope of Japan's business activities, world peace and prosperity are indispensable for Japan's own peace and prosperity. Accordingly, Japan should take the initiative in reinforcing the postwar international economic system. The private business sector advocates harmonious relations with the world beyond Japan's borders. It is high time for Japanese business to act according to the concept of "live and let live."

Indeed, Japanese firms have taken to considering the question as to whether consumer interests have in the past received their due in Japan. This has been part of a broader effort to reexamine the relationship between business activity and social responsibility. Most recently, some Japanese business figures have been concerned about finding means of living together harmoniously with business communities overseas. These individuals have adopted the term *kyosei* (economic symbiosis) to describe their efforts.

Such concerns come in response to harsh foreign criticism of the "aggressive" Japanese business practices used to expand market share at any cost. The results of Japanese business practices in some cases have been to create unstable market conditions undermining local competitors. Although continued competition is desirable, Japanese firms need to adapt to local business environments.

In a variety of ways, then, Japan has been providing evidence of a growing interest in playing a constructive global role. Japan seeks to carve out such a role by emphasizing cooperation with other advanced industrialized economies within institutions that can address the increasingly complex problems of the post–Cold War world. Although Japanese attitudes, institutions, and policies will continue to change, this process inevitably will be a gradual one. As Japan adapts to new circumstances, it also will be important for other countries to recognize the depth and significance of Japan's international contributions.

Notes

1. *Yomiuri Shimbun,* January 27, 1992.
2. The Japanese government has created five consecutive Commissions on Administrative Reform in the last twenty years. The third commission, established in 1990, created the Subcommittee on Japan in the World to examine the basic philosophy of Japanese foreign policy at a time of growing international expectations that Japan would play a larger global role. The subcommittee produced an interim report in June 1991 calling for Japan to champion freedom and democracy in a peaceful and prosperous international community. It called for Japan to work for peace through a strengthened United Nations, international economic policy coordination, the promotion of market economies, and the resolution of global issues.

The subcommittee also called for Japanese government administrative reform to encourage greater outward orientation, enabling Japan to act more decisively and rapidly in its foreign policy. The government accepted these proposals and committed itself to pursue these recommendations.

Part 2

Security Issues

5

Prospects for U.S.-Japanese Security Cooperation

Norman D. Levin

Many observers have noted a central paradox in current U.S.-Japan relations: by many measurements the bilateral relationship is the closest and arguably the most mutually beneficial of any existing in the world today; yet the relationship is under greater assault and challenge. During many periods, acrimony suggests a fragility in the relationship that belies its importance to both nations. This paradox affects the security side of the relationship as well, with close, harmonious, and mutually advantageous working relationships juxtaposed against growing doubts on both sides of the Pacific about the wisdom and benefits of continued close association. Understanding the policy choices available to Japan's foreign policy makers requires an appreciation of the dynamics in Japan-U.S. relations. And any assessment of the prospects for future security cooperation between Japan and the United States must address both sides of the situation: the factors holding the relationship together as well as those pushing it apart.

At a time when national priorities are changing almost everywhere as leadership adjusts to radically different international and domestic conditions, it is important to return to first principles. Hence, this chapter reviews the underlying conditions, interests, and values that provided the basis for security cooperation in the past. It then examines the recent changes and their effect on these underlying foundations. The chapter concludes with an assessment of the prospects for security cooperation between Japan and the United States and the requirements for keeping the relationship intact for the coming decade.

Past Bases for Security Cooperation

The foundation for U.S.-Japan security cooperation is the Security Treaty between the two countries, which reflected the conditions existing at the time Japan regained its independence from the United States in the early

71

1950s. These included a Japan that was too weak to defend itself against external danger, a threatening security environment and a sense of vulnerability among the Japanese leadership, a domestic and regional environment distrustful of Japan and hostile to Japanese rearmament, a critical need for Japanese economic reconstruction, and the bipolar structure of international politics with the United States locked in global competition with the Soviet Union.

Japanese interests in this environment were clear: economic reconstruction, international political rehabilitation, and ensuring national security. Japanese leaders adopted a two-pronged strategy to meet these interests: (1) to concentrate on expanding foreign markets for Japanese exports to foster economic development, while nurturing Japanese industries and gaining control over high-value-added technologies critical to Japanese industrial competitiveness; and (2) to minimize military expenditures and maintain a low political profile, relying on the United States to guarantee Japan's external security. U.S. threefold interests were equally clear: (1) to prevent communist expansion and domination of the Asia Pacific region by any hostile power or group of powers; (2) to maintain U.S. access to and through the region; and (3) to foster the spread of market-oriented economies and liberal democratic political systems throughout the region. The United States tried to achieve these interests through the strategy of containment, with all of its regional assistance and defense pact accoutrements.

Their respective national strategies provided Japan and the United States strong incentives for cooperation. On the Japanese side, the U.S. role both in facilitating access to markets and technology and protecting against foreign intimidation made close ties with the United States a matter of paramount strategic importance. On the U.S. side, Japan's importance as a bulwark against communist expansion and as an Asian showcase of the virtues of free markets and liberal democracy made Japan important to U.S. global strategy. The revised (1960) Security Treaty between Japan and the United States formally codified these fundamental common interests.

The Mutual Security Treaty does much more than this, however. Formally titled the "Treaty of Mutual Cooperation and Security Between the United States of America and Japan," the treaty articulates a set of values that underpin the alliance. The preamble stresses in its first paragraph the desire of both countries to "uphold the principles of democracy, individual liberty, and the rule of law." It calls for "closer economic cooperation" and joint efforts to "promote conditions of economic stability and well-being" in both countries; and it reaffirms a mutual belief "in the purposes and principles of the Charter of the United Nations" and the commonly shared desire "to live in peace with all peoples and governments." The treaty goes on to stipulate that both countries will settle international disputes by peaceful means "in such a manner that international peace and security and justice are not endangered" (Article I) and will contribute toward the further development of peaceful international relations "by strengthening their free institutions, by bringing about a better understanding of the principles upon which these institutions are founded, and by promoting conditions of stability and well-being" (Article II).[1]

Subsequent articles in the treaty commit Japan and the United States to pursue economic collaboration and to strengthen security cooperation. It is worthwhile stressing that the treaty provides a comprehensive basis for the crucial relationship that has developed. For this reason, the treaty may be as relevant to the relationship today as it was in 1960. The treaty's emphasis on common values—and joint action to uphold these values—illustrates why the Security Treaty may be the most often cited and least understood document in U.S.-Japan relations. Far from simply swapping a U.S. defense commitment for access to Japanese bases, as critics often charge, the treaty articulates the rationale for a close and comprehensive alliance. Indeed, it provides a framework defining the fundamental bilateral ties of the two countries.[2] In this sense, the drafters of the treaty may have understood something better than many people today: that "threats" may come and go but values are enduring.

They also understood something else: their shared interest in regional security. This is reflected in the preamble's emphasis on the two countries' "common concern" with "the maintenance of international peace and security in the Far East," as well as in the repeated, explicit linkages thereafter between the "security of Japan" and "the maintenance of international peace and security in the Far East." Indeed, the Japanese provision of military facilities to the United States is described precisely in these terms: "For the purpose of contributing to the security of Japan and the maintenance of international peace and security in the Far East . . ." (Article 6). This description suggests a role for the Security Treaty of importance today but inherent from the beginning: maintaining regional stability. The drumbeat of concern about the "global" Soviet threat for the last couple of decades tended to obscure this facet of the treaty.

It is interesting to note, in this regard, that U.S. and Japanese definitions of threat—and of the severity of defined threats—have not always been identical. Indeed, at different times in the postwar period, Japanese and U.S. threat evaluations have diverged in important respects concerning all the communist powers: the Soviet Union, China, North Korea, and Vietnam. In the most notable instance, Japan successfully pursued its interests in China—through its "separation of politics and economics" policy—at a time when the United States was trying hard to isolate Beijing.[3] What has been crucial for U.S.-Japan security cooperation has not been that Japanese and U.S. threat perceptions are identical, but that they are sufficiently overlapping to undergird a sense of broad common interests.

Japan is surrounded by potential antagonists and has no "natural" allies. Together with its dependence on imported resources, these factors contributed in the postwar period to a strong and seemingly perpetual sense of vulnerability transcending any single, particular "threat." The United States, for its part, also has tended to view Asia as an uncertain and dangerous place—again, quite apart from the Soviet threat—requiring a substantial U.S. military presence. These shared perceptions have facilitated cooperative endeavors.

Although the bases for Japan-U.S. security cooperation are rooted in historical conditions, they also evolve over time. One criticism often made of the Security Treaty, for example, is that it is asymmetrical: The United States is required to defend Japan, but the Japanese are under no formal obligation to defend the United States. This criticism has merit.[4] Nevertheless, it is important to recognize the growth in Japanese security policies throughout the last two decades.[5] This growth has come in three main areas:

1. *Japanese defense efforts.* In response to strong U.S. pressures, Japan has significantly improved the capabilities of the Self-Defense Forces and assumed expanded responsibilities (to a distance of 1,000 nautical miles) for Japan's air and naval defense. New Japanese capabilities have significantly strengthened the SDF's ability to defend Japanese territory and the immediately surrounding areas, freeing up the United States—at a time of pressing demands and constrained resources—to focus on other defense priorities.

2. *U.S.-Japan military interactions.* Building on the "Guidelines on U.S.-Japan Defense Cooperation," formally adopted in 1978, Japan has significantly expanded its participation in joint operational planning and military exercises: it has increased its financial support for the U.S. military presence in Japan to the point where Japanese support now totals more than $3 billion annually, the largest contribution ever made by any U.S. ally and around 75 percent of total nonlabor U.S. costs. Japan has agreed to allow the transfer of military technology to the United States, and it has permitted U.S. military deployments, thereby improving Washington's ability to operate throughout the region and as far away as the Gulf. Defense industrial cooperation has grown in similar fashion, from U.S. military and commercial sales to licensed production of U.S. systems and now to full coproduction.[6] In the process, U.S.-Japan security cooperation has become increasingly close and taken on a global dimension.

3. *Broader Japanese international contributions.* Finally, also partly in response to U.S. pressures, Japanese leaders have broadened

their horizons: they have supported the United States on most major international political issues for the past two decades; they have endorsed U.S. positions on terrorism and arms control; and they have substantially increased their foreign economic assistance, a growing share of which is being allocated to countries deemed strategically important to the United States. With the principal exception of nuclear arms control, there is virtually no major international negotiation today in which Japan is not a participant, invariably in ways supportive of broad U.S. interests.

The point is not that Japan has dramatically changed its security policies. These policies show a fundamental underlying continuity throughout the postwar period: the nonmilitary components of security continue to be emphasized; the basic framework that has structured Japan's defense policies remains intact; and the Self-Defense Forces continue to be constrained by political, resource, and other limitations. Rather, the point is that Japanese policies have evolved over time. And with this evolution has come significantly expanded U.S.-Japan interaction. In the process, a greater sense of shared beliefs and habits of cooperation have developed that contribute to the effort to achieve common interests.

The Tokyo Declaration on the U.S.-Japan Global Partnership promulgated by President Bush and Prime Minister Kiichi Miyazawa in January 1992, potentially an important document, is a case in point. As recently as little more than a decade ago a Japanese prime minister was under assault for having used the word "alliance" to describe Japan's relations with the United States. Yet Miyazawa, in the Tokyo Declaration, was touting the "highly productive and mutually beneficial relationship of close political, security, economic, scientific, and cultural cooperation" achieved between the countries over the years; emphasizing the "shared principles" and "enduring values" of "political and economic freedom, democracy, the rule of law, and respect for human rights" that underpin this cooperation; and committing Japan to "create an even closer partnership" with the United States based on these principles and values that reflect both countries' acceptance of their "special responsibility" for building a "just, peaceful, and prosperous world."

The Tokyo Declaration does more, though, than merely symbolize how far Japan has come. It also reinforces the effort to contain bilateral economic tensions and create a basis for development of a broader "global partnership." As defined in the declaration, such a partnership has a broad mandate: maintaining world peace and security; promoting development of the world economy; supporting the worldwide trend to democratization and market-oriented economies; and meeting the new set of transnational challenges. This mandate is backed, moreover, by "action plans" in both political/security and economic/trade areas covering an ambitious range of

issues: addressing the proliferation of advanced weapons; promoting democratization and economic reform; enhancing cooperation on development assistance; strengthening regional political dialogue and economic
cooperation; promoting bilateral defense cooperation and interoperability;
enhancing cooperation on global environmental matters; cooperating on
international drug, refugee, and humanitarian issues; bringing the Uruguay
Round of trade negotiations to a successful conclusion; reinvigorating the
Structural Impediments Initiative; and enhancing bilateral trade and investment (to name just the more significant). Unquestionably, these ambitions will not be easy to fulfill, a fact reflected no doubt in the action
plans' general lack of specificity. But the ongoing process of seeking policy complementarity must itself be considered a basis for future security
cooperation.

Finally, the objective growth of interdependence bolsters the basis for
U.S.-Japan cooperation. Put simply, the two countries have become so
critical to each other's well-being that they can afford not to cooperate
only at considerable cost to themselves. Economically, access to U.S. markets is essential to Japan's economic health, and Japanese purchases of
U.S. Treasury bonds are indispensable to finance the U.S. budget deficit.
Politically, the demise of the Cold War has brought to the surface a new
set of international "threats"—massive internal instabilities in important
parts of the world, potential domination of critical regions by hostile local
powers, the proliferation of lethal and sophisticated weapons, environmental deterioration, and global disaster relief operations—which impinge
on both Japanese and U.S. interests and cannot be solved by unilateral action. Such interdependence reinforces the awareness of common interests
and constrains centrifugal pressures in the bilateral relationship.

To summarize, for the last forty years Japan and the United States
have significantly broadened the scope and deepened the extent of their
security cooperation. It is misleading, therefore, to imagine that the end of
the Cold War leaves Japanese policymakers free to pursue policies entirely
independently of the United States. Inevitably, managing the Japan-U.S.
relationship will continue to be Japan's most crucial foreign policy task.

Recent Changes

The multiple bases for U.S.-Japan security cooperation are currently undergoing considerable challenge as a result of changes in the global, bilateral, and domestic environments. Cutting across the many changes of the
past several years are three broad global trends directly affecting the
prospects for U.S.-Japan cooperation.[7]

The first, as is well appreciated by now, is the disintegration of the
Soviet Union. This, in turn, is part of a larger international communist crisis.

Among other consequences, this crisis has precipitated the radical transformation of Eastern Europe, the collapse of any global communist threat, and a formal end to the bipolar structure of international politics. The political and economic collapse of the Soviet Union has ramifications throughout Asia, constraining the ability of any successor state to use military force and intensifying the difficulties for Asia's remaining communist powers.

After more than four decades of nearly singular focus on preventing communist expansion, the United States is now left with neither a global rival nor a clear external threat. This new global context has created enormous uncertainty about appropriate long-term U.S. goals and weakened public support for continued U.S. assumption of a heavy international burden. At the same time, the Soviet collapse has freed the United States to focus greater attention on its domestic problems, the state of the economy, international competitiveness, and quality of life issues.

In Japan, the effect of the disintegration of the Soviet Union has been less pronounced. Historical animosities and continuing unresolved bilateral issues contribute to maintaining the chill in Russia-Japan relations. Few people expect a dramatic improvement in the short term, and a combination of power and proximity make Russia a long-term strategic concern to Japanese leaders. Nonetheless, the effect of Soviet disintegration has been significant: by removing the global communist challenge and transforming the bipolar international system, it has lowered public threat perceptions, weakened the domestic consensus supporting expanded U.S.-Japan military interactions, and bolstered Japanese voices urging the government to "say no" to the United States on trade and burden-sharing issues.

The second broad trend is the relative change in the balance of economic power between Japan and the United States. Japanese growth itself is part of a broader relative shift of economic power to the Pacific. In 1960, for example, the combined gross national products of China, Japan, South Korea, and Taiwan were roughly half those of France, West Germany, and the United Kingdom; by 1980, the four Asian countries surpassed those of the three Europeans, and could surpass the United States in combined GNP by the end of the decade.[8] U.S. trade across the Pacific now exceeds that across the Atlantic by around 50 percent, with East Asia accounting for more than one-third of total U.S. foreign commerce.[9] Trade patterns are matched by U.S.-Asian investment flows, which now total more than $150 billion. This shift in relative economic power has exacerbated anxieties in the United States over long-term U.S. competitiveness. It also has strengthened the image of Asian countries—first and foremost Japan—as rivals, if not "threats," rather than as security partners. This economic rivalry is particularly evident in the area of defense technology competition, where there is fear of a loss of U.S. preeminence; this contributes to growing calls in the United States for more restrictive policies toward technology transfers.

The third trend is the increasing primacy of domestic politics. This global trend stems partly from crises in the former communist countries and partly from a growing struggle between nationalism and interdependence. Although the dominant economic trend is toward the latter, interdependence is a two-edged sword: although it bolsters the impetus toward cooperation, it also weakens national control over economies. The globalization of major industries and internationalization of capital flows increasingly have challenged national boundaries, producing stronger pressures for a nationalist response. These forces have strengthened insular tendencies in the United States and fostered a political backlash against foreign aid and overseas spending.

The United States recently announced plans to reduce military spending by $50 billion over the next five years and to reduce the U.S. military force structure by roughly 25 percent globally. The Bush administration plans to reduce the military share of the federal budget to below 16 percent, the lowest level in more than fifty years, and to 3.4 percent of GNP, the lowest level since before the attack on Pearl Harbor.[10]

The Congress, however, favors even larger cuts. Current congressional proposals range from military cuts of $74 billion to $231 billion over the next five years.[11] Although U.S. force drawdowns from Asia have been modest relative to those from Europe, and are likely to remain so according to the Bush administration's plans, budget cuts of this magnitude would inevitably affect U.S. regional military capabilities as well. Perhaps even more important, they could cut into U.S. reinforcement capabilities and call into question the credibility of continuing U.S. defense commitments. Reduced U.S. military deployments could seriously undermine the fundamental tenet of U.S.-Japan security relations. Even if such drastic cuts are not implemented, the growing emphasis on domestic priorities will increase pressures on Japan and other U.S. Asian allies for expanded burden-sharing efforts that may not be politically sustainable within those countries.

At the same time, changes in public attitudes in both Japan and the United States indicate disturbing trends. Clearly there remains a certain dualism in public opinion, with indications of respect, trust, and admiration mixed with more negative images in both countries. Nevertheless, repeated polls suggest a significant erosion in feelings of friendliness. In the United States, a Times-Mirror survey found the proportion of people holding a favorable view of Japan fell from 70 percent in May 1987 to 56 percent in May 1990.[12] A Gallup poll in October and November 1990 for the Chicago Council on Foreign Relations found a full 60 percent of the U.S. public, and 63 percent of U.S. leaders, regarded Japan's economic power as a "critical threat" to the United States.[13]

There is a similar dualism on the Japanese side, with widespread recognition of the crucial importance of the U.S.-Japan relationship mixed with increasingly negative images of the United States. These images portray a fat and lazy United States unable to get its economic house in order and increasingly prone to blame others for its own difficulties. Such images have fed an incipient anti-U.S. nationalism, as one high-profile report suggested, and have begun to weaken support for cooperation with the United States.[14] They have also adversely affected public attitudes toward the security relationship: according to a 1991 Japanese government survey, the percentage of Japanese who regard the U.S.-Japan Security Treaty as either "useful" or "rather useful" fell from 71 percent in 1984 to 63 percent in 1991. Not surprising, the percentage of Japanese who want to protect Japan's security "with both the Self-Defense Forces and the U.S.-Japan Security Treaty as at present" fell from nearly 70 percent in 1984 to 62 percent in 1991, whereas those favoring abrogation of the treaty (in combination with either a strengthening or reduction of the Self-Defense Forces) rose from 12 percent to nearly 18 percent.[15]

In addition to these global and attitudinal changes, there may be a change of thought about the security relationship itself, at least in the United States. In the 1950s and 1960s, Japan sought to ensure a U.S. defense guarantee while limiting Japan's own obligations, essentially to maximize U.S. contributions and minimize those of Japan. Throughout the 1970s and 1980s, as noted above, Japanese leaders evinced a willingness to accept greater burdens, making defense the "happy" part of the U.S.-Japan relationship. But it did not alter Japan's fundamental orientation: do the least required to maintain close relations while pleading special circumstances as reasons to avoid larger responsibilities. This attitude produced what some have called the "if only" syndrome—"if only we didn't have Article 9," "if only Nakasone were Prime Minister," "if only the LDP had a broader support basis," "if only . . ."—which has been frequently used to rationalize Japanese inaction.[16] The United States tolerated Japanese foot-dragging in exchange for dominant leadership authority and gradually increased Japanese burden-sharing. Today something of a reversal of the traditional positions may be seen, with the United States seeking to maximize Japanese contributions to the alliance while minimizing its own responsibilities. The question is the extent to which Japan is prepared to assume significantly greater responsibility itself for the health of the alliance.

Prospects for Future Security Cooperation

If this new era is one of reduced danger of global conflict, it is also an era of enormous uncertainties. Nowhere is this more true than in Asia, where the domestic difficulties of the world's major remaining communist countries make their future particularly problematic and where the roles and relationships of emerging regional powers remain to be determined. The United States is currently struggling to adapt to the new era in timely ways to maintain global and regional stability. But there is considerable confusion in the United States about desirable long-term U.S. goals and appropriate national strategies for achieving them. In Japan there appears somewhat greater satisfaction with the status quo and less internal pressures to change long-standing policies. But even here one senses substantial ferment, as Japanese leaders perceive the need for new approaches and grope for ways to define more satisfying roles and responses. Clearly, the prospects for U.S.-Japan security cooperation hinge critically on how attitudes evolve and how the internal debates are resolved in each country.

Although the future is murky, at least a few things can be said about the bases for cooperation. First among those bases that have underpinned cooperation in the past, clearly the greatest changes have been in the objective environmental conditions. Of the five conditions identified in the beginning of this chapter, three have been fundamentally transformed (Japan is no longer weak, it has recovered from wartime devastation, and the Cold War is over) and one has been significantly altered (the external threat is far less salient today). Only one, antimilitarism, remains a major determining factor. These changes suggest that the 1990s will be a time of significant adjustment in U.S.-Japan security relations.

Important aspects of continuity should not be overlooked, however. Although Japan is no longer too weak to defend itself against external danger, its unique and largely self-imposed limitations constrain its ability to provide single-handedly for its own defense. This is most obvious in the nuclear area, where Japan lacks any deterrent or second-strike capability, and it is also true regarding Japan's conventional capabilities: the Self-Defense Forces remain uniquely unbalanced, for example, with no "offensive" weapons or power projection capabilities, and shackled by a host of political, technical, operational, and resource limitations.

The threat of Soviet aggression has now disappeared, but Japan nevertheless remains surrounded by potential antagonists and is still dependent on imported resources from distant and unstable parts of the world. The prospect of nuclear weapons on the Korean peninsula highlights the danger. Regional instability, together with the unique limitations mentioned above, reinforces the continuing Japanese sense of vulnerability.

The bipolar structure of international politics has ended, and with it the ideological competition between the superpowers, but, nonetheless, uncertainties remain about the future of the states of the former Soviet Union and the communist states of Asia. Potentially adverse developments, such as an explosion on the Korean peninsula or a fracturing of China, remain concerns in both Washington and Tokyo.

Despite dramatic changes in the external environment, basic U.S. and Japanese interests have remained more fixed, reflecting the fact that although a country's policies change in response to changing conditions, its fundamental national interests tend to have a more enduring quality. Assuming that the core environment is roughly as characterized above, the United States will probably continue to pursue—albeit at reduced levels of military forces—its historical interests: preventing domination of the Asia Pacific region by any hostile power or combination of powers, assuring U.S. access to and through the region, and fostering the spread of market-oriented economies open to U.S. exports and the growth of democratic values and institutions. If anything, the importance of these interests may even increase in certain respects, given the growing uncertainties. But two new interests are likely to be added to this historical list and to receive much greater emphasis than in the past: strengthening U.S. competitive capabilities and controlling nuclear and other weapons proliferation.

For Japan, intrinsic vulnerabilities will dictate continued pursuit of an open international trading system and association with the West. The uncertain security prospects of Northeast Asia and Japan's continuing geostrategic isolation will also necessitate continued focus—although undoubtedly at slower rates of growth—on improving Japanese military capabilities and securing Japan's national defense. Except in the unlikely event that Japan moves toward a Gaullist set of policies, which itself supposes a major change in U.S.-Japan relations, Tokyo is likely to seek continued military ties with the United States.

In sum, environmental conditions and national interests will probably provide a continuing basis for security cooperation between Japan and the United States. Both sides will have ample regional security concerns to justify continued cooperation, and neither will want to risk uprooting the foundation not only for U.S.-Japan relations, but also for the stability and security of the entire region. Given the reality of interdependence, moreover, neither will be able to address the new set of international issues without the other's cooperation. The role that security ties play in maximizing incentives to resolve bilateral economic frictions will give an additional, if perhaps somewhat diminished, support for continued cooperation.

U.S.-Japan security ties—like the broader U.S.-Japan relationship—are nonetheless facing a rocky road. The collapse of the Soviet Union has not only removed the sense of shared threat that gave immediacy to bilateral security cooperation, but it also has generated a whole new set of national preoccupations. Moreover, U.S. views toward Japan are experiencing a new and potentially dangerous volatility. The growing perception of Japan as a "threat" and potential "enemy" increasingly compares with earlier U.S. perceptions of the former Soviet Union and exacerbates the task of maintaining close cooperative relations. Such views are rogue factors in future U.S. security policy toward Japan. Whether the United States can constructively address legitimate problems affecting its global competitiveness and develop a basis for sustaining active international engagement in a world without a clear and indisputable external threat is a question affecting U.S. security involvement in the world more broadly.

On the Japanese side, the removal of the Soviet threat is undermining public support for a continued military buildup and diminishing tolerance for the more intrusive aspects (military bases and exercises, for example) of the U.S. military presence. Demographic and socioeconomic changes in Japan are increasing pressures on available resources. A renaissance of Japanese nationalism on both sides of the political spectrum is once again polarizing the defense debate. At a minimum, these changes will create a more complex Japanese political environment constraining the expansion of U.S.-Japan security cooperation. At a maximum, they could call into question Japan's fundamental orientation. Major efforts will thus be required by both sides to maintain the security relationship. A number of steps in particular are essential.

First, the U.S.-Japan Security Treaty should be maintained. The treaty has been demonstrably successful in meeting both Japanese and U.S. interests for the past four decades at relatively little cost to either side. It continues to provide a strong foundation for sustaining close relations as well as a flexible tool for responding to the uncertainties of the new era. Beyond this, the treaty plays important environment-shaping and hedging roles that should be candidly acknowledged: it anchors the United States in the region, a position that restrains Asia's communist states from adventurist actions and prevents a potential "vacuum" of power; it facilitates pursuit of regional tension reduction and arms control measures; it obviates the need for Japan to develop a fully independent military capability and thus reassures Asian states nervous about Japanese rearmament; it facilitates the political integration of Japan into the region and greater Japanese contributions to regional security; and it minimizes the possibility of political realignments that could be highly disruptive to regional stability. The treaty is not an absolute prerequisite for healthy bilateral relations, but recent changes in public attitudes on both sides of the Pacific suggest how much harder this objective would be to achieve in its absence.

Second, the treaty should be invigorated by bolstering its mutuality. Reducing asymmetries is an important first step. Japan is tiring of being presented with faits accomplis while being blamed for what it regards as U.S. problems; the United States is tiring of the perceived one-sidedness of bilateral security relations. Criticisms on the Japanese side that the United States is unwilling to share decisionmaking authority with Japan— only the burdens that flow from unilateral U.S. decisions—will continue, and Washington will complain that Tokyo is unwilling to assume responsibility for making decisions that involve increased Japanese burdens. Addressing such criticisms will require meaningful consultations, greater policy flexibility, and a more balanced division of labor. Increases in Japanese cost-sharing for the U.S. military presence in Japan have been significant and should be continued. At the same time, however, other burden-sharing issues besides purely financial ones should be pursued, such as prepositioning supplies and equipment in Japan for regional contingencies and improving integration of the U.S.-Japan communications infrastructure, which would be important in the event of a sudden crisis.

Third, Japan and the United States will need to move the relationship beyond the Security Treaty and develop a greater sense of common purpose. The leadership in both countries will need to seek ways to cooperate in maintaining a successful world order, including concerns about nuclear and ballistic missile proliferation, encouraging the spread of open markets, and fostering democracy and human rights, if the relationship is to prosper. Asia itself is facing potentially dramatic change, including a possible fracturing of the Russian republic, instability or possible systemic change in China, and unification or a violent explosion on the Korean peninsula. Whether Japan and the United States share perspectives on these issues and agree on how to share "global responsibilities" remains uncertain. New modalities for cooperation and ways to embed Japan and the United States in larger regional political and security relationships are needed. Determining common interests on these issues and working out concrete means for pooling resources is not only a prerequisite for sharing responsibilities, it is also a critical tool for justifying the continued security connection.

Finally, both sides need to demonstrate learning. Japan and the United States have each had unfortunate historical experiences in developing and sustaining a positive role in world affairs. Neither has much historical experience in operating as a genuine "equal." In the case of the United States, the challenge will be to avoid a return to isolationism and narrow economic nationalism while devising policies that both meet U.S. interests and allow for diversity. For Japan, the task will be to resist mercantilism and xenophobia while overcoming the insular "if only" mentality and contributing real ideas and solutions to regional and global problems. In both cases, the paramount need will be for leadership. The ultimate prospects for U.S.-Japan security cooperation hinge on whether and how this leadership is demonstrated.

Notes

1. The text of the treaty may be found in U.S. Department of State, "Security Treaty Between the United States of America and Japan," in *United States Treaties and Other International Agreements,* vol. 11 (Washington, D.C.: U.S. Government Printing Office, 1961), pp. 1633–1635. For a similar point about the treaty's emphasis on values, see Masashi Nishihara, "New Roles for the Japan-U.S. Security Treaty," *Japan Review of International Affairs* (Spring–Summer 1991): 24–26.

2. Yukio Kashiyama, "To Avoid the 'Coming War'—A First Hand Observation of U.S.-Japan Relations," East Asian Institute report, Columbia University, New York, December 1991, p. 3.

3. Mike Mochizuki, "Japan and the Strategic Quadrangle," in Seweryn Bialer and Michael Mandelbaum, eds., *The Politics of the Strategic Quadrangle: The United States, the Soviet Union, Japan and China in East Asia* (Boulder, Colo.: Westview Press, 1990), p. 3.

4. Although the United States pressed hard throughout the 1950s for expanded Japanese contributions to U.S. and Western security (see, for example, the 1954 U.S.-Japan Mutual Defense Assistance Agreement, which stressed the need for increased Japanese "support of the defense . . . of the free world"), Japan restricted itself to a gradual and incremental military buildup geared solely to Japan's immediate territorial defense. Even in the revised Security Treaty of 1960, Japanese obligations to contribute to the defense of the United States were limited to "armed attacks against either Party in the territories under the administration of Japan" (Article V). The absence of greater reciprocity—and the difficulty many Japanese have in conceiving of security in other than narrow, self-centered terms—continues to plague U.S.-Japan relations, as seen most acutely in the case of the Gulf War and Japan's groping for a policy concerning participation in international peacekeeping efforts.

5. For a more elaborate treatment, see Norman D. Levin, "Japan's Changing Defense Posture," Report N-2739, Office of the Secretary of Defense, The RAND Corporation, June 1988.

6. I. M. Destler and Michael Nacht, "Beyond Mutual Recrimination," *International Security* (Winter 1990/91): 96–97.

7. For more elaborate treatment of these and other trends, see Norman D. Levin, "Security Trends and U.S.-ROK Military Planning in the 1990s," Report N-3312 Net Assessment, Under Secretary of Defense for Policy, The RAND Corporation, 1991; and Norman D. Levin, "The Strategic Dimensions of Japanese Foreign Policy," in Gerald Curtis, ed., *Japanese Foreign Policy in the Post–Cold War World: Coping with Change* (Armonk, N.Y.: M.E. Sharpe, forthcoming).

8. Charles Wolf et al., "Long-Term Economic and Military Trends, 1950–2010," Report N-2757-USDP, Under Secretary of Defense for Policy, The RAND Corporation, April 1989, p. 7.

9. Richard Solomon, "The Promise of Pacific Cooperation," *Current Policy*, no. 1208 (Washington, D.C.: U.S. Department of State, October 1989).

10. This information comes from a statement by Secretary of Defense Dick Cheney before the Armed Services Committee in connection with the FY 1993 budget for the Department of Defense. Department of Defense, Washington, D.C., January 31, 1992.

11. *Los Angeles Times*, February 26, 1992.

12. *Washington Post*, September 19, 1990.

13. The decreasing regard for Japan was one of the major themes to emerge from this comprehensive survey of U.S. attitudes toward global issues. Ed Rielly, *American Public Opinion and U.S. Foreign Policy 1991* (Chicago: The Chicago Council on Foreign Relations, 1991), p. 7.

14. The report was prepared by Professors Seizaburo Sato and Shinichi Kitaoka for the Japan International Affairs Institute, a research institute run under the auspices of Japan's Foreign Ministry. A summary of the report is in *Yomiuri Shinbun*, March 18, 1991.

15. "Jieitai, boei mondai ni kansuru seron chosa" (Public opinion polls concerning the issues of the Self-Defense Forces and defense), *Boei Antenna* (July 1991): 35.

16. Michael Blaker, "Evaluating Japanese Diplomatic Performance," in Curtis, *Japanese Foreign Policy*.

6

Northeast Asia
and Japanese Security

Masashi Nishihara

During this century, international relations in the Asia Pacific region have been determined primarily by four powers: China, Japan, Russia or the former Soviet Union, and the United States. The collapse of the Soviet empire is likely to force Russia to play a low-key role for a while. Hence, the key strategic relations today involve the China-Japan-U.S. triangle.

Japanese are conscious of the need to play an active role on the global scene. The United States has been pushing Japan in this direction, particularly after the Gulf War. If the United States should move away from its forward deployment policy and withdraw most of its forces from the region, Japan's role might well increase significantly. Major new Japanese deployments, in turn, would create rivalry between Japan and China, destabilizing the regional security environment. Taiwan and South Korea, also emerging as new powers in Northeast Asia, add a new level of complexity to the already complicated power relations.

Taiwan, with the world's largest holdings of exchange reserves and more foreign trade than China, is economically integrating itself with Hong Kong and major parts of China's Pacific coast. Indeed, high economic growth in the western Pacific, perhaps eventually stretching from Russia's Maritime Province (Sakhalin), down to Indonesia, will benefit the region's security environment. Sustained economic growth will tend to generate economic interdependence, thereby restraining political tensions among countries in the area. Other developments, however, are disconcerting: in particular, the volatility of the Korean peninsula, with the world's heaviest concentration of hostile forces deployed along the demilitarized zone. The peninsula long has been a stage for major power competition. Hence, developments on the Korean peninsula will have important effects on relations among the major regional powers.

By examining in greater detail the concerns of the region's key actors, these new complexities become more understandable.

"Democratic" Russia

The new Russian federation—geographically identical with the former Soviet Union as far as East Asia is concerned—is emerging today as a friendly and cooperative power. Moscow recognized South Korea in September 1990 and improved relations with Japan despite the lack of significant progress on the disputes over the islands off Hokkaido.

Former Soviet President Mikhail Gorbachev visited Beijing in May 1989, normalizing relations with China. His visits to Tokyo and Seoul in April 1991 and the decision by his successor, Boris Yeltsin, to open Vladivostok to foreign commercial activities after January 1992 have also helped improve Moscow's image in Asia. Since late 1991, Russia has been a full member of the semi-official Pacific Economic Cooperation Council (PECC).

Japan and other Asian powers believe that the Russian military threat in the region has declined. Economic chaos and shortages of fuel and parts apparently are forcing the reduction of Russian military flights and naval activities as well as the closing down of bases in Vietnam. Confusion in the military chain of command and the decline of morale among both officers and the Red Army rank and file further weaken Moscow's military capabilities. Both Japanese and U.S. authorities maintain, nonetheless, that Russia has not reduced its capabilities, but has in fact added to its advanced weaponry.[1]

With the weakening of its military instruments of power, Moscow will develop its Asia Pacific diplomacy with greater vigor than in the past. The region is an attractive high-growth economic area, particularly when compared to Moscow's problems in the Caucasus, the Baltics, and Central Asia, where it is being blocked by the emergence of independent republics.

Nevertheless, Russia's entry into the Asia Pacific region may not proceed smoothly. To allay Asian fears of a revival of Russian military power, Moscow must convert its military-industrial complex into civilian production. Territorial disputes with Japan need to be resolved. Russia also faces difficult relations with North Korea and Vietnam, its former allies, to whom Russia has stopped providing oil and other commodities at subsidized prices since January 1991.

Furthermore, it is not certain that Russia's democratic transformation will proceed smoothly or that conservative forces will not regain ascendancy. Even if economic restructuring proves successful, Russian leaders might attempt to resume their country's military dominance in the region. In any case, for some time to come Russia will be so preoccupied with internal difficulties that it will not pose a serious threat to its neighbors. For now it has almost dropped out of the regional power game.

China: Dynamic and Unpredictable

In the aftermath of the Tiananmen Square incident in June 1989, the major powers tried to isolate China. China has, however, managed to end its isolation by tightening internal control, promoting economic open-door policies, and pursuing vigorous diplomatic initiatives. China's strategy now seems to be to resist U.S. "hegemony" by fostering close relations with Japan and other Asian countries while preparing to blunt Japan's political influence in the region.

China must also contend with the possibility that the rise of ethnic nationalism in the former Soviet Union will stimulate similar sentiment in China's own outer regions such as Inner Mongolia, Xinjiang-Uigur, and Tibet. Authorities in Beijing have, therefore, strengthened internal security measures in these regions. Added to the uncertainty of China's future is the potential of nationalist movements.

Deng Xiaoping and his reformist supporters have so far successfully gained the upper hand in their power struggle with hardliners and are pushing economic open-door policies. The leadership has been able to tame the high inflation of the late 1980s, the economy is growing at a rate of 7 to 10 percent annually, and foreign trade and foreign investment are expanding. In 1990, China's exports were 17 percent of GNP, and its imports were 15 percent.[2] Now further integrated into the world economy, China can promote economic democratization. China, however, faces numerous problems of adjustment to the market system: inefficient state enterprises that compete with private firms and the growing income gap between urban and rural areas are two examples.

The aging Chinese leadership has been able thus far to maintain tight political control while freeing up the economy. Party hardliners, however, fear that economic reform will lead to weaker central control and stronger demands for political democratization. They are also concerned about the reported emergence of economic "warlordism," with rising independence among the economically dynamic provinces. Fujian and Guangdong are becoming more closely tied to Taiwan and Hong Kong, respectively. Party conservatives also condemn Western nations for fomenting "peaceful evolution" against the communist system by advocating economic pluralism and human rights. Guangdong is said to be like "a colony of Hong Kong" and too rich for Beijing to control.[3] Guangdong's gross product is $31 billion, compared with Singapore's $35 billion and Hong Kong's $70 billion. Central control over these provinces has declined.

Elections held in Hong Kong last year gave a victory to the anti-Beijing party. Beijing charges the party with "meddling in mainland politics" by supporting political dissidents in China. The Beijing government is already trying to consolidate its political control in Hong Kong by intimidating the democratic opposition forces.

The potential for unstable relations between China and Taiwan, despite their shared pragmatic diplomacy—as well as between Beijing and Hong Kong—will continue.[4] The international status of Taiwan and Hong Kong was enhanced in October 1991 when both gained membership in the Asia Pacific Economic Cooperation (APEC) forum. Despite the success of Taiwan's ruling party over the Democratic Progressive Party (DPP) in elections in December 1991 for representatives of the Republic of China's National Assembly, the popularity of the DPP platform, which advocates an independent Republic of Taiwan, may increase in the future. With the admission of the two Koreas, the Baltics, and other former Soviet republics into the United Nations, Taiwan is increasingly prone to seek international recognition as a sovereign political community.

To the frustration of the Chinese leadership, Western powers, particularly the United States, regulate their links with China according to the nature of China's relations with Hong Kong and Taiwan. Hence, China often is isolated internationally as a result of what Chinese leaders see as interference in internal Chinese affairs. Indeed, China acts under a different set of rules or values from those followed by other powers. China so far has shown no interest in reducing its nuclear stockpiles in response to Washington and Moscow's agreement to reduce strategic nuclear weapons through the Strategic Arms Reduction Treaty and cut back tactical nuclear weapons. In fact, in May 1992, China conducted nuclear tests; the Chinese defense budget has increased more than 12–18 percent per annum for the past few years; China is said to be contemplating the construction of a helicopter carrier of 48,000 tons and interested in purchasing a half-completed carrier from Ukraine; Beijing bought air tankers from Israel; and Beijing has continued to supply arms to the repressive military regime in Myanmar (Burma), as it did to the Pol Pot forces in Cambodia. China's acquisition of these new weapons could make it a formidable regional power, affecting the naval balance in the region.

Japan Searching for a New Role

The end of the Cold War affected Japanese security policy as well as its foreign policy. As the Soviet military threat declined, Japan reduced its budget for arms procurement and delayed procurement programs, although its overall defense budget increased at the rate of 3.5 percent or so due to higher personnel costs. Increasingly active on the diplomatic scene, Japan also launched a national debate on what role Japan should play internationally.

Japan's current search for a larger global political role is not a new phenomenon. In 1983, for instance, Prime Minister Yasuhiro Nakasone attempted to increase the Japanese role in international security by taking a stand in support of the U.S. deployment of intermediate-range nuclear missiles in Europe to balance the Soviet SS-20 missiles that year. The end of the Cold War, however, further stimulated Tokyo to expand its role in international security issues; and in this regard, the government often expresses its aspiration to become a permanent member of the UN Security Council.

When the Soviet Union, under Gorbachev, applied "new thinking" to its policy toward Asia, Tokyo changed its policy toward Moscow, because to improve relations with Moscow would enhance a Japanese role in world affairs. Japan now extends economic aid to Russia through both multilateral and bilateral frameworks and, gradually, has modified its long-held policy of linking the scale of economic cooperation to the return of the disputed islands of Japan.

How soon the territorial disputes will be solved remains to be seen. Soon after the ill-fated coup in Moscow in August 1991, the Yeltsin government stated that "law and justice" should be applied to the solution of the territorial issue. The four islands off Hokkaido were occupied by Soviet forces in August 1945 after Japan surrendered to the Allied Powers. Japan has since maintained that Moscow's occupation of the islands is illegal. Because of the islands dispute, the two countries have not yet signed a peace treaty four decades after the end of World War II. An early solution of the territorial disputes seems unlikely because Yeltsin fears that returning the islands to Japan would inflame opposition from Russian military and other nationalist groups, thereby weakening his domestic position.

Japan is likely to limit its economic aid to Russia until the four islands are returned. Since the Group of Seven (G-7) summit held in Texas in 1990, Tokyo has been trying to mobilize the support of the G-7 behind its territorial claims, thus putting international pressure on Moscow. These efforts also reflect a more active Japanese diplomacy.

Japan also has been using its influence on the Korean peninsula. When Gorbachev decided to recognize South Korea, Pyongyang responded by seeking to normalize relations with Japan. Talks began in January 1991. North Korea, in desperate need of Japanese economic aid, seeks to reduce its international isolation. Progress in Tokyo-Pyongyang relations, however, has stalled over several issues, notably North Korea's alleged development of nuclear capabilities.

Given the uncertain security environment on the Korean peninsula and in China, Japan is moving cautiously in redefining its regional role. Japan's defense posture remains cautious, but in June 1992 it made a historic breakthrough by adopting a law that allows its Self-Defense Forces to serve overseas under UN peacekeeping operations. The Japanese Peace Keeping Operations law prohibits Japanese forces from engaging in dangerous missions, such as supervising cease-fires and demobilizing warring forces. It does allow them, however, to participate in such missions as constructing roads and bridges, monitoring elections, and police patrolling.

Thus, the Gulf War had a significant impact on Japan's future security role. Japan's inability to send any personnel, even civilian personnel, to the Gulf during the war embarrassed those Japanese who felt that their country ought to be sharing risks with other like-minded nations in seeking international security. The prevailing interpretation of the constitution prevented any member of the Self-Defense Forces, even military doctors, from participating in the efforts of the UN-supported coalition forces. The Kaifu government failed even to use Japanese civilian ships and airplanes to provide logistical support. But as a result of the new PKO law, Tokyo may have an expanded role in international security issues. Nevertheless, national debates on Japan's global role triggered by the Gulf War intensified interparty cleavages in Japan. The Social Democratic Party (formerly known in English as the Japan Socialist Party), the largest opposition party, led the opposition to government efforts to enact the law that allows the SDF to be used overseas.

The Economically Troubled United States

The end of the Cold War has placed the United States in an awkward position. The collapse of the Soviet Union has left the United States as the sole superpower, but economic problems make it difficult to act like one. In 1990, the U.S. trade deficit was $124 billion and its budget deficit amounted to $166 billion. Economic troubles may not allow the United States to maintain its overseas military presence or its international leadership.

The perceived decline of the Russian military threat plus economic recession in the United States strengthen the argument among a growing number in the United States that their country can and should reduce its commitments abroad. The Pentagon's 1990 document, *A Strategic Framework for the Asian Pacific Rim*, announced a three-stage plan for readjustment of troop deployments in the region.[5] The United States has already terminated B-52 deployments in Guam and closed some Marine Corps facilities in Okinawa, and it is promoting defense burden-sharing with East Asian allies to a greater extent than before.

Although the Pentagon is conscious of financial strains, it upholds a forward defense strategy. The document cited above maintains that the United States should stay in the Asia Pacific region. President Bush's trip to Australia, Singapore, South Korea, and Japan in January 1992 also brought that message to Asians. An assistant secretary of defense, James R. Lilley, stated in Singapore in February 1992 that it is wrong "to mistake the American troop reductions in the Philippines, Japan, and Korea as an indication of American withdrawal from the region."[6]

Because the United States trades more with Asia than with Europe— more than a third of total U.S. trade—it is likely to continue its military presence to buttress its economic interests. The United States will, therefore, probably retain its strategy for forward defense in the Asia Pacific region. The aircraft carrier, *Midway*, deployed for many years in the Yoko-suka, Japan, base, has been replaced by a newer and stronger carrier, *Independence*. Some of the functions served by the Clark and Subic bases in the Philippines are being handled at facilities in other Asian countries.

Diplomatically, the United States worked hard, consulting closely with Japan and South Korea, to prevent North Korea's development of nuclear weapons. However, tensions between Washington and Beijing over such issues as China's secret sales of long-range missiles to Iran and Syria and suspected assistance to Pakistan's nuclear development have hampered efforts to improve U.S.-China economic ties. U.S. displeasure with the events in Tiananmen Square in June 1989 led to economic and other sanctions against China. China's waning strategic value to the United States, given the emergence of a closer U.S.-Russia partnership, results in these frictions assuming greater significance than was the case in the 1970s and 1980s.

Is a Power Vacuum Emerging?

As the discussion above suggests, relations among the four major powers in the Asia Pacific region are undergoing a fundamental transformation. Russia is no longer a major actor, Japan aspires to more active economic and political roles, and although the United States is still the major Pacific power, its security commitment may weaken as a result of economic troubles. China may then wish to assert itself as the region's dominant actor. Under these circumstances, is a power vacuum emerging?

Japan, Russia, and the United States do not perceive a power vacuum in the region. Russia today expresses its desire to join many Western organizations and has become a member of the newly formed North Atlantic Cooperation Council, which works closely with NATO. Russia has also been accepted into the International Monetary Fund. Russian President Boris Yeltsin claims that Moscow considers Japan "a potential ally." To a degree unimaginable just three years ago, Japan, Russia, and the United States today share democratic political values, although the longevity of Russia's commitment to democracy remains to be established. Despite formidable territorial problems between Moscow and Tokyo, the two have ceased exchanging hostile remarks. The salience of military confidence-building measures and naval arms control has given way to that of humanitarian and economic assistance from Japan and the United States to Russia. In these circumstances, the balance-of-power calculus (and the notion of a power vacuum) appears to be in suspension.

The United States is adjusting to the post–Cold War era by reducing its defense budget, nuclear deployments, and troops overseas. Japan has likewise cut its appropriation for arms procurement programs. Neither of the two consider that a power vacuum requiring a military buildup has been created as a result of the collapse of the Soviet Union.

China, however, is an exception in this regard. The Chinese feel threatened by what they regard as a U.S. "conspiracy for a peaceful evolution" and consider that they must weaken the U.S. position in East Asia and the Western Pacific. Chinese leaders have often expressed displeasure with what they perceive as U.S. hegemony in the wake of the Gulf War. They have strongly resisted the U.S. interventionist posture over human rights issues. Furthermore, hoping to check U.S. influence in the region, President Yang Shangkun, during his visit to Malaysia in January 1992, expressed China's support for Malaysian Prime Minister Mahathir Mohamad's proposed East Asian Economic Caucus, a structure that would not include the United States.

U.S. officials maintain that the United States will stay out of Asian territorial disputes. This U.S. policy leaves China free to pursue its territorial claims. In February 1992, after China established a dominant position over Vietnam in September 1991 and the United States closed its bases in the Philippines in December of that year, China expanded its claims to the territorial waters of the Senkaku Islands, over which Japan maintains effective control, and the South China Sea islands, which are being contested by several countries in the region. China appears ready to protect by force its own territorial interests, a move that could create new tensions with Japan and other Asian countries in the future.

China fears that Japan is becoming a military power and has expressed concern about Japan having sent minesweepers to the Gulf in April 1991 and its plan to send its troops overseas as part of UN peacekeeping operations. A recent article in the *Beijing Review* reported that "Japan has become more active and independent in conducting its foreign policy in an attempt to fill the vacancy in the Asian-Pacific region left by the withdrawal of U.S. and Russian influences."[7] The Chinese tend to perceive, first, that a power vacuum has been created and, second, that Japan is moving to fill it.

The Korean Peninsula and the Four Powers

The Volatile Korean Peninsula

The Korean peninsula remains the most volatile spot in the region. Talks at the prime ministerial level aimed at unifying the two Koreas have yet to secure peace there. Unification will be a difficult process, and a growing number of South Koreans fear that an abrupt collapse of the North Korean political system and a swift attempt at unification would be disruptive to South Korea.

One of the obstacles to the improvement of north-south relations is North Korea's nuclear development. The joint declaration issued on December 31, 1991, ensured that the peninsula would be nuclear-free and that the two Koreas would have mutual inspection of nuclear facilities. The declaration became effective on February 19, 1992, when the two prime ministers met in Pyongyang. Under a reconciliation accord, both sides pledged to honor mutual nonaggression. Yet, few signs indicate that the two sides have improved their mutual trust.

On January 30, North Korea, a signatory to the Nuclear Non-Proliferation Treaty (NPT), agreed to observe Article III of the treaty, which requires a signatory to conclude a safeguard agreement with the International Atomic Energy Agency. Just before an IAEA team went to Pyongyang, the North Korean government admitted that it had, in fact, experimented with producing plutonium, which can be used for military purposes. The IAEA reported that North Korea's construction of the buildings in question seemed to serve more than experimental purposes.

South Korea continues to suspect North Korean intentions. U.S. military analysts have been suggesting that North Korea could develop nuclear weapons within a few years, perhaps as early as 1993.[8] North Korea is reportedly transferring nuclear materials into secret underground tunnels in Yongbyon, 90 kilometers north of Pyongyang, probably to avoid international inspections or to avoid U.S. surgical strikes.[9] The U.S. government, in the meantime, has taken out all ground-based tactical nuclear weapons from South Korea and canceled an annual large-scale exercise ("Team Spirit") with South Korea for 1992. North Korea's response so far has not gone beyond the exchange of accords with South Korea. Its promise to implement mutual test inspections has not yet been put into effect.

As they have in the past, developments on the peninsula also involve the four major powers. Russia is the only nation among the four major powers in the region that has official contacts with both North and South Korea. Its relations with Pyongyang have been sharply reduced, however, due to Russia's termination of economic support, particularly oil supplies, and to ideological differences. The Moscow-Pyongyang military pact, signed in 1961, appears virtually defunct. Thus, China now seems more trusted by North Korean leaders than is Russia.

For South Korea, however, "democratic" Russia is politically more acceptable than is anti-democratic China. Yet, economically, South Korea finds it more advantageous to work with China than with Russia. Thus, China's influence over South Korea may become larger than Russia's before too long. In fact, China may well be speculating that if the two Koreas should develop their dialogue, it could increase its own influence over the entire Korean peninsula. China can probably act as an interlocutor for the two Koreas more effectively than can Russia. In this regard, China may be impressed with its opportunities for influence given the U.S. withdrawal of ground-based tactical nuclear weapons from South Korea as well as the U.S. cancellation of the Team Spirit exercises. Japan also seeks to influence North Korea through its economic aid, trade, and investment. Japan's role in the South Korean economy is clearly important.

South Korea today conducts a complicated but skillful diplomacy. It finds itself in a much better position in the international community than does its northern counterpart. Seoul wants to improve its relations with the north on its own terms: it has rejected the idea of a conference among the four external powers plus the two Koreas. It wants to ensure that Japanese payment of "war reparations" to Pyongyang would not jeopardize the process of unification. It resists the U.S. suggestion that the south is perhaps making more concessions toward the north than necessary. Over the longer term, therefore, Japanese and U.S. influence may decrease over the peninsula.

Unification Scenarios

It remains unclear just how Korea might be unified. The north has for some time proposed a Korean confederation in which the two Koreas would retain their respective political systems. The south regards this as unrealistic. When the south applied for a separate UN membership in fall 1991, the north quickly modified its position and also applied for a UN seat, although it still favors some form of confederation. A German model for unification is not likely for the peninsula because North Koreans are not likely to rebel against Kim Il Sung or his son to seek a better life. Bitter antipathy persists, and South Koreans do not want to carry a heavy burden in reconstructing the economy of the north, as West Germans are doing for former East Germans. The means of unification may emerge after Kim Il Sung leaves the political scene.

The Market Economy Tide

In Asia, communist countries such as China initiated market principles to strengthen their economies long before Gorbachev introduced market reforms into the Soviet economy. China adopted an open-door policy in the early 1980s, and Vietnam followed suit in 1986. In this sense, the impact of perestroika and glasnost has not been as great in these countries as in the East European economies. Yet with Mongolia and Russia moving toward market economies, the reform process in Asian communist countries is speeding up. Even North Korea is setting up special economic zones with ports open to Western economic activities to attract foreign investment and earn more hard currency.

Communist regimes in Northeast Asia cannot resist the attraction of market economies, despite their fears that economic decentralization will undermine the regimes' ideological foundations. China's Fujian and Guangdong Provinces now are "contaminated" by the capitalism of Taiwan and Hong Kong. Shandong Province is also being influenced by capitalist South Korea. The successful capitalist economies in the Western Pacific are integrating coastal parts of mainland China, a process that may spread to North Korea.

The Tumen River delta development project was officially taken up in Ulan Bator in July 1991 by the UN Development Program for the six countries of Northeast Asia: China, Japan, Mongolia, North Korea, South Korea, and Russia. The project, encompassing the boundaries of North Korea, Russia, and China's Jilin Province, is designed to promote economic interdependence among these countries, thereby contributing to regional stability.[10] Such development also would serve the Japan Sea littoral states. Another ambitious project aims at boosting the economies of the Japan Sea Rim by developing the Maritime Province and Sakhalin. Both these projects will depend primarily on Japanese, South Korean, and U.S. capital and technology. Successful development of these areas could lead to a Far Eastern republic seceding from Russia.

The trend of subregional economic integration between the offshore nations and the coastal zones of continental Asia will contribute to the improvement of political relations among them. Tighter economic interdependence could push forward the process of Korean unification as well as improvement in China-Taiwan and China-Hong Kong relations.

Such trends could undermine the remaining two communist regimes in Northeast Asia, leading to political instability along with the spread of market economies. The rise of large market economies on the continent might then induce Japan, South Korea, and Taiwan to place less stress on their respective political and security dependence upon the United States.

Territorial Issues: A New Source of Tension

The optimistic prospect of subregional economic development programs has to be balanced by a new source of regional tensions that has surfaced since February 1992, that of territorial issues. Japan is involved in all such issues: in addition to territorial disputes with Russia, Japan recently has developed tensions with South Korea over the latter's use of the waters around the disputed northern territories, as well as with China and Taiwan over the Senkaku Islands, located north of Taiwan.

Tokyo wants Seoul tacitly to recognize Japanese claims to the Northern Territories by abstaining from obtaining fishing permits from Moscow. Japan's dispute with China is more complicated. The Chinese Territorial Waters law, promulgated on February 25, 1992, apparently resulted from heated debates between anti–Deng Xiaoping hardliners and pro-Deng reformists within the People's Congress.[11] The law, which specifically mentions the Senkaku Islands as part of China and allows the government to use force in protecting them, was a victory for the hardliners. Internal power struggles are thus involved, and it will be difficult to withdraw the law.

Japan's territorial concerns involving South Korea and China are compounded by historical animosities. As a legacy of Japanese colonialism and military expansionism, Koreans and Chinese remain largely hostile to Japan today. Hence, Tokyo's protests over territorial issues may not be effective, and a firm Japanese line risks damaging overall bilateral relations. The Japanese government has emphasized the overriding importance of maintaining good political and economic relations with China and South Korea, but leading members of the ruling Liberal Democratic Party demand a tougher line.[12] Territorial issues, then, not only complicate Japan-Russia relations, but could also encourage Japanese hardliners to demand a stronger military capability to defend Japan's territories.

Prospects for Japan's Security Role

Emerging security trends in Northeast Asia pose several complex problems for Japan. On the one hand, the decline of Russian military capabilities and the end of Cold War tensions between Washington and Moscow have improved Japan's security environment. On the other hand, uncertainties in Russia, China, and the Korean peninsula make the Japanese apprehensive.

Joint economic development projects such as the Tumen River delta project can work to improve the climate of regional cooperation, which would help Japan's security environment. Should such projects result in strengthening Japan's already dominant economic role, however, they might invite political backlash.

Japan's neighbors will continue to welcome a Japanese policy of developing military capabilities of only a defensive nature. These countries understand Japan's potential to develop formidable military power based on high technology armaments. China would also like to limit Japan's regional political role, and South and North Korea express suspicion about Japanese military capabilities. It is crucial to regional stability, therefore, that Japan retain only a defensive military posture.

Japan's security role in Northeast Asia will respond to U.S. policies. If for financial reasons the U.S. military role should decline in the region, or should Tokyo lose faith in the credibility of the U.S. security guarantee, Japan might be tempted to increase its military capabilities. The worst scenario for Japanese security would combine U.S. abrogation of its security treaties with both South Korea and Japan, along with unification of a

Korea hostile to Japan and possessing nuclear weapons and long-range missiles capable of targeting Tokyo. Thus, the U.S.-Japan Security Treaty continues to play a critical role in stabilizing the region by providing a nuclear umbrella for Japan and discouraging Japan from developing an offensive military posture, including nuclear arms.

As Japan begins to play a larger political role in the region, a Japan-China rivalry could develop. Therefore, closer dialogue on security matters between the two countries is essential. China's strategic interest will be to contain the regional influence of both Japan and the United States while continuing to derive economic benefits from its contacts with them. For the Chinese, it remains unclear whether those strategic interests are better served by strong Japan-U.S. relations or a rift in those ties. For now, China could easily contain a politically and militarily independent Japan. In the longer term, however, China would face problems in managing a stronger Japan.

Japan is apt to be caught between Chinese and U.S. diplomacies. When the United States gets tough with Japan on economic issues, and when China criticizes Japan's wartime conduct, Tokyo will feel isolated and may be tempted to follow nationalistic policies. China will probably seek "friendship" with Japan, partly to encourage Tokyo to loosen ties with Washington. It will be up to Japan and the United States to strengthen their relations to further their mutual regional interests. For some time to come, the triangular relations among China, Japan, and the United States are likely to be the dominant factors affecting Japanese foreign and security policies.

Notes

Views expressed here are those of the author and do not necessarily represent those of the Japanese Defense Agency with which he is affiliated.

1. U.S. Department of Defense, *Military Forces in Transition, 1991* (Washington, D.C.: U.S. Government Printing Office, 1991), p. 5; Japan, Defense Agency, *Defense of Japan, 1991* (Tokyo: Japan Times, 1991), pp. 29–30.

2. Comparable Japanese figures are 9.7 percent and 7.9 percent, respectively, and U.S. figures are 7.2 percent and 9.2 percent, respectively. *Japan 1992: An International Comparison* (Tokyo: Keizai Koho Center, 1992), p. 30.

3. Frank Gibney, Jr., "A World Apart," *Newsweek*, February 1, 1992, pp. 8–12.

4. Frederick Chien, "A View from Taipei," *Foreign Affairs* 70, no. 5 (Winter 1991/92): 93–103.

5. U.S. Department of Defense, *A Strategic Framework for the Asian Pacific Rim: Looking Toward the 21st Century* (Washington, D.C.: U.S. Government Printing Office, 1990).

6. James R. Lilley, "Tides," speech given at the First Asia-Pacific Defense Conference, Singapore, February 2, 1992.

7. Lin Xiaoguang, "Japan Seeks Greater Role in the World," *Beijing Review* 35, nos. 5–6 (February 1992): 10.

8. *Sankei Shimbun*, March 6, 1992, morning edition.

9. Reported in *Washington Post*, February 21, 1992. Quoted in *Sankei Shimbun*, February 22, 1992, evening edition.

10. Lincoln Kaye, "Hinterland of Hope," *Far Eastern Economic Review*, January 16, 1992, pp. 16–17.

11. *Sankei Shimbun*, February 27, 1992, morning edition.

12. *Sankei Shimbun*, March 7, 1992, morning edition.

7

Japan and the Future of Collective Security

Kenneth B. Pyle

In the autumn of 1945, as the U.S. occupation of Japan began, John Emmerson, a young foreign service officer, prepared to move into the requisitioned office of a Japanese corporate executive. Emmerson later recalled arriving "just as a Mitsui junior executive was clearing the last items from his desk." As he left, the Japanese "pointed to a map on the wall depicting Japan's Co-Prosperity Sphere. 'There it is,' he said smiling. 'We tried. See what you can do with it!'"[1] For the next half-century what the United States "did with Asia" was largely determined by the Cold War, although the broad goals of the United States were fundamentally the same ones it had pursued throughout the twentieth century, namely to maintain a stable balance of power in which no other country became so strong as to dominate the region, to preserve free trade patterns in the region so that it would be open to U.S. trade and investment, and to promote the evolution of democratic politics as the surest way to preserve a peaceful region.

In the 1990s, Asia is again on the threshold of a new era. The sudden end of the Cold War, the emergence of Japan as a regional and global economic superpower, and the relentless economic dynamism of the Pacific Basin are creating a new distribution of economic and political power and raising an entirely new set of issues affecting the fundamental structure of international relations in the region. These developments, above all, raise issues for the Japan-U.S. relationship in Asia, where for forty years the bilateral security pact and the growth of economic interdependence between the two countries have been a cornerstone of the structure of international relations.

The end of the Cold War requires a new definition of security in the Pacific (and in the world), one that takes into account the changed distribution of economic and political power in the region and identifies new institutions to manage this new distribution of power. What will be especially distinctive about any new world (and Pacific) order is the linkage between security and economic concerns. Accordingly, Japan's emergence as the leading economic power in the East Asia region—as trader, investor, aid-giver, and financier—makes essential the restructuring of bilateral Japan-U.S. relations as a foundation of a new Pacific order. The issue has not been systematically and forcefully addressed by either Washington or Tokyo. This chapter looks at the task of creating a new regional order and the roles that Japan and the United States might play in its organization. It examines Japanese responses to the concept of collective security in this century and recent changes of policy on this issue among countries in the region.

In an age of upheaval it is useful to approach such fundamental change from the perspective of history. Asia has previously experienced two great transformations of its organizing structure of regional politics in this century. Both came at the end of world wars, both were achieved through U.S. leadership, and both shaped the fundamental nature of U.S.-Japan relations for the succeeding decades. Both, however, ultimately failed to integrate Japan into a regional structure of international relations.

The Failure of the Washington Treaty System

The first transformation in regional politics came about after World War I had destroyed the imperialist balance of power in East Asia. At the Washington conference of 1921–1922, the United States attempted to reorganize the region on the basis of Wilsonian principles and to constrain the Japanese effort to secure preeminence in the region. The United States insisted on the termination of the U.K.-Japan alliance, believing that Japan was using it as a cover for its imperialist expansion at China's expense. The alliance was replaced with vague multilateral treaties in which the powers promised to consult if any threat to security arose. They promised to respect the open door and territorial integrity of China, they agreed to advance their interests through economic rather than military competition, and they concluded a treaty limiting naval armament.

The Washington system was a regional expression of the framework of international affairs formulated in the Covenant of the League of Nations and subsequently elaborated in such treaties as the Pact of Paris in 1928. It represented a commitment on the part of the powers to engage in multilateral consultation and cooperation to maintain regional stability. Japan was a founding member of the League of Nations, seeking the international recognition that such participation brought; but despite its status as a permanent member of the council it was from the start skeptical of the concept of collective security.

A new generation of influential political figures such as Fumimaro Konoe saw the League of Nations as part of a U.K.-U.S. effort to preserve the status quo, pitting the "have nations" (*moteru kuni*) against the "have-not nations" (*motazaru kuni*). Late developing countries such as Japan were condemned "to remain forever subordinate to the advanced nations" and, unless something were done to allow Japan "equal access to the markets and natural resources of the colonial areas," Japan, the young Konoe wrote in 1918, would be forced "to destroy the status quo for the sake of self-preservation."[2] Japan, the only great power not submitting a draft proposal for the League, never took an active role in the new organization. Rejection of the racial equality clause convinced Japan that its interests were not likely to be represented in the League. By 1928, the low level of Japanese participation in the personnel of the secretariat was indicative of its negative attitude toward this institution of collective security: the Japanese contributed 5 members; Italians, 23; French, 100; Swiss, 126; and British, 143.[3]

The Washington system failed to enhance international security because the United States, after establishing the system, ultimately failed to support it, much less give it leadership. Japan was never fully assimilated into the new order. Because it obliged Japan to withdraw its troops from Siberia, return the Shandong concession to China, and abandon its ambitious naval building plan, Shigenori Togo, who later served as foreign minister in the Tojo cabinet, described it as a "second Triple Intervention."[4] Shigeru Yoshida, a post–World War II prime minister, subsequently saw the dissolution of the U.K.-Japan alliance as destabilizing Japanese diplomacy and allowing China to play one power against another: "Without the stabilizing influence of the Alliance, our military men saw fit to overrun Manchuria and China; the Second World War started . . . and everyone knows what happened to us."[5] Although for a time induced to cooperate in the Washington Treaty System, Japan's fundamental objective of seeking preeminence in the region remained constant. Japanese planners reasoned that military and economic security were indivisible, that without unimpeded access to the region's resources and markets Japan would remain vulnerable. By the end of the 1920s, powerful domestic forces opposing the status quo as contrary to Japan's national aspirations rather easily outflanked the internationalists who wanted to cooperate with the Western powers to advance Japan's industrial interests. Japan denounced the Washington system and embarked on its own effort to establish a new regional order.

Japan's Abstention from the Postwar Order in Asia

The second great structural transformation of international relations in the Pacific was the establishment of the Pax Americana after World War II. Having eliminated the Japanese challenge, the United States sought to prevent the Soviet Union from achieving total hegemony in Eurasia through strategies of containment and deterrence that entailed the forward deployment of U.S. forces, the organization of a complex system of collective security arrangements, and massive aid and development programs designed to stabilize the region and promote democratic politics.

Again, in this new structure of Asian politics, Japan was not satisfactorily integrated—this time by its own choice. In 1950, John Foster Dulles and the State Department tried to establish a regional security organization similar to the North Atlantic Treaty Organization in the Pacific. Dulles proposed to Japan and other countries a Pacific pact, a regional defense alliance that would facilitate Japanese rearmament but keep it under international control. The pact would initially include Australia, Japan, New Zealand, the Philippines, the United States, and, perhaps, Indonesia. Dulles believed that such an alliance, permitted under Article 51 of the UN Charter, would internationalize Japanese military forces and "ease reconciliation" with the Japanese constitution. Dulles was prepared to offer guarantees and to override the objections of other Asian countries to secure their acquiescence to Japanese remilitarization and entry into a regional security organization.

Prime Minister Yoshida, however, was unwilling to participate in such a multilateral Pacific security system, which he realized would draw Japan into Cold War politics, force Japan to expend its limited and precious resources on remilitarization, and postpone the full economic and social recovery of the Japanese people. Instead, he was determined to use the circumstances of the Cold War to Japan's maximum advantage and to pursue relentlessly a narrowly defined sense of economic self-interest. He overrode the objections of other Japanese leaders, both conservatives and right-wing socialists, who advocated rearmament as a necessary response to the beginning of the Cold War in Asia. Instead, Yoshida contrived to trade bases on Japanese soil for a U.S. guarantee of Japanese security and keep Japan as lightly armed as possible so that the nation could concentrate all its energies on economic growth.

This policy, the Yoshida Doctrine, was carried on and elaborated by his successors.[6] As Yoshida confided in 1952 to an attentive young aide,

> The day [for rearmament] will come naturally when our livelihood recovers. It may seem devious [*zurui*], but let the Americans handle our security until then. It is indeed our Heaven-bestowed good fortune that the constitution bans arms. If the Americans complain, the constitution gives us a perfect justification [*chanto shita riyu ni naru*]. The politicians who want to amend it are fools.[7]

The young aide to whom Yoshida confided these views was Kiichi Miyazawa, who recorded his mentor's views in his 1956 book, *Tokyo-Washington no mitsudan* (Secret conversations in Tokyo and Washington).

It thus became an idée fixe of postwar Japanese diplomacy—it was an essential corollary of the Yoshida Doctrine—to avoid any collective security commitments. The constitution, as Yoshida here confided, gave a pretext for a narrow, self-interested foreign policy. Unlike Konrad Adenauer, chancellor of the Federal Republic of Germany, with whom Yoshida is often compared—who sought West German entry into NATO as a way of integrating his country with the rest of Europe, anchoring the Federal Republic to the West, and reducing concern over the German question—Yoshida was too much of a nationalist to favor anything but economic ties with Asia. Whereas Adenauer anguished over Germany's war crimes and took a positive attitude toward reparations for Israel, Yoshida resisted payment of reparations to Asian countries as "meaningless" unless they served Japan's self-interest by promoting sources of food and raw materials and establishing markets for Japanese products.[8] As a consequence, in the postwar period, until quite recently Japan's relations with the rest of Asia have been distant and largely limited to trade.

Yoshida and his successors built an elaborate set of policies to avoid involvement in international political-strategic issues and prevent Japan's being drawn into any overseas commitments whatsoever: in 1954 when, under U.S. pressure, the Self-Defense Forces were organized, the upper house of the Diet passed a unanimous resolution opposing the overseas dispatch of the SDF, a position the government had previously asserted on many occasions. Thereafter it became the set position of the government for nearly four decades that the constitution did not permit deployment of the SDF abroad, nor did it permit participation in collective self-defense or collective security arrangements. The Japanese government insisted that although Article 51 of the UN Charter recognized the right of nations to collective security, Japan's constitution did not permit such a right for Japan. Even though the constitution's preamble stated that the Japanese people had "determined to preserve our security and existence, trusting in the justice and faith of the peace-loving peoples of the world," Tokyo adopted the position that although it would rely on other nations to defend Japan, it would undertake no reciprocal obligations. In effect, Japan would be a special ward of the international community. It was a position precisely the opposite of collective security.

Contrary to what has been commonly assumed, the adoption of a position diametrically opposed to collective security was not forced on Japanese leaders by the imposed constitution. On the contrary, the U.S. drafters explicitly held that the constitution put no roadblocks in the way of Japan's full participation in collective security arrangements. At the time the constitution was drafted, Yoshida and other cabinet members expressed concern that Article 9 might prevent Japan's membership in the United Nations, because of the obligation of all members to make armed forces available to the UN Security Council. But Colonel Charles Kades, who was in charge of drafting the constitution, held that "it certainly was not an objective of the Occupation to put any obstacle in the way of Japan becoming a full-fledged member of the United Nations."[9] The Ashida amendments to the constitution provided the flexibility to participate in collective security arrangements if the government chose. Yoshida, however, wanted to avoid this alternative. When the nation subsequently applied for membership in the United Nations, Foreign Minister Katsuo Okazaki stated ambiguously that Japan would abide by the obligations in the UN charter "by all means at its disposal."[10]

After he left office, Yoshida came to regret the course he had set for the nation at this critical juncture. He seemed implicitly to acknowledge the dissembling way in which he had used Article 9 as a pretext to evade U.S. pressure to participate more fully in Japan's own defense and in collective security arrangements. He wrote in 1963:

> In my recent travels, I have met with leaders of other countries who have recovered from war and are contributing to world peace and prosperity. I feel Japan should be contributing too. For an independent Japan, which is among the first rank countries in economics, technology, and learning, to continue to be dependent on another country is a deformity [*katawa*] of the state. . . . For Japan, a member of the United Nations and expecting its benefits, to avoid support of its peacekeeping mechanisms is selfish behavior. This is unacceptable in international society. I myself cannot escape responsibility for the use of the Constitution as a pretext [*tatemae*] for this way of conducting national policy.[11]

Nevertheless, by the time Yoshida left office in 1954 the fundamental foreign policy course had been set: Japan would pursue an economics-first policy and a narrowly defined sense of its own self-interest. Yoshida's successors elaborated the Yoshida Doctrine by adopting the Three Non-Nuclear Principles, the three principles proscribing arms and military technology exports, and the 1 percent of GNP limitation on defense spending. Without these policies and their apparent constitutional sanction, the pressure on Japan to contribute in a direct military way to the Cold War effort would have been almost irresistible. (For example, over the course of the war, South Korea sent more than 300,000 troops to Vietnam, whereas Japan was able to avoid direct military involvement.)

This particular form of isolationism and the foreign policy that underlay it were a brilliant success. Japan could rely on its alliance with the United States to guarantee its security and maintain the international free trade order while Tokyo was free to follow policies of economic nationalism. As former Foreign Minister Sunao Sonoda told an Australian political scientist in 1975: "The Americans were always asking us to do this and to do that, to take over part of the burden of their Far Eastern policies. But all their efforts were sabotaged by one Japanese Cabinet after another."[12] The great power of the United States and its preoccupation with the Cold War, the conservative Kanji Nishio wrote in 1988, allowed Japan "to conduct a diplomacy that exploited and totally used the U.S. Even if Japan was asked to take some responsibility, we could get away with avoiding it and simply pursue our own economic interests."[13] Masataka Kosaka, a leading conservative theorist of the Liberal Democratic Party, admitted that the Japanese concept of "comprehensive security," which attempted to broaden the definition of security to include such items as foreign aid and earthquake and disaster relief and, therefore, to draw attention away from purely military aspects of defense, "has actually been an excuse, even a lie, to avoid greater defense efforts."[14]

Minimalist Interpretations of the Constitution

Following the war in the Gulf, President Bush told Prime Minister Kaifu at their California summit in April 1991 that he thought "most Americans understand the constitutional constraints on Japan."[15] It seems clear, however, that Article 9 has often been used cynically and interpreted by the conservative mainstream leadership to suit their political needs and their fundamental definition of Japanese national purpose—which was to concentrate exclusively on economic development. Interpretations have been political rather than legal judgments. That is possible because Japan's conservative and stodgy Supreme Court, whose judges are appointed by the Cabinet, has sidestepped every opportunity to interpret Article 9, declaring it a "political question." As a consequence, a political consensus of the LDP in effect determines the meaning of Article 9. Minimalist interpretations of what the constitution permits have been offered to avoid being drawn into collective security arrangements or the domestic controversy and disruption that would attend a more active foreign policy.

The growth of Japanese power, the end of the Cold War, and Japan's limited commitment to the Gulf coalition have made an issue of the minimalist interpretations of Article 9. For example, Masamichi Inoki, the moderate, scholarly, and widely respected former head of the National Defense Academy, currently head of a research institute on security problems, observed in the midst of the Gulf crisis that Japan, when it wanted to maintain a low posture in international politics and avoid actions expected of it by the international community, frequently resorted to what he called "the devious [*zurui*] measure of using the Constitution as a pretext." In uncharacteristically strong language, he condemned it as "a despicable way of escaping responsibility" (*kitanai nigeguchi*). Inoki, who does not favor constitutional revision, argued that the SDF should participate in UN peacekeeping forces. Under the constitution, he said, Japan possesses the full right of participating in collective security arrangements. This right was implied in joining the United Nations in 1956.[16]

The advantage of maintaining a low posture in international affairs since World War II has been the ability not only to concentrate exclusively on economic growth but also to avoid the extreme internal political divisions that an active foreign policy would engender. For most of the postwar period there has been a tacit agreement between the conservative mainstream and the left-wing progressive camp to avoid the divisive issues of rearmament and constitutional reinterpretation. Japan alone among advanced industrial nations has been shielded from the social stresses of an active foreign policy. But the cost of this low-posture policy is becoming increasingly clear.

The Yoshida strategy began as a means of handling the international politics of the Cold War and the domestic politics of pacifism. But as the years of its success lengthened, many of the institutions and processes required for an active and independent foreign policy were left undeveloped. Whereas the Ministry of Finance (MOF), the Ministry of International Trade and Industry, the Economic Planning Agency (EPA), and, on some issues, big business dominated the formulation of foreign policy, the growth of institutions of autonomous policymaking in the security field was stunted. Institutions of intelligence gathering, strategic thinking, crisis management, policy implementation, and, of course, the armed forces went undeveloped.

But a more costly and basic result of the moratorium that Japan has enjoyed is the state of internal Japanese opinion. As a result of the Yoshida strategy, the conservatives abnegated the responsibilities of leadership in a democracy to inform and educate its citizenry. The debate over Japan's role in the Gulf demonstrated the divisions—parochialism and isolationism—that sway Japanese views, even among the elite. The opposition to a more positive foreign policy—one that accepts collective security commitments—is less ideological today than it was in the past. Instead, opposition to the government's wholly innocuous United Nations Peace Cooperation bill in fall 1990, which would have permitted the dispatch of personnel to the Gulf, came from a mixture of complacency, anti-U.S. nationalism, and residual distrust of a situation in which the postwar restraints on an expanded military are removed. Decades of shunning collective security arrangements, accommodating left-wing opinion, and minimalist interpretations of the constitution have left Japanese opinion adrift and reactive in its attitudes toward post–Cold War foreign policy. The Gulf crisis demonstrated once again that the capacity for Japan itself to change, develop policies transcending its own narrow self-interest, and play a role of international leadership in a way that would satisfy world expectations is severely limited by the institutional legacies of the postwar experience.

In fall 1991, after assuming the prime ministership, Kiichi Miyazawa, acceding to international criticism and to pressure from the Takeshita faction to which he owed his election, gave his support to legislation that authorized dispatch of Self-Defense Forces abroad to participate in UN peacekeeping operations. The legislation, which gained Diet approval in June 1992, set five conditions for participation: a cease-fire agreement must exist, a Japanese role must be accepted by parties directly involved in conflicts, the UN force must be neutral, the Self-Defense Forces must be withdrawn once a truce collapses, and personnel would be allowed to use arms only in self-defense. Blithely altering his long-held position, Miyazawa said the dispatch of the SDF overseas would not be unconstitutional because they would have no intention of using force. He altered his stance, but it was the quintessence of the Yoshida strategy: He offered a pragmatic, minimalist concession in response to strong foreign pressure.

The Re-Asianization of Japan

One role of leadership is emerging that will follow almost naturally from the trajectory of the postwar Japanese state. That is the role of leadership of Asia's emergence as the world's most dynamic economic region. This role is developing almost ineluctably from the needs of the Japanese economy, international political-economic trends, and the predilections of Japan's dominant postwar institutions and their bureaucratic and business leadership. The implications of this development for the United States and the international system are substantial.

A remarkable convergence of developments in the mid-1980s provided the opportunity for Japan's evolution as the core economy of an increasingly cohesive and interdependent region. Since 1985, Japan has acquired an impressive array of economic tools that make it possible to establish economic leadership in the region—foreign aid, commercial loans, technology transfer, direct investment, and preferential access to the Japanese market.

Japan is today undergoing a process of re-Asianization. After deliberately remaining aloof from Asia for four decades, Japan is now focusing its attention on the region, a process driven by Japan's economic interests. In the last few years a Japanese strategy has begun to take shape that seeks to develop a more cohesive and interdependent region under a low-key Japanese leadership. With the facilitation of the government, Japanese corporations are integrating the region into an increasingly interdependent system of trade, finance, and production. This strategy involves the coordinated use of what MITI calls "the trinity" (*sanmi-ittai*) of trade, aid, and investment.

As Japanese economic power in Asia becomes more marked, the Japan-U.S. alliance as presently constituted will become still more paradoxical. The United States will confront in a stark way the need for a coherent policy that acknowledges the new distribution of power and integrates new strategic and economic realities. It appears that the U.S. security system will be keeping order for an economically and technologically thriving region dominated by Japan. Such an arrangement is of questionable stability. Despite the fact that U.S. forces have been in Japan not only for the defense of Japan but also to serve U.S. interests, it is unlikely that U.S. opinion will continue to support the maintenance of more than 40,000 military personnel in Japan, even though under an agreement signed in 1991 the Japanese government will assume by 1995 approximately half the cost of keeping U.S. bases and forces in Japan. The U.S. public is not likely to accept indefinitely a role akin to mercenaries, especially while running more than a $40 billion trade deficit with Japan and while trade friction grows unabated.

The end of the Cold War has vitiated the original purposes of the alliance, and it is now seen principally as a means of preventing the emergence of an independent Japanese military. To assign the Mutual Security Treaty the purpose of containing Japanese power and influence in the Pacific will not square with the prevailing nationalist mood in Japan. The day is likely to arrive when Japan will reject the anomaly of financing foreign bases that are there in large part to "contain" Japan, particularly when this situation contributes to a politically deferential and dependent foreign policy. If incrementalism at best, or drift at worst, continues to characterize the anomalous situation in U.S.-Japan relations, the alliance will continue to weaken in a way that is tantamount to its termination—with all the consequences of destabilizing the region and great power relations in the post–Cold War world.

Some astute observers in Japan fear that an end to the alliance would have consequences similar to those of the termination of the U.K.-Japan alliance (1902–1923). The veteran diplomat and strategist Hisahiko Okazaki observed in 1990:

> Japan's past militarism arose from the fact that the Anglo-Japanese alliance . . . fell apart. . . . In the early years of Japan's modernization the British navy ruled the seas, providing Japan with great security. . . . But the alliance collapsed, and the Japanese had to defend themselves without outside help. When a country has to guarantee its own security, it tends to go too far for fear of falling short. And Japan did just that. Today, similarly Japan won't become militaristic as long as it has an alliance with the United States. But if Washington decides to cut the tie, I predict that in just six months we'll revert to militarism.[17]

So dire a forecast needs no acceptance to conclude that the situation requires the establishment of a new U.S.-Japan equilibrium, a comprehensive revision of the alliance based on clearly defined new purposes, and a realistic process of achieving it.

The New Internationalism

Although Japan is divided, adrift, and reactive in its post–Cold War foreign policy, and the dominant impulse is to favor an extension of the Yoshida Doctrine—a concentration on economic goals, a modest security role, and reliance on the U.S. alliance—nonetheless, a constituency is growing in Japan for cooperation with the United States in a more responsible international role. Cooperation in the establishment of a new multilateral security arrangement in the Pacific would appeal to what can be called a new internationalism that is stirring among the Japanese elites.

This new internationalism does not grow out of any fundamental liberalism (there is not a whiff of Wilsonian idealism in this) but rather from a broadened conception of Japan's own national interest. It is a new kind of nationalism or, as one Japanese political analyst called it, an "international nationalism."[18] In the mainstream of the LDP, in major ministries, and among leaders of big business involved in international trade, there is a dawning recognition that so great is Japan's stake in the stability of the international political-economic order, that now more than ever, to be a Japanese nationalist is to be, in a certain sense, an internationalist. The view that is beginning to take shape is that, having caught up with the West after a century-long struggle and having a confident vision of Japan's future economic and technological prowess, Japan's own interest is no longer best served by narrow mercantilist policies and a passive role in international organizations.

There are three fundamental tenets of this broadened conception of Japan's national interest. First, it is in Japan's national interest to give support and leadership to the institutions of a liberal international economic order. (Free trade is the ideology of the strong.) Second, Japan must of its own initiative and to its own advantage reform its institutions to bring them into harmony with international norms and expectations. Finally, the Japanese people must develop a new global consciousness, a more liberal nationalism that is respectful of other national traditions and that will provide popular support for a more responsible international role, including participation in collective security arrangements. These were goals that Prime Minister Yasuhiro Nakasone pursued with limited success during his five-year term (1982–1987). He was attacked on all sides: by the bureaucracy for overriding its prerogatives in trying to revise its narrow policies of self-interest; by the mainline conservatives, who wished to hold to the successful Yoshida policies of the past; by the left wing, which saw him undermining the constitutional limits on Japanese foreign policy; and by neonationalists such as Shintaro Ishihara, who regarded his plans as too deferential to the wishes of the United States.

In the 1990s, leadership of the new internationalism is being taken up by younger, tough-minded LDP leaders, most notably Ichiro Ozawa —probably the most interesting political figure in the party. During the Kaifu administration, as secretary-general of the party, Ozawa was the de facto author of the UN Peace Cooperation bill, insisting that SDF members participate without giving up their status as members of the military. Although the bill failed, he believed that introducing it and forcing debate on the constitutionality of sending SDF personnel to co-operate with international peacekeeping efforts was in itself a political achievement. In June 1991, Ozawa was chosen to head a special LDP study group on Japan's role in international society, and he said he wanted to use this position to lead a fundamental debate on constitu-tional matters. Ozawa stressed that Japan's identity as a nation was the issue. Was Japanese exceptionalism still viable? In a 1990 newspaper interview, Ozawa said, "We have to decide whether to say 'Japan is spe-cial and we can only offer money' or devise more comprehensive assis-tance through the U.N. that does not go beyond the bounds of the con-stitution. I believe the former would isolate us from the international community."[19]

In short, the internationalist point of view is still in a formative stage; and, as has once again been demonstrated by the Gulf crisis and its after-math, this view clearly does not yet constitute a national consensus. Nor is it likely to do so for some time. Except in response to outside pressure, there is to date neither sufficient political will, nor the necessary institu-tions, nor the values and cultural resources that would impel Japan to abandon the highly successful but narrowly self-interested policies of the past and assume a self-generated role of international leadership, even though its own long-term interest lies in such a course.

Japan's New Interest
in Multilateral Security in the Pacific

Among internationalists there has been considerable interest in a new multilateralism in Pacific security concerns. This interest has received some tentative encouragement in the region. More than is often realized, the countries of Southeast Asia (in contrast to the countries of North-east Asia) are increasingly prepared to accept an enhanced Japanese se-curity role, provided that the United States remains centrally involved even at a reduced level. In April 1991, when Prime Minister Kaifu met Thai Prime Minister Anand Panyarachun, the latter said that Thailand hoped Japan would play a multifaceted role and not restrict itself solely to economic activities.[20] A year earlier the Thai prime minister had surprised Japanese officials by proposing joint Thai-Japanese naval exercises.

Also in April 1991, the Philippines defense secretary proposed to members of the LDP that Asia establish a regional security system.[21] In the previous month, Indonesian President Suharto told Michio Watanabe, a senior LDP politician (now foreign minister), that Indonesia would understand if Japan were to send its armed forces on overseas peacekeeping missions. Singapore's new prime minister said the same.[22] At about the same time, Malaysia tried to persuade Japan to take the lead in forming a new East Asia economic group, demonstrating receptivity to a more active Japanese leadership in the region. Kaifu responded cautiously to these indications. In May 1991, on a visit to Southeast Asia, he asserted that Japan would play a greater political role in the region. This was accepted as "only natural" by Malaysian leaders and by the new prime minister of Singapore, who said that this role should be exercised within the framework of the U.S. security system.

With these encouraging signs of support, the Japanese made further soundings. The head of the LDP's national security division, Koji Kakizawa, in a lecture at the National Defense Academy in the spring of 1991, called for the creation of an Asian peacekeeping force:

> We have to think of discharging our responsibility to the world instead of just concentrating our efforts in developing our own economy as we did in the past; we need to apply an internationalist concept to the SDF.
>
> By bringing an "international outlook" to the SDF, I mean we should enable the SDF to build up mutual trust with other armed services in the region. This could be done through joint military exercises or through personnel exchanges with the armed forces of our neighboring Asian countries. This is one aspect of internationalization. Another is to permit the SDF to shoulder part of the responsibility for maintaining peace and security in the Asia-Pacific region. The formation of an Asian peacekeeping force under U.N. auspices, I think is the first step toward such internationalization.[23]

Kakizawa concluded that if participation in such an Asian peacekeeping force was regarded as unconstitutional, then it was time to revise the constitution.

At about the same time, in May 1991, Nakasone engaged in a dialogue with Masataka Kosaka in which he blamed the disarray in Japanese foreign policy on the Yoshida strategy.[24] Reflecting on the shambles of Japan's international position after the utter failure to formulate policies during the Gulf War, former Prime Minister Nakasone traced the cause back to Yoshida's handling of defense policy in the 1950s and the "irresponsible" course on which it set Japanese policy and opinion. In a long and sober dialogue with Kosaka, published in May 1991, Nakasone observed that

in my view, Yoshida at that time should have said [to the Japanese peo-
ple] that even though Japan is impoverished it is wrong if a people do not
defend their own country; it will not do to continue this way; and once
we recover our economic capability we must have commensurate military power in order to carry out our international responsibilities.
Yoshida bears a heavy responsibility for his failure to say these things.
. . . Thus when I became prime minister, I said "we must extricate our-
selves from the Yoshida system."[25]

As a consequence of this policy, according to Nakasone, the Japanese people were sheltered from the reality of international politics; the debate on
the Gulf War turned on superficial issues of how much money was sufficient to contribute, whether the Self-Defense Forces should be dispatched,
and what they should be permitted to do. What was necessary was "to return to the fundamental issues of Yoshida's day"—namely, the question of
what constituted the fundamental obligations of a nation-state—which had
been decided wrongly. Strong leadership, Nakasone concluded, was
required to reeducate the Japanese people and to wean them from the politics of "prevarication" (*gomakashi*), "escapism" (*tohishugi*), and "ostrich-
like pacifism." He again advocated activist policies and especially urged
the formation of an Asian version of the Conference on Security and
Cooperation in Europe.[26]

In July 1991, abruptly and evidently with little warning to other countries, Foreign Minister Taro Nakayama launched a trial balloon. At a meeting with the ASEAN foreign ministers, he proposed establishing a forum
for security matters, an annual meeting at which ASEAN and interested
parties—Australia, Canada, the EC, Japan, New Zealand, South Korea,
and the United States—could exchange views about security problems in
the Asia Pacific region. The proposal, which had previously been set forth
in different forms by Australia, Canada, and Russia, got a polite rebuff
from the United States, and Japan beat a hasty retreat. But among Japanese
leadership there is now a growing interest in multilateral security organizations and the issue of Japanese participation in collective security
arrangements.

The UN peacekeeping law stimulated a prolonged and intense debate
on Japan's role in collective security arrangements. The law, which passed
the Diet on June 15, 1992, ended the ban on sending SDF troops abroad,
but limited such deployment to logistical and humanitarian support, monitoring elections, and providing aid in civil administration. Under a com-
promise required to gain sufficient Diet support, a section of the law
entailing SDF involvement in armed missions, such as monitoring cease-
fires, disarming combatants, and patrolling buffer zones, was frozen for
the time being. Thus, in its final form, the law was an innocuous and min-
imal response to the international criticism of Japan's inaction during the
Gulf crisis.

A New Regional Order

Despite the fact that Japan in several ways is displacing U.S. leadership in the region, the United States, as the provider of security and the primary market for exports from the region, and enjoying the legitimacy that comes from having won the Cold War, retains critical elements of leadership. For the time being, Japanese policy favors a continuation of the U.S. security role as essential to maintain the stability of the region required for Japanese economic interests. Although U.S. decline is presumed, the security role is still needed. This dependence on the alliance implies resentment over the continued deference to U.S. political leadership, but Japan grudgingly for the time being pays that price. The point that needs to be emphasized is that the United States still has the ability to shape the institutional structure of a new regional order.

Among important sectors of the Japanese leadership, a clear trend is developing toward reinterpreting the constitution to provide room for a more activist foreign policy, particularly to allow participation in collective security arrangements. Interpretations of Article 9 have always been political rather than legal judgments, reflecting a consensus within the LDP. Throughout the Cold War, Article 9 was used as a cover for a low-posture foreign policy that allowed the government to maintain domestic peace and pursue mercantilist policies abroad. But this is now changing as a result of the end of the Cold War, the international criticism of Japan's failure to contribute adequately to the international system, and the Japanese ambition for a seat on the UN Security Council. Young leaders such as Ozawa are saying that it is time to end the sophistry (what he calls *gomakashi*). The draft report of the Ozawa commission on Japan's international role recommended on February 20, 1992, that the constitution be reinterpreted to permit an "active pacifism" (*nodoteki heiwashugi*) that would sanction a role for the SDF in collective security arrangements.[27] Even Miyazawa, the last of Yoshida's disciples, seems to see the handwriting on the wall. In a newspaper interview in October 1991, he said,

> I'm not in favor of revision, but it's good for there to be a thorough discussion of whether things are right the way they are. I asked Ozawa Ichiro to debate this question [in the Commission he chairs on Japan's international role]. . . . I have my own position [about Article 9] that I've developed over a long period, but it's important for the young generation to rethink these issues, and I won't stop them.[28]

Although it is apparent that the constitution will not be revised, given the state of Japanese public opinion, a more flexible interpretation of Article 9 is likely to emerge in the not too distant future.

In light of the trends cited—Japan's growing engagement in Asia, the window of opportunity in terms of leverage that the United States still maintains, and the signs of a new receptivity to collective security arrangements—the time may be ripe for planning a new international order in East Asia that weaves Japan into a multilateral context. The United States should strive to build an integrated security community in Asia that would link economic and security interests and responsibilities and be less exclusively dependent on U.S. resources than in the Cold War era. Such a framework should not significantly limit U.S. flexibility, nor should it promote an unwanted military growth among Asian nations, including Japan. On the contrary, it would be a U.S. effort to shape Japan's inevitably greater political role in the region. To try to keep Japan as an abnormal country by containing it through the bilateral alliance will become more difficult over time and will assure continued conflict with Japanese pride and its steadily growing nationalist mood. Across a wide spectrum in Japan, there is increasing impatience with a deferential foreign policy and a growing will to exert leadership in the region, even though there is no agreement on quite how this should be done.

In the short run, if the Japanese sense that the United States would prefer Japan simply to put up more money for bases and foreign aid, then the Japanese system, given its inclination and inertia, at this point will fall into line. Many members of the conservative political elite, probably a majority, will welcome a continuation of this arrangement. For the time being, it provides the regional stability necessary for Japanese economic interests, and it reassures other Asian nations that Japan's growing economic influence will not be translated into military power. Nonetheless, it stretches credulity to expect such an anomalous arrangement to be durable in the new era.

U.S. initiative in establishing a realistic new U.S.-Japan equilibrium is necessary while Washington still maintains substantial leverage and while Tokyo is still divided, adrift, and reactive in its post–Cold War foreign policy. This undertaking will challenge U.S. leadership capacity because of its many dimensions. It will entail executive branch leadership and the articulation of a coherent new Japan policy based on conditions in the post–Cold War world. It will require the mobilization of considerable U.S. resources to analyze the Japanese political-economic system and devise new policies in the interest of nudging it toward a new foreign policy consensus. Above all, the path to a successful new Japan policy must inevitably lead through domestic policies that will revive U.S. economic competitiveness.

Without U.S. initiative, an effective renewal of the alliance is not likely. Historically embedded obstacles keep Japan from taking the lead. Except in response to outside pressure, the political will, the necessary institutions, or the values and cultural resources do not exist to impel Japan to abandon its heretofore highly successful but narrowly self-generated vision of its world role. At the same time, there is a Japanese constituency for a more active international role. As demonstrated by the Gulf crisis, this view is not yet a national consensus, nor is it likely to be so for some time. Nevertheless, because it is still only partially formed, the new internationalism is tractable and susceptible to effective U.S. leadership.

A revised alliance will have both global and regional implications, including U.S. support and encouragement of a more prominent Japanese role in multilateral organizations, including the United Nations, International Monetary Fund, and World Bank. In the short run, the alliance can be made more reciprocal and equal by forging much closer cooperation on official aid projects. Joint efforts, for example, to facilitate the stability of the former Eastern bloc countries and their integration into the world economy, as opposed to narrowly self-interested allocation of aid for commercial purposes, are appropriate to both U.S. and Japanese long-range interests.

A central purpose of the revised alliance would be cooperation in building a new structure of international relations in the Pacific and articulating its motivating spirit. Japan must play a more responsible role in regional collective security arrangements. Unless Japan is assimilated into a regional security structure, the likelihood of its adopting a more independent role—reflecting its burgeoning economic power, its robust self-confidence, and the unraveling of the U.S.-Japan alliance—will grow dramatically during the decade of the 1990s. Minimalist interpretations of Article 9, which were tolerable during the Cold War, will be less persuasive both at home and abroad under the new conditions.

As for the United States, the end of the Cold War, the growing economic strength of the Pacific countries, and the urgency of domestic renewal will all generate pressure to reduce the U.S. presence in the region. In short, the time has come to ponder the shape of a new security order in the western Pacific that is less exclusively dependent on U.S. resources. The U.S. Department of Defense has already set in motion a decrease in the size of U.S. forces, but this decision appears driven by budgetary exigencies rather than a new strategic vision. The new conditions in Asia suggest that Washington's approach to Asia Pacific security should be rethought, with greater emphasis on multilateral arrangements, mutuality, consensus, and local contribution. Thought should be given to increased cooperation and coordination with Japan and other countries of the region, resulting in common military doctrine and coordinated training. Some initial steps in this direction have, in fact, already been taken in the 1980s: Greater Japanese responsibility for defense of its sea-lanes and an increased level and sophistication of joint military training with forces from the United States and other Pacific nations are examples. In light of new conditions, moving substantially beyond these steps is appropriate. A reduced U.S. presence might lead to new forms of security maintenance, internationalized defense of sea-lanes, joint use of bases, and other innovative arrangements.

The United States retains a good deal of leverage, and there is an internationalist constituency in Japan that is susceptible to U.S. leadership. Rather than attempting an indefinite containment of Japanese pride and power through a continuation of the security treaty in its present form, greater realism dictates U.S. initiatives—while the United States is in a position to guide and shape the process—to form a multilateral organization of which a revised U.S.-Japan alliance would serve as the core. Such an organization would link economic and security interests and responsibilities, and be less exclusively dependent on U.S. resources than in the Cold War era, and still leave the United States with decisive power and leverage as a balancer. By weaving a responsible Japanese security role into a multilateral context, the goal of preventing an independent Japanese "power projection capability" would be achieved through positive measures rather than an effort to contain Japan solely through the current bilateral relationship, which is of questionable stability.

Notes

The author expresses appreciation to the American Enterprise Institute for permission to include material originally presented in his book, Kenneth B. Pyle, *The Japanese Question: Power and Purpose in a New Era* (Washington, D.C.: AEI Press, 1992).

1. The incident is recounted in Michael Schaller, *The American Occupation of Japan: The Origins of the Cold War in Asia* (Oxford: Oxford University Press, 1985), p. vii.

2. See Teiji Yabe, *Konoe Fumimaro* (Tokyo: Kobundo, 1952); and Yoshitake Oka, *Konoe Fumimaro: A Political Biography*, Shumpei Okamoto and Patricia Murray, trans. (Tokyo: University of Tokyo, 1983).

3. Masatoshi Matsushita, *Japan in the League of Nations* (New York: Columbia University Press, 1929), p. 119.

4. See Shigeharu Matsumoto, *Showashi e no ichi shogen* (A testimony on the history of the Showa era) (Tokyo: Mainichi shimbunsha, 1986), p. 303.

5. John Dower, *Empire and Aftermath: Yoshida Shigeru and the Japanese Experience, 1878–1954* (Cambridge, Mass.: Harvard University Press, 1979), p. 36.

6. Kenneth B. Pyle, "Japan, the World, and the Twenty-first Century," in *The Political Economy of Japan: Vol. 2, The Changing International Context*, Takashi Inoguchi and Daniel I. Okimoto, eds. (Stanford, Calif.: Stanford University Press, 1988), pp. 446–486.

7. Kiichi Miyazawa, *Tokyo-Washington no mitsudan* (Secret conversations in Tokyo and Washington) (Tokyo: Jitsugyo no Nihon sha, 1956), p. 160.

8. Hideo Otake, *Adenaua to Yoshida Shigeru* (Shigeru Yoshida and Adenauer) (Tokyo: Chuo koronsha, 1986), p. 328.

9. Charles Kades, "The American Role in Revising Japan's Imperial Constitution," *Political Science Quarterly* (Summer 1989): 237.

10. *Japan Times*, October 20, 1990, p. 2.

11. Shigeru Yoshida, *Sekai to Nippon* (Japan and the world) (Tokyo: Bancho shobo, 1963), pp. 202–203.

12. John Welfield, *An Empire in Eclipse* (London: Athlone Press, 1988), p. 251.

13. Kanji Nishio, "Senryaku toshite no 'sakoku' e no ishi" (A closed country as a strategy), *Seiron* (January 1988).

14. Richard Solomon and Masataka Kosaka, *The Soviet Far East Military Buildup* (Dover, Mass.: Auburn House, 1986), p. 136.

15. *New York Times*, April 5, 1991.

16. Inoki is quoted in Soichiro Tahara, "Nippon no fumie" (A test of Japan's beliefs), *Bungei Shunju*, October 1990.

17. Hisahiko Okazaki and Seizaburo Sato, "Nihon wa kokusaiteki sekinin o do hatatsu no ka" (How should Japan discharge its international responsibility?), *Gaiko Forum*, October 1990. See translation in *Japan Echo* 18, no. 1 (Spring 1991).

18. Hideo Otake, "Nakasone seiji no ideorogi" (The ideology of Nakasone politics), *Leviathan* (Autumn 1987): 83.

19. *Japan Economic Journal*, November 3, 1990.

20. See Hisahiko Okazaki, "Ajia shokoku e no hairyo" (Consideration for the countries of Asia), *Voice* (July 1991).

21. *Japan Times*, April 4, 1991.

22. *The Economist*, March 9, 1991.

23. *Japan Times*, April 17, 1991.

24. Yasuhiro Nakasone and Masataka Kosaka, "Atarashii Nippon no kokka senryaku" (A new Japanese national strategy), *Voice* (May 1991).

25. Ibid.

26. Ibid.

27. *Asahi Shimbun*, February 21, 1992.

28. Ibid, October 8, 1991.

Part 3

Political Economy Issues

8

Japan's Changing Political Economy

Kent E. Calder

The twilight of the Cold War and the birth of a new global political era have constituted a period of unusual drama and flux even in Japan, with its appearance of eternal resistance to any sort of change. Within three years starting in spring 1989, Japan had four prime ministers—a more rapidly revolving door than even the French Third Republic could typically boast. The media have been spewing forth an endless stream of juicy scandals— Recruit; the Uno sex scandals; the Nomura, Fuji, and IBJ banking scandals; Kyowa; Itoman; and Sagawa Kyubin, to name a few prominent ones. The ruling Liberal Democratic Party lost full control of the National Diet for the first time since 1955.[1]

Amidst this ferment, there has been heated discussion of the need for more thoroughgoing political reform. Several major politicians—Toshiki Kaifu, Tsutomu Hata, and, in certain respects, even Ichiro Ozawa—have seriously backed electoral reform in Japan's cumbersome multimember electoral district system. Prime Minister Kaifu abruptly fell from office in the fall of 1991 over precisely this issue. Judicial rulings have generated pressure to redress discrepancies between the value of urban and rural votes, with reapportionment gradually occurring as a consequence.

To be sure, there are sharply conflicting interpretations of this recent turbulence. Journalist Karel van Wolferen, for example, views it as business as usual; financial and political scandals for him simply show the incestuous corruption that has long been and continues to be rampant in a static, elite-dominated system that is fundamentally incapable of change.[2] Seen in historical and integrated political-economic perspective, however, there are clearly major ingredients of transition that could well produce a substantially different Japanese political system—and a significantly different Japanese international political role—by the end of this decade.

As Chalmers Johnson persuasively argues, the political and economic evolution of contemporary Japan are deeply related.[3] But such interrelationship is not a simple matter of persistent political dominance over

121

economics. When economic forces are unusually powerful and politically insistent, they can prove catalytic in reshaping the political world. Economic pressures expressed through particular interests played a key role during Great Britain's transition after the 1848 rejection of the protectionist Corn Laws and they may do so again in Japan.[4]

To understand the pressures for political transformation that are currently at work in Japan, it is important to understand the economic and political forces that created conservative one-party dominance in 1955 and have since sustained it.[5]

Contrary to van Wolferen's historically naive but recently influential stereotype of static, unchanging Japanese politics, the first postwar decade (1945–1955) was extremely fluid, involving a socialist cabinet, two coalition cabinets, and numerous rival parties vying for power. The dynamic variables outside Japanese politics, which ultimately forced it into the post-1955 configuration of one-party dominance, were two-fold: (1) U.S. pressure for stability, flowing from Cold War geopolitical exigencies such as the fall of China in 1949; and (2) desire of the domestic business world for stability so as to facilitate the rapid debt-based heavy industrialization that began with the Korean War (1950–1953).

U.S. pressure led, through such mechanisms as the Showa Denko scandal and the Red Purge, to the dominance of U.S. protégé Shigeru Yoshida as prime minister for an extended period (1948–1954). But it did so within the context of a political system comprised of rival conservative and, from 1951 to 1955, rival socialist parties as well.[6] For the increasingly debt-reliant big-business world, this fluid political environment was too precarious and unpredictable, especially following the sudden resignation of Yoshida in December 1954 and the recreation of a unified Socialist Party two months later. The result was strong, insistent big-business pressure for a conservative merger that would presumably stabilize the political scene. Such a conservative union materialized with the creation of the LDP in October 1955.

Through the dynamic of "crisis and compensation"—by which the ruling conservatives have strategically compensated pivotal constituencies such as small business, agriculture, the elderly, and citizens of depressed regions for past or prospective support in periods when their preeminence was most tenuous—this one-party conservative dominance has continued to this day.[7] But the economic and strategic circumstances that led to and long sustained conservative dominance have now sharply changed, calling its long-term viability into question. Indeed, it is precisely the prospect of future political fluidity, and the dynamic, shifting economic interests underlying Japan's dominant conservative coalition, that have provoked the political turmoil as well as many of the scandal revelations of recent years. Far from being static, as the revisionists contend, the current Japanese political scene is intensely dynamic and under strong and deepening pressures for major reconfiguration.

The waning of the Cold War has undermined the geostrategic rationale on the part of the United States, which has continued since the mid-1950s, for U.S. support of one-party conservative dominance in Japan. The United States simply no longer needs an LDP-dominated Japan as an "unsinkable aircraft carrier" against the Russians in the same way as the Reagan administration felt it did in the mid-1980s. More important, fundamental changes in Japanese industrial structure and corporate finance have made such one-party dominance less critical for the Japanese big-business world than was true even a decade ago. This emerging reality is reflected in the uninhibited—indeed, at times rather scathing—recent criticism of LDP political scandals and inefficient subsidy policies by the top leadership of Keidanren (the Federation of Business Organizations, Japan's most powerful business group), including its chairman, Gaishi Hiraiwa.

One-party conservative dominance is becoming less important for the big-business world than it was during the high growth period because industry itself is less capital intensive and because individual firms find themselves less precariously reliant on debt than was formerly the case. In 1976, for example, the ratio of shareholders equity to total capitalization in Japanese manufacturing was only 13.7 percent, or roughly one part equity to seven parts debt; ten years later, the average equity component in total capitalization had more than doubled.[8] The huge steel, shipbuilding, and petrochemical combinats of the 1960s and 1970s, which often cost billions of dollars to build, have been replaced at the heart of the Japanese economy by integrated-circuit fabrication plants only one-fifth as expensive per unit. And Japanese manufacturing firms that once lived from hand to mouth as part of the "bicycle economy" (their survival—or staying upright—required continuous, rapid forward movement) have themselves become affluent. Industrial giants such as Toyota Motors and Matsushita Electric generate $2 to 4 billion annually in current profit[9] and sit atop huge cash hoards in the tens of billions of dollars that are invested globally. Economic efficiency, rather than the stable, persistent dominance of a single political party, is increasingly becoming their priority concern.

Japanese business, like its counterparts in conservative political ranks around the world, still includes some deeply politicized firms, particularly among regional construction companies and other local bodies. Such local business interests in the past fifteen years have become increasingly important financially to LDP politicians, as changes in fund-raising laws have placed a premium for the politicians on recruiting large numbers of individual and small-business donors.[10] But the concerns of these politicized local business interests are diverging from the preoccupations of the big-business mainstream. Japan's largest firms, increasingly multinational in their operations, have much broader concerns than simply keeping the LDP in power within Japan itself.

The aging of Japanese society, together with broader quality of life issues in a nation that very nearly "has it all" in narrow monetary terms, further deepen the emerging LDP dilemma and increase the impending likelihood of major political transition in Japan. The increase in the number of aged Japanese threatens to escalate welfare-related budgetary claims against the Japanese state, which would otherwise be available for politically efficacious distributive spending, as has been true since the onset of high growth in the 1950s. Japan is currently aging more rapidly than any other major nation in the world, with the number of Japanese over sixty-five likely to double to more than twenty-five million before the end of this decade.[11] This expanding community of elderly will have needs conflicting with the "compensation politics" demands for construction contracts and other largesse that arise from the LDP's traditional constituencies.

Ongoing social change, even apart from aging, also has major prospective implications for politics. In 1950, 48 percent of Japanese employment was rural; that figure has declined to 7 percent today.[12] The role of women in Japanese society is likewise changing rapidly. A new generation of citizens that does not remember war or occupation is moving into leadership positions. Japanese are becoming somewhat more cosmopolitan—eleven million traveled abroad in 1990.

What these changes add up to is a Japanese electorate that is more urban, more fluid and critical (especially women), and more internationally conscious than that of the past. The highly inefficient structure of small-scale manufacturing, distribution, and agriculture, together with the related political constituencies that have profoundly affected Japanese politics and policy since the 1950s, surely remain, nevertheless. Japan's electorate is much more volatile and manifests less one-party loyalty than was true until the late 1970s. There was enough pent-up frustration within the country to give Japan's remarkably inarticulate opposition party a sweeping victory in the 1989 Upper House election and to force resignation of two LDP prime ministers enmeshed in scandal during that same tumultuous year. At the same time, there is enough ambivalence about the opposition's capacity to give the ruling LDP a major victory in the 1992 Upper House elections.

Implications for International Engagement

The foregoing analysis suggests the presence of important domestic supports, at the level of interest-group structure and popular opinion, for a foreign policy that is markedly more internationally cooperative—indeed, activist in its cooperation—on a range of pressing global issues than such policy typically has been. With Japanese economic interests much more deeply engaged abroad today than was true even seven or eight years ago (new direct foreign investment soared from $12 billion in 1985 to $68 billion in 1989, and portfolio investment totaled close to $300 billion in the latter year), incentives for global responsiveness certainly exist at that level as well. The problem is clearly the intermediate variable—the structure of a still remarkably feudal, parochial, and fractious political system that immobilizes a potentially important contributor to international political and economic affairs.

Three particular structural difficulties inhibit Japan from playing a more active international role. The first constraint is the faction-ridden and grassroots-dominated character of the ruling Liberal Democratic Party, shaped profoundly by Japan's distinctive multimember district electoral system. Under this system, between two and five candidates are elected in virtually all Japanese electoral districts.[13] Voters, however, vote for a single candidate rather than a party slate. The system, whose only remote functional parallels elsewhere in the democratic world are in Ireland and Finland,[14] has three important policy implications. First, it encourages candidates to make narrow special-interest appeals and, once in office, binds them closely to interest groups; the system makes it possible to be elected with as little as 10–15 percent of the vote. Second, the need intensively to cultivate small numbers of constituents forces politicians to spend as much as three days a week in their districts, leaving less time for foreign affairs activities and other forms of active involvement in national policy formation. Finally, the electoral system forces candidates of large parties like the ruling LDP into competition with one another at the grassroots level, thus virtually assuring persistence of a factional system that makes any prime minister's authority, and even tenure in office, a precarious matter indeed.

A second structural difficulty of Japanese domestic politics, to which Karel von Wolferen correctly points,[15] is the salience of complex personal networks (*jinmyaku*) in the Japanese decisionmaking process. This pattern has become more and more pronounced throughout the last two decades. These complex networks clearly slow the pace of decisionmaking and make policymakers loathe to accept clear responsibility for controversial policy outcomes, found so frequently in the foreign policy area. It is often far easier to shift the burden of decisions, especially fundamentally unpopular foreign policy decisions, to third parties than to jeopardize finely calibrated personal networks of domestic political ties by accepting responsibility directly.

A final structural factor complicating Japan's assumption of a more proactive international political role is the inadequacy of the Japanese bureaucratic structure, whatever the intellectual strengths of its talented bureaucrats as individuals might be. Part of the problem, especially critical in emerging sectors such as telematics and international finance, is the omnipresent reality of ambiguous, overlapping spheres of jurisdiction; the regulatory spheres of major Japanese ministries were legally specified in the early 1950s and have not since been fundamentally changed, despite major shifts in economic structure.[16] The difficulties for policymaking that these ambiguities create are compounded by the partisanship generated by lifetime employment commitments in the bureaucracy and the absence of a powerful central executive, which in presidential systems like that in the United States can operate to suppress or mediate intragovernmental rivalry. These domestic constraints have combined to make Japan a "reactive state" in foreign policy, even when Japanese interests—and the aspirations of the Japanese people—would be better served by activism and when Japan has the power resources in international affairs to behave more proactively.[17] If these domestic constraints were removed, the foregoing pages suggest, Japan would play a considerably more active role in international affairs than is currently the case.

The manifest linkage between the multimember district electoral system and the factional, particularistic, distributive orientation of Japanese politics and policymaking suggest the great importance, from the standpoint of encouraging a more proactive Japanese role in world affairs, of domestic electoral reform. Although the Japanese electoral system clearly promotes intense interaction between national parliamentarians and the grassroots, as discussed above, it leaves them poorly prepared and with little time to think systematically about international affairs, precisely because of those domestic political preoccupations. Proposals such as that of LDP electoral reform commission chairman Tsutomu Hata to Prime Minister Kaifu in fall 1991, which would have created numerous single-member districts in the Lower House of the Japanese Diet, could have important, positive long-term consequences for foreign policy, if implemented. Despite considerable opposition from older Dietmen lacking confidence in their ability to compete under new electoral rules, the support of consumers and international business ultimately is likely to result in major electoral changes.

Interpersonal networks have long been central in Japanese politics. But they have become especially constraining for policy for the past decade or two, as the share of second- and third-generation Dietmen (members whose fathers and grandfathers preceded them in the Diet) has risen to more than one-third of all Lower House members from the ruling Liberal Democratic Party.[18] Electoral reform should weaken these networks and thereby create greater freedom for policymakers from interest-group pressure by decreasing the power of incumbents in the Diet. As a practical matter, of course, neither the advantages of incumbency nor the importance of established personal networks will disappear. The lowered salience of factional rivalries that electoral reform would likely induce, however, should give Japanese policymaking more flexibility.

Provided electoral reform toward a single-member district system for the Lower House is achieved, the most important structural prerequisite for a more proactive Japanese foreign policy is building the new bureaucratic institutions for leadership. In this regard, the early post–World War II

experience of the United States in creating an organizationally sophisticated National Security Council, Central Intelligence Agency, and Executive Office of the President may be relevant,[19] although Japan's emerging
international role will obviously be somewhat different, and in no sense
as dominant or as militarily oriented as was that of the United States after
1945. Japan clearly needs better independent intelligence information, especially in the political-military area, as the evolution of the Kuwait crisis,
which broke just thirteen days before Prime Minister Kaifu's scheduled
visit to the Middle East, clearly showed. A lack of adequate independent
capacity to evaluate fast-breaking events in the crisis was, indeed, a factor in Kaifu's anguished, abrupt decision to cancel his trip, almost on the
eve of departure.[20]

One of the most pressing structural problems of the Japanese foreign
policy apparatus in the 1990s is the need for a significantly expanded Ministry of Foreign Affairs (MOFA) on the one hand, and for a larger and
more powerful Prime Minister's Office on the other. With only 4,400
career employees (60 percent of whom are serving abroad), the Japanese
Foreign Ministry remains smaller than those of Canada and Italy, one-half
the size of Britain's and less than one-third the size of that of the United
States. It has been growing in recent years by only 2 to 3 percent annually, at most.[21]

The Japanese foreign aid bureaucracy is also remarkably small and
only slowly expanding. In 1988, for example, Japan had 1,539 personnel
serving in its foreign-aid disbursement institutions (the Overseas Economic Cooperation Fund and the Japan International Cooperation Agency)
compared to the 4,695 who disburse a roughly equivalent amount of aid
in the United States. Japan's foreign aid disbursement staff has grown less
than one-third as fast as the ODA budget, year in and year out, ever since
the mid-1970s.[22] The need for additional diplomats and foreign-aid pro-
fessionals is especially pressing for Japan, as their responsibilities lie,
more disproportionately than for ministries such as MITI and MOF, in the
political realm. Japanese foreign policymaking in this area has been especially underdeveloped since World War II.

The failure of both the Ministry of Foreign Affairs and foreign-aid
agencies, themselves closely related to MOFA, to expand together with
Japan's broadening global role is a result of the ministry's vulnerable domestic political position. In sharp contrast to its rivals, MOF and MITI,
MOFA lacks any significant regulatory power over business; indeed, it has
no domestic jurisdiction at all. Reflecting its weakness vis-à-vis dominant
economic forces, MOFA has very few former members currently serving
in the Diet—only four in 1988 as compared to thirty-four for MOF and
nine for MITI.[23] In 1992, a former MOFA official, Koichi Kato, served as
chief cabinet secretary of the Miyazawa cabinet. But this degree of prominence for an ex-MOFA official was virtually unprecedented since the

mid-1950s, when Yoshida, long-time ambassador to the Court of St. James's, left the prime ministership. MOFA today simply lacks the domestic political influence to expand its institutional size and scope of responsibilities. The adverse implications for Japan's diplomatic potential are inevitable under these circumstances.

The other major ministries obviously have different conceptions about how the Japanese government should cope with its new global responsibilities. MITI has been aggressively expanding its international economic diplomacy, in part with the aid of extra-budgetary funds from its sponsorship of bicycle racing that are beyond the control of the Ministry of Finance. MOF has worked through multilateral financial institutions, such as the International Monetary Fund and the Asian Development Bank, as well as a complex network of semigovernment bodies largely financed by private banks, securities firms, and insurance companies.

Fortunately, MOF has recently agreed to a 1,000-member expansion of the Foreign Ministry,[24] spurred by the demonstrable logistical problems that MOFA has incurred in coping with its spiraling global responsibilities. Many of the new diplomats are to be lateral appointments from business, with the maximum age of entry being raised from twenty-eight to thirty-three. These steps should help to cover more adequately MOFA's responsibilities, but more needs to be done.

Given the current salience of the major ministries such as MOFA, MITI, and MOF in Japanese foreign policymaking, together with Japan's standing as a parliamentary rather than a presidential system of government, it is unlikely that the Office of the Prime Minister in Japan will ever come to fully equal that of the White House in the United States in stature. But the experience of U.S. foreign policymaking for the past five decades does suggest the potential value to Japan, from the standpoint of efficient, coordinated global power projection and rapid reaction to foreign crises, of a centralized foreign policy office to which the chief of government has direct access. In this sense the efforts of former Prime Minister Nakasone during the mid-1980s to expand the functions of the prime ministerial office, or *kantei*, were farsighted Japanese efforts that could make a proactive diplomacy easier to achieve.

Nakasone's successors have failed to build on his efforts to strengthen the *kantei*. While in office, Nakasone employed a powerful chief cabinet secretary, Masaharu Gotoda, who was both a top official of the dominant Tanaka/Takeshita faction of the ruling LDP and a respected former Home Ministry bureaucrat. Gotoda thus centralized two of Japan's most influential policy networks. Subsequent prime ministers have not reproduced these critical political ingredients. No recent cabinet has combined Nakasone's state-oriented future vision and the administrative talents of a Gotoda. Under Prime Minister Kaifu (1989–1991), when a powerful *kantei* might have been especially useful because of the Gulf crisis, the bureau-cracy resisted such a development, and Kaifu did not have the leverage to overcome its opposition. Many political analysts suggest that the full emergence of a "presidential-style" *kantei* in Japan, if it ever occurs, will have to wait for the emergence of a geostrategically oriented prime minis-ter unconstrained by factional politics—perhaps after a major electoral re-form in the middle to late 1990s. Some younger leaders in the powerful Takeshita faction of the LDP, such as prime ministerial aspirant Ichiro Ozawa, who served as secretary general of the LDP during the Gulf crisis, are reportedly convinced of the importance of a more powerful *kantei.*

Multilateral institutions will likely be an increasingly important area for Japanese global leadership in years to come, provided sticky issues of voting rights can be resolved or at least finessed. Yet Japan remains grossly underrepresented at the multilaterals on the professional staff level. In 1991, for example, Japan contributed 11.4 percent of the entire UN budget—considerably more than any nation other than the United States—yet provided only 3.6 percent of its staff. It provided fewer UN staffers than Britain, which contributed little more than one-third as much as did Japan in support of UN activities.[25] Certainly the appointment in the early 1990s of Japanese nationals to head the UN High Commission on Refugees, the World Health Organization, and the UN Transitional Au-thority in Cambodia were important steps toward a more substantive Japanese role in the multilaterals. But serious problems of midlevel staffing remain.

Given the pressing need for more qualified Japanese foreign policy specialists, both in Japanese and multilateral organizations, training also remains an important requisite for an expanded Japanese international role. Much of this training can, and perhaps should, be undertaken in foreign institutions. But there is also a need to expand relevant facilities within Japan. Language facilities, area studies institutes, and organizations en-gaging in more general international relations research, especially in the political-military area, are all urgent priorities.

As Washington evolved from a foreign affairs backwater to a global power center when the 1930s gave way to the 1940s, and when the Cold War waxed in intensity during the 1950s and 1960s, that capital city began to develop an intellectual support structure for the policy process, tran-scending government itself. Tokyo will also soon need an analogue. This is the complex but important network of think tanks, semigovernmental agencies, and lobbying organizations that generates so many of the con-crete policy proposals that have helped to make U.S. policymaking pro-active in those issue areas where the United States lacks the power re-sources to prevail otherwise.[26] Such bodies as the International Institute for Global Peace, chaired by former Prime Minister Nakasone and housing numerous staffers seconded from government agencies as well as businessmen, will no doubt need to expand in scale and grow in importance as Japan's global stakes and role on the world scene surge beyond current levels.

Notes

The author expresses special appreciation to Edna Lloyd and Marianne Donath for their help in the preparation of this chapter.

1. Since 1989, the LDP has lacked control of the Upper House—the House of Councillors. Between 1976 and 1980, it lacked full control of some committees in the Lower House, but it had full numerical control of both houses.

2. For a succinct, relatively recent statement of van Wolferen's provocative argument, see Karel van Wolferen, "The Japan Problem Revisited," *Foreign Affairs* (Fall 1990): 42–45. See also Karel van Wolferen, *The Enigma of Japanese Power* (New York: Vintage Books, 1990).

3. Chalmers Johnson, *MITI and the Japanese Miracle* (Stanford, Calif.: Stanford University Press, 1982), esp. pp. 3–34.

4. On the process of domestic political transition, see, for example, Norman Gash, *Politics in the Age of Peel* (New York: W.W. Norton and Company, 1953).

5. For a more detailed explication, see Kent E. Calder, *Crisis and Compensation: Political Stability and Public Policy in Japan* (Princeton, N.J.: Princeton University Press, 1988), pp. 117–126.

6. See John Dower, *Empire and Aftermath: Yoshida Shigeru and the Japanese Experience, 1878–1954* (Cambridge, Mass.: Harvard University Council on East Asian Studies, 1979); and Calder, *Crisis and Compensation*, pp. 71–126.

7. For elaboration of the argument, see Calder, *Crisis and Compensation*, esp. pp. 156–230.

8. The equity total capitalization ratio in Japanese manufacturing had risen by 1986 to 28.1 percent. See Okurasho Shoken Kyoku, *Hojin Kigyo Tokei Nenpo* (Yearbook of corporate statistics) (Tokyo: Okurasho Insatsu Kyoku), various issues.

9. Toyota's expected current profit for January 1992 was ¥615 billion, and Matsushita's for March 1992 was ¥265 billion. See Tōyō Keizai Shinpōsa, *Japan Company Handbook* (Summer 1991): 680, 775.

10. See Gerald Curtis, *The Japanese Way of Politics* (New York: Columbia University Press, 1988), esp. pp. 176–191.

11. Keizai Koho Center, *Japan 1992: An International Comparison* (Tokyo: Keizai Koho Center, 1992), p. 8.

12. Ibid., p. 20.

13. The only exception is the Amami Oshima island constituency off southern Kyushu, which elects only a single candidate, as under the typical UK-U.S. system.

14. For comparative details, as well as broader analysis of systemic implications, see Calder, *Crisis and Compensation*, pp. 61–170.

15. See van Wolferen, *Enigma of Japanese Power*.

16. On the operational difficulties these overlapping jurisdictions create in formulating proactive foreign economic policies that would demonstrably be in Japan's international interest, see Kent E. Calder, *International Pressure and Domestic Policy Response: Japanese Informatics Policy in the 1980s,* Research

Monograph Series, no. 57 (Princeton, N.J.: Princeton University Center of International Studies, 1989).

17. For a more detailed presentation of this structuralist argument, see Kent E. Calder, "Japanese Foreign Economic Policy: Explaining the Reactive State," *World Politics* (July 1988): 517–541.

18. See, for example, Koichi Kishimoto, *Nihon no Gikai Seiji* (Japan's parliamentary politics) (Tokyo: Gyosei Mondai Kenkyu Jo, 1983), p. 233.

19. See, for example, Bradley H. Patterson, *The Ring of Power: The White House Staff and Its Expanding Role in Government* (New York: Basic Books, 1988).

20. On Japanese foreign policymaking of this period, see Kent E. Calder, "Japan in 1990: Limits to Change," *Asian Survey* 31, no. 1 (January 1991): 21–35.

21. Japan's Foreign Ministry currently has about 4,400 career officials, compared with 15,900 for the United States, 8,100 for Britain, 6,600 each for France and Germany, and 4,600 for Canada. See *The Economist*, December 7, 1991, p. 38.

22. Robert M. Orr, Jr., *The Emergence of Japan's Foreign Aid Power* (New York: Columbia University Press, 1990), p. 50.

23. Fuji Seikei Shimbun Sha, *Kokkai Yoran* (Diet almanac), 1989 edition (Tokyo: Fuji Seikei Shimbun Sha, 1988).

24. *Japan Times Weekly*, December 7, 1991.

25. Keizai Koho Center, *Japan 1992: An International Comparison*, p. 96.

26. On the contemporary role of think tanks in the U.S. policy process, see James A. Smith, *The Idea Brokers: Think Tanks and the Rise of the New Policy Elite* (New York: The Free Press, 1991).

9

Japanese Trade and Investment Issues

Edward J. Lincoln

Japanese trade and investment behavior lies at the core of shaping the nation's global role during the 1990s. A huge wave of investment abroad has pushed the nation to a closer relationship with the outside world and increased foreign perceptions of Japan as a world power. But both the new investment relationship as well as continuing trade developments imply that Japan will face serious problems in exercising a larger world role. A rising aysmmetry on investment and a continuing disparity on trade—with Japan absorbing fewer foreign products than other industrial nations—create an environment in which the Japanese government may not face a positive response to its efforts to play a larger policy role. Dealing with these problems could be the most difficult task facing Japan as it shifts its global orientation.

On the trade front, some progress has taken place in the statistical measures of import penetration, imports' share of gross domestic product (GDP) and manufactured imports as a share of GDP, making Japan somewhat less different from other major industrial nations than it has been in the past. Nevertheless, major differences remain, and a key question for the rest of the 1990s will be the extent to which progress continues.

This chapter discusses both the important new developments in Japan's investment position (and the problems that they engender), and the continuing developments on trade. The purpose here is to highlight the key economic variables, the ways in which they are evolving, and the current status of research concerning their importance, as well as, finally, to offer some thoughts on how trade and investment affects Japan's future role in world affairs.

The conclusion is cautious: investment has played an important role in breaking down Japan's strong insularity by pushing firms and individuals to deal with international issues to an extent that they have avoided in the past; but the asymmetries on trade and investment remain and create an unfavorable international image for the nation. Real improvement has occurred on manufactured import penetration and intra-industry trade—trade of goods within the same industry—which should ameliorate some of the negative image of the past. But Japanese behavior continues to appear substantially different from that of other nations. So long as the rest of the world perceives Japan as less receptive to imports and inward investment than other nations, Japan's ability to play a leading role on both economic and political matters in the world will be impeded.

Investment

Underlying the transformation of Japan's economic relationship with the world has been the nation's rapid rise as an important international investor over the course of the 1980s. It is Japan's physical presence through investment that provides a major source of the recognition within and outside of Japan that the nation should play a more active role in world affairs. Although growth in investment has slowed in the 1990s, additions to the already large amounts of investment will continue. On a net basis, the current-account surpluses that imply a net outflow of capital are likely to continue for most or all of the rest of this decade. On a gross basis (even if foreigners buy more Japanese assets than the reverse, Japanese ownership of foreign assets still will be rising), sizable additions to ownership of foreign assests—especially in the form of manufacturing and other corporate activities abroad—will also continue. Driven by the close relationship with the rest of the world that investment implies, Japan will certainly play a larger role in international economics and politics for the rest of the decade. Japan's investment position, however, also poses a variety of problems that could seriously hinder a smooth integration of Japan into world affairs.

Why is investment so important? During the earlier postwar period, Japan's main economic interaction with the outside world was carried out through merchandise trade. This form of interaction requires relatively little economic intimacy between the nation or the society and the outside world. Imports were heavily channeled through a limited number of Japanese general trading companies, manufactured imports faced stiff barriers, and foreign firms often settled for arms-length licensing arrangements because direct investment was difficult. Exports also relied heavily on a few large trading companies. Adapting exports for foreign markets was an activity that required a relatively shallow understanding of foreign cultures and political systems that could be relayed through those trading companies and a small handful of other corporate representatives abroad. International economic behavior was thus entirely consistent with the array of political and social aspects of Japan's insularity.

Investment, on the other hand, requires extensive understanding and interaction with the world. To put the matter at an elemental level, the management of workers in Tennessee requires far more interaction or understanding than does the export of cars from Japan to the United States. Successful investments require an understanding of foreign cultures, legal systems, and political systems, as well as a tolerance and acceptance of diverse ethnic and racial groups. Because of the rise in investment, Japanese society now faces the necessity of developing this understanding. Furthermore, foreign investment requires much more personnel input by the Japanese themselves. The number of Japanese managers and their families living abroad will increase rapidly—another substantial change for the society.

A final aspect of the importance of investment comes from foreign perceptions of Japan. The United States views Japan today as a more important nation than it did in the early 1980s because of the visible presence of Japanese investment. Perceiving Japan as more important and involved has led to the increase in expectations that Japan should or will play an increasingly active role in international policymaking, both economic and political.

Several factors have been responsible for the epochal shift in Japan's investment posture, most of them related to the completion of the century-long process of catching up with the industrialized world. When economic catch-up ended in the 1970s, the pace of investment moderated in the economy, yielding the slower growth rates in GNP that have characterized Japan since 1974. The desire to save, however, did not moderate as much as investment, producing a surplus of savings over investment in the private sector. During the rest of the 1970s, the government absorbed those private-sector savings by increasing the government deficit, a traditional Keynesian response to surplus savings.

During the 1980s, however, the government aggressively reduced and eliminated its deficits. On a national-income account basis, which includes local government and social security in the combined government sector, a government deficit of 5.5 percent of GNP in 1978 was reversed to a surplus of 3 percent by the end of the 1980s, representing a large 8.5 percentage-point shift in this key macroeconomic variable.[1] The outside world replaced the government as the absorber of surplus savings. During the 1980s, Japan exported capital to the rest of the world, a phenomenon caused by running a current-account surplus.[2] Table 9.1 presents basic data on Japan's current-account balances for the 1980s, with a shift from a deficit of almost $11 billion in 1980 to a peak surplus of $87 billion in 1987. The corresponding net flow of capital to the rest of the world made Japan the largest net creditor in the world by late in the decade, and, by the end of 1990, the nation's net credit position was $328 billion (from only $11 billion in 1980).[3] Japan had become the greatest creditor nation the world has ever known.

This aspect of Japan's new position has been well publicized, especially because the Japanese feel a sense of superiority due to the simultaneous move of the United States to the position of the world's largest net debtor. A much more interesting and important aspect of Japan's credit position is less frequently discussed, however. The macroeconomic changes discussed above made necessary an extensive process of financial deregulation in the economy to accommodate the changes in financial flows associated with the long-term shift in private-sector savings and investment, the government deficit, and the net outflow of investment to the rest of the world. Deregulation made possible far larger gross flows of capital across Japan's borders, and the most important aspect of changes in the 1980s has been the enormous increase in Japan's gross investment in the world.

Table 9.2 shows the long-term capital transactions in the balance of payments. Gross long-term capital outflow (the change in long-term assets), which was only $10.8 billion in 1980, has been more than $100 billion every year from 1986, peaking at $192.1 billion in 1989. Even though long-term transactions do not capture all forms of capital flow, these figures are indicative of the enormous change that has occurred in the size of gross capital outflow.

These annual flows have produced a dramatic increase in the cumulative value of Japanese ownership of foreign assets. In 1980, the cumulative value of all Japanese investments overseas was only $150 billion. By 1990, the total was $1.9 trillion, for an average annual growth rate of 29 percent over the course of the decade.[4] In the space of ten years, Japan had moved from being a relatively minor world investor to being one of the largest. What characterizes investment as a whole also characterizes direct investment (in which the investor's stake represents at least a degree of managerial control). From a cumulative value of only $19.6 billion in 1980, direct investment totaled $201 billion by 1990, generating a 26 percent average annual growth rate for the decade, roughly equaling the growth rate in total external assets.[5]

The motivation for foreign direct investment involves more than the financial deregulation that has affected investment in general, although capital controls were certainly the major explanation for low levels of direct investment abroad in the earlier postwar period through the late 1970s. For the 1980s, the increase in direct investment is related to two other important factors: a fear of foreign protection and the rising value of the yen.

During the 1980s, Japanese foreign direct investment experienced a relative shift in location away from developing countries and toward the industrialized world. In 1980, 27 percent of cumulative Japanese direct investment abroad was located in North America, and by 1989 that share had jumped to 43 percent. Similarly, investment in Europe expanded from 12 percent to 18 percent of the total in the same time period.[6] Investment in both North America and Europe has been motivated by a perception that these areas were becoming more protectionist. Surmounting protectionist barriers through investment has been a time-honored pattern for all investing nations, and Japan is no exception.

Table 9.1 Japan's Balance of Payments: Current-Account Detail (in $ billions)

| | Current-Account Balance | Merchandise Trade Balance | Services | | | | | | | |
| | | | Total Balance | Travel | | Transportation | | Net Investment Income | Patent Royalties | |
				Net	Debits	Net	Debits		Net	Credits
1980	-10.7	2.1	-11.3	-3.9	-4.6	-4.3	-17.3	0.9	-1.0	0.4
1981	4.8	20.0	-13.6	-3.9	-4.6	-3.2	-18.5	-0.8	-1.2	0.5
1982	6.9	18.1	-9.8	-3.4	-4.1	-3.4	-16.7	1.7	-1.2	0.6
1983	20.8	31.5	-9.1	-3.6	-4.4	-3.3	-15.5	3.1	-1.4	0.6
1984	35.0	44.3	-7.7	-3.6	-4.6	-3.0	-15.9	4.2	-1.6	0.7
1985	49.2	56.0	-5.2	-3.7	-4.8	-2.6	-15.1	6.8	-1.6	0.7
1986	85.8	92.8	-4.9	-5.8	-7.2	-2.5	-13.9	9.5	-2.3	0.9
1987	87.0	96.4	-5.7	-8.6	-10.8	-6.1	-19.1	16.7	-2.5	1.3
1988	79.6	95.0	-11.3	-15.8	-18.7	-7.4	-23.0	21.0	-3.4	1.6
1989	57.2	76.9	-15.5	-19.3	-22.5	-7.8	-25.8	23.4	-3.3	2.0
1990	35.8	63.5	-22.3	-21.4	-24.9	-9.5	-27.6	23.2	-3.6	2.5
1991	72.6	103.3	-18.2	-20.5	-23.9	-10.5	-29.9	26.7	-3.2	2.9

Source: Bank of Japan, International Department, *Balance of Payments Monthly* (Tokyo: Bank of Japan, January and December 1991), pp. 7–8, 29–30, 36, 42, 47–48.

Table 9.2 Japan's Balance of Payments: Capital Flow Detail (in $ billions)

	Net	Long-term Capital Flow						Net Short-Term Capital Flow	Errors and Omissions
		Total	Change in Assets				Change in Liabilities		
			Direct Investment	Loans	Securities				
					Total	Bonds			
1980	2.3	-10.8	-2.4	-2.6	-3.8	-3.0	13.1	3.1	-3.1
1981	-9.7	-22.8	-4.9	-5.1	-8.8	-5.8	13.1	2.3	0.5
1982	-15.0	-27.4	-4.5	-7.9	-9.7	-6.1	12.4	-1.6	4.7
1983	-17.7	-32.5	-3.6	-8.4	-16.0	-12.5	14.8	0.0	2.1
1984	-49.7	-56.8	-6.0	-11.9	-30.8	-26.8	7.1	-4.3	3.7
1985	-64.5	-81.8	-6.5	-10.4	-59.8	-53.5	17.3	-0.9	-4.0
1986	-131.5	-132.1	-14.5	-9.3	-102.0	-93.0	0.6	-1.6	2.5
1987	-136.5	-132.8	-19.5	-16.2	-87.8	-72.9	-3.7	23.9	3.9
1988	-130.9	-149.9	-34.2	-15.2	-86.9	-85.8	18.9	19.5	2.8
1989	-89.2	-192.1	-44.1	-22.5	-113.2	-94.1	102.9	20.8	-22.0
1990	-43.6	-120.8	-48.0	-22.2	-39.7	-29.0	77.2	21.5	-20.9
1991	36.6	-121.9	-31.2	-13.5	-74.3	-68.2	158.5	-26.4	-6.5

Note: Money leaving the country is indicated by negative values; that entering by positive values. Hence, a negative number under any of the categories for Change in Assets implies a flow of money abroad to purchase more assets (a transaction that one might normally associate with a positive number).

Source: Bank of Japan, International Department, *Balance of Payments Monthly* (Tokyo: Bank of Japan, March and December 1991), pp. 7–8, 59–60, 65.

Sharp appreciation of the yen between 1985 and 1987 (and rough stability at the higher level since 1987) provides another motivation. Throughout the postwar period, Japanese manufacturing generally operated with an assumption that production at home was more efficient (yielded lower production costs and higher quality) than local production abroad. The exceptions were natural resource development, which was dictated by the location of the resources, and cotton textiles, which provided the first wave of Japanese foreign direct investment in the 1970s. Production at home allowed smaller inventories of work in progress, closer communication among all units of production, and an emphasis on the substitution of capital for labor in response to rising wages—a process that yielded higher product quality in the form of lower defects in assembly. Japanese determination to keep production at home had limits, however, and the appreciation of the yen after 1985 exceeded what marginal producers could counter through substitution of capital for labor. The Japanese government and press in the late 1980s stressed how well industry was able to cope with yen appreciation, but that is not the point. Economics stresses the concept of the margin; Toyota might have been able to cope with an even stronger appreciation of the yen in the late 1980s, but some producers could not. Faced with a loss of international price competitiveness, these industries began a major effort to relocate production abroad, chiefly to Southeast Asia. For the first half of the 1980s, the cumulative value of manufacturing investment abroad grew at an average annual rate of 14 percent and then expanded sharply to 28 percent in the second half of the decade.[7]

Some industries not only relocated production abroad, but they began to increase sales back to Japan. Traditionally, Japanese foreign investment in manufacturing was intended to supply either local markets or third markets and not to manufacture products for shipment back to Japan. Survey data on Japanese manufacturing subsidiaries operating in Southeast Asia, though, show that the share of output destined back to Japan increased moderately from 11 percent in 1983 to 16 percent in 1989.[8] This shift is small, but at least indicative of the alteration of perceptions about the acceptability of manufacturing abroad for the Japanese market.

The high overall outflow of capital in the late 1980s was produced to some extent by the financial "bubbles" in Japan. Rising real estate and stock market values gave investors greater collateral to use to finance purchases overseas. The collapse of those bubbles should lead to a diminished flow of new investment to the rest of the world. Indeed, in 1991, the gross outflow of long-term capital from Japan to the rest of the world was $121.9 billion, down 36 percent from the $192.1 billion peak of 1989 and slightly lower than the flows in any year since 1986, as shown in Table 9.2.

Even without the financial bubbles, the fact that one motivation for Japanese foreign investment was a portfolio adjustment in response to deregulation—with investors making up for the earlier limitations on foreign investment—argues in favor of smaller investment flows in the 1990s. A substantially lower gross flow of capital from Japan may characterize the rest of the 1990s, but it is just as important to recognize that these reduced levels should remain substantially above what prevailed prior to 1985, and they certainly will not become negative.

Balance-of-payments data for 1991 indicate an unusual net inflow of long-term capital for the year, leading some commentators to speak of the Japanese ending their wave of foreign investment and pulling their money home. This has not happened on either a net or gross basis. That the current-account surplus was higher in 1991 meant that the overall net of capital from Japan to the rest of the world actually increased. The confusion here stems from looking only at the long-term capital account, which is only one form of possible capital flow. The full balance-of-payments picture shows the long-term capital inflow more than offset by a combination of a net short-term capital outflow, increased foreign exchange holdings of the government, and a sharp increase in private monetary holdings (mainly bank accounts abroad).

Furthermore, the net inflow of long-term capital in 1991 came from a sharp rise in foreigners' investment in Japan, not from a decline in Japanese investment abroad. Gross long-term capital inflow more than doubled, from $77.2 billion in 1990 to $158.5 billion in 1991 (Table 9.2), largely on the strength of a surge of foreign portfolio investment in the Japanese stock market.[9]

The rationale for continued substantial flows of capital during the rest of the 1990s rests on several features of the Japanese economy. First, the financial deregulation that characterized the 1980s will not be reversed. Several embarrassing financial scandals plagued Japan throughout 1990–1991, but they have not led to any serious effort to reimpose barriers on the flow of investment overseas. Second, unlike the first half of the 1980s, there is little prospect that the yen will weaken in the 1990s, so that the cost motivation for direct investment overseas will continue. Third, and most important, Japan is facing the beginning of a long-term demographic shift with strong implications for the economy. The population in the 15- to 64-year-old age bracket—the main pool from which the labor force is drawn—will start falling from 1996, according to current projections. In sharp contrast, this segment of the population was still rising at 1 percent per year as of the mid-1980s. A sustained reduction in this population growth rate did not set in until 1988, and now growth will diminish rapidly each year until it reaches zero in 1995, with absolute decline setting in from 1996. Unlike the overall population projections for the next century, this forecast is quite certain; all of the people who will be in this age segment in the late 1990s have already been born.[10] If broader population projections are correct (showing that the total population will begin shrinking starting in 2006), a declining labor pool will continue for the foreseeable future.

A falling labor-force pool will continue the pressure Japanese firms will feel to engage in overseas investment. Unable to find workers at home, firms must expand overseas if they intend to grow. The pressure that population change imposes on the labor force could be offset partially by rising labor-force participation rates, but a major change in participation seems unlikely at this time. A relatively high proportion of women, for example, are already in the labor force in Japan (compared to other industrial nations). Furthermore, demographic change will impose demands on the allocation of labor, with rising employment in health care and other services for the elderly, which will also strengthen the labor pressures on the manufacturing sector.

The demographic shift could well be the most important change affecting Japan's economic behavior over the next several decades, and this imposes a variety of other considerations. Will society accept more foreign workers in the domestic economy? Will household savings shrink, eliminating the imbalance between private-sector savings and investment (and thereby reducing or eliminating the current-account surplus)? Some Japanese authors see impending disaster for the nation, as the falling population leads to a stagnant economy, an inflow of foreigners, and even (the ultimate threat) foreign purchase of faltering Japanese companies.[11] Journalist Bill Emmott has also sketched a scenario in which demographic change is a primary factor in eliminating the current-account surplus.[12]

The substantial drop in the current-account surplus from 1987 to 1990 (Table 9.1) would also seem to belie its continuation during the 1990s, but one must consider the composition of the change. Much of the drop in those years came in services transactions. The merchandise trade surplus dropped by only about one-third from its peak of $96.4 million in 1987 to $63.5 billion in 1990 (compared to the two-thirds drop in the current-account balance); in 1990 it was actually higher than in 1985. The negative shift in the services accounts was driven principally by the enormous surge in personal travel-related expenditures as a wave of Japanese chose to travel abroad. The travel and transportation accounts combined went from a deficit of $16.1 billion to a deficit of $39.5 billion over these years—a $23.4 billion deterioration. This negative impact was more than sufficient to outweigh the rapidly increasing net surplus on income from investment. The surge in travel may now be over; travel-related expenditures will remain at a high level, but will not grow at the rate of the past several years (because this, too, has been affected by a kind of portfolio shift that may have run its course). The 1991 figures seem to bear this out, with the sum of travel and transportation remaining somewhat constant from the previous year, albeit affected by a temporary drop in travel caused by the 1991 Gulf War.

As the growth rate of foreign travel-related expenditures diminishes, the inexorable rise in investment income in the services portion of the current account that is the result of the cumulative current-account surpluses will act to reduce the overall services deficit. Furthermore, the merchandise trade surplus is rising again. The large scale of plant and equipment investment in the late 1980s brought installation of new equipment that allowed substantial cost reductions in manufacturing, in turn helping to maintain the international price competitiveness of many industries despite the strengthening of the yen. When domestic economic growth slowed in 1991, manufacturers responded in traditional fashion, pushing exports to compensate for domestic sluggishness. As a result, the merchandise trade balance in 1991 (on a balance-of-payments basis) jumped to $103.3 billion from $63.5 billion the previous year.

Japanese government predictions of a current-account surplus on the order of 2 percent of gross domestic product during the rest of the decade is quite probable. After the turn of the century, demographics may have a strong enough impact on reducing domestic savings and increasing government expenditures—mainly through net deficits in the social security account—so that the current-account surpluses will diminish or disappear. But this prospect remains a number of years in the future.

Even an elimination of the current-account surplus during the later 1990s could take place in the context of continued sizable capital outflows, which in this case would be offset by capital inflows. If Japan's importance in the world and the pressures on the nation to play a more active role in the world are motivated by its presence abroad as an investor, then elimination of the current-account surplus per se does not imply a diminishing of those pressures or of Japan's involvement in the outside world.

As noted above, managing assets or workers overseas will have an inherently liberalizing impact on this very insular nation. The investment dimension has, however, also added new problems and issues that could obstruct Japan's emergence as an effective international power. First among these problems is the asymmetry involved in investment, a problem that parallels trade problems. In the past decade an explosive burst of investment by Japanese firms and individuals in the outside world has taken place that has not been matched by a comparable rise in foreign investment in Japan. Whereas the cumulative value of Japanese direct investment abroad grew at a 29 percent annual rate in the 1980s, direct investment by foreigners in Japan grew at only a 12 percent rate. As a result of the decade-long differential in growth rates, the flow of new direct investment from Japan in 1990 was $48 billion, whereas the inflow was only $1.8 billion.[13] By the end of 1990, this wide disparity in the growth of outward and inward investment meant that the cumulative value of Japanese investment abroad was twenty times larger than that of foreign investment in Japan.

Official barriers to inward direct investment were severe in the 1950s and 1960s, but were lowered in a number of steps beginning in 1968 and extending through 1980. Although informal negative pressures may still affect some investments, official investment barriers are no longer part of the bilateral negotiating agenda. Nevertheless, the legacy of the past continues to haunt the present. Had there been no barriers to inward investment in the 1950s and 1960s, then the asymmetry that now characterizes cumulative investment might not have arisen. But it has arisen and creates an imbalance in vested interests.

Politically, one can think of direct investments as a form of hostage taking (or vested-interest building). Foreign firms investing in the local economy develop economic interests that would be harmed by deteriorating economic relations. Those firms then act as a moderating influence on their own governments. The American Chamber of Commerce in Japan (ACCJ), for example, has long been regarded as a voice of moderation on U.S. policy on Japan. But Japan has far too few such foreign hostages benefiting from a presence in its economy who can speak up in their own countries to moderate anti-Japan sentiments. In particular, despite the behavior of the ACCJ, U.S. politicians do not operate with a strong perception of vital U.S. economic interests in Japan that would be jeopardized by worsening bilateral relations.

The importance of direct investments in producing hostages is evident when one considers the role subsidiaries play in generating business for U.S. firms. World sales by the foreign subsidiaries of U.S. firms were three times larger than direct exports from the United States in the mid-1980s. But because of the limited amount of foreign direct investment in Japan, this ratio does not characterize the U.S. bilateral experience, in which subsidiary sales only roughly equal U.S. exports.[14]

Furthermore, European, Japanese, and U.S. firms all prefer majority ownership of foreign subsidiaries. Worldwide, 75 percent of sales of subsidiaries of U.S. firms are from majority-owned operations. Japanese majority-owned operations abroad generate an even higher 85 percent of total sales of their foreign subsidiaries. This tendency does not characterize the U.S. experience in Japan, however, where only 40 percent of sales are by majority-owned subsidiaries—another legacy of a past in which establishment of majority-owned subsidiaries was extremely difficult.[15]

If the world pattern for sales and ownership applied to the U.S. presence in Japan, then U.S. firms would be more of a voice of moderation in Washington policymaking. Until such time as the patterns change, through a major expansion of foreign investment in Japan, the nation faces a problem.

Even today, national treatment for foreign investment in Japan does not mean that ease of entry for investment is equal to that in other countries. A principal means for investing around the world has been the takeover of local firms. Japan stands out in international comparison as a nation where few foreign takeovers occur. The Japanese argue that mergers and acquisitions are not part of their culture, and that national treatment implies foreign firms must adapt to local conditions. Nevertheless, another serious asymmetry has developed. Not engaging in takeovers may be a Japanese trait, but Japanese firms have proven to be eager to engage in such behavior abroad. In 1990, Japanese firms acquired 464 firms abroad and 306 firms at home, whereas foreign acquisitions of firms in Japan totaled only 17.[16] These figures represent a serious deterioration from 1985, when Japanese acquisitions abroad totaled a much smaller figure of 100, and foreign acquisitions in Japan were a somewhat larger 26.[17] In contrast, foreigners purchased between 125 and 264 U.S. firms each year from 1982 to 1987. Domestic merger and acquisition activity in Japan in total does not appear to be substantially less than that in the United States.[18]

The problem here is not the lack of *hostile* takeovers by foreigners in Japan, but the lack of *friendly* takeovers. Japanese firms do not appear actively to seek foreign firms as potential purchasers. To the extent that this attitude is deeply ingrained in Japanese business mentality, rather than imposed by government, the prognosis for the future is not particularly bright.[19] The government could, however, use moral suasion or administrative guidance to try to boost the market for foreign takeovers and inward investment in general.

Import Behavior

The international institutional framework governing (noncommunist bloc) trade and investment in the postwar era—embodied principally in the General Agreement on Tariffs and Trade—was established without Japanese participation. Once Japan was included within the system in 1955, the government regarded the GATT as an international public good. It was a framework supplying a "good"—more open access to foreign markets—to all participants, which Japan could consume without making any real contribution itself (in the form of market opening at home). That behavior was tolerated by the United States in the 1950s, but for the past thirty years Japan has been under pressure from many of its trading partners to reduce its trade barriers.

Despite many years of market-opening measures, during the 1980s Japan's import behavior continued to appear to be more protectionist than that of other nations. This impression that Japan remained less open than other nations led to increased dissatisfaction on the part of key trading partners, especially the United States.

Evaluation of the trade behavior of Japan was the subject of the book *Japan's Unequal Trade* by Lincoln, which looked at a variety of issues related to market access in Japan.[20] One of the initial efforts of the research for that book was to look at the simple ratio of manufactured imports to GDP in Japan and other countries, as a measure of the actual penetration of the economy by imports. This ratio obviously varies considerably with a variety of economic factors—population, income levels, and the existence of such special institutional arrangements as the European Community—but a number of econometric studies have now identified Japan as an outlier even when these factors are included. The ratio of manufactured imports to GDP has been unusually low in Japan, and it failed to rise over time even as Japan lowered official trade barriers.

Intra-industry trade has been the other major distinctive feature of Japanese trade. The simple theory of comparative advantage explains why nations export some products and import others; it does not explain why a nation would both export and import similar products. A large portion of trade, however, especially among industrial nations, is in the form of exports and imports of products falling within the same industry classification. The United States, for example, is the world's largest exporter of office equipment and also the world's largest importer of office equipment. Economic explanations of why this trade takes place rest on a combination of two factors: product differentiation (office equipment includes a wide variety of individual products that are not entirely similar) and economies of scale (through which firms can lower their average cost per unit by increasing production to supply export markets as well as the domestic market).

All nations engage in intra-industry trade to some extent, but national experience varies widely. Economists have found that the extent of intra-industry trade tends to rise as trade barriers fall, as nations achieve higher levels of industrialization, as they simply become larger economically, and as they converge in terms of income levels. From the 1960s to the 1980s, Japan moved upward in all of these measures, moving from being an economically small developing country to being a large, advanced, industrial nation closer in size and per capita income to its major industrial trading partners. Contrary to the observed results for other nations, however, intra-industry trade did not expand for Japan. The index number for intra-industry trade in manufactured products for Japan was thirty-two in 1970 and actually declined somewhat to twenty-six by 1985.[21] This level was less than half that of the United States in 1985, fifty-four, and even farther below the European nations.

Since the publication of *Japan's Unequal Trade*, a variety of other studies have appeared concerning Japanese trade behavior. Not all statistical studies have agreed that Japanese trade behavior has been unusual, although most of these were published prior to 1990. Two recent Australian efforts have focused specifically on the intra-industry trade question. Working with a general trade model, Philip Lowe tests again whether convergence of resource endowments and factor composition (relative endowments of land, labor, and capital), increasing economic size, and convergence of economic size lead to higher levels of intra-industry trade. His model pools cross-section and annual time series data for bilateral country pairs from 1965 to 1985. Although his work was intended as a general test of intra-industry trade behavior, without a specific focus on Japan, he finds Japanese intra-industry trade behavior to be significantly lower than predicted from the late 1970s to 1985.[22]

John Ravenhill, in another Australian study of Japanese intra-industry trade, also finds that Japanese patterns are contrary to expectations. He concludes that the biggest improvement in intra-industry performance by Japan in the late 1980s did not come in the advanced products that commonly characterize such trade among industrial nations, but rather in material or labor-intensive products. That is, intra-industry trade appears to be increasing mainly in those industries that are in decline in Japan, not those at the core of the manufacturing sector.[23]

Research in the United States has recently turned to investigation of the role of the Japanese vertical and horizontal business groupings—*keiretsu*—as a possible explanation for the observed differences in import and intra-industry trade behavior. The horizontal groupings involve a variety of ties among firms in different industries, with group membership related to the prewar large business groups (*zaibatsu*). With some intragroup equity ties and some dependence on loans from group banks, plus a variety of periodic meetings of group corporate executives, the argument is that loyalty to the group causes member firms to skew their purchases toward other group members.

The vertical groupings involve relations between major manufacturers and either their parts suppliers or their distributors. These ties tend to be tighter and longer lasting than those in the U.S. corporate world. Although long-term dealings may yield some economic benefits (such as enhanced communication between manufacturers and parts suppliers, or higher quality control),[24] the ties seem to go beyond the purely economic. The fact that retiring employees often end up with the firm's parts suppliers or distributers, or that managers of the various group firms spend long hours drinking or playing golf together, suggests that personal relationships add a distinctly noneconomic dimension to preservation of ties within these groups.[25]

Economist Robert Lawrence began his investigation using an econometric model of international trade patterns to which he added data on the share of industry output originating from firms with vertical or horizontal *keiretsu* ties. He found that a larger presence of *keiretsu*—either vertical or horizontal—in an industry is negatively associated with imports of products in that industry category.[26] Economist Marcus Noland has now extended this work. He also finds that horizontal groupings have a negative impact on imports, although the evidence is not as strong as in the Law-rence research.[27] Both of these studies suggest that the vertical *keiretsu* may have an efficiency impact, because they are associated with both lower imports and higher exports (which one would expect if vertical *keiretsu* structures made Japanese manufacturers more competitive). This research, however, should be regarded as only in an early phase, with fur-ther arguments expected on both sides.

One of the criticisms leveled by numerous Japanese government offi-cials against some of these studies has been that import behavior was changing rapidly in the middle to late 1980s and that these changes are not reflected in the statistical data used in most of the published studies. Since 1985, the appreciation of the yen against the dollar has stimulated a rapid expansion of manufactured imports. From 1985 to 1990, manufactured im-ports expanded at an average annual rate of 26 percent. Within that ex-pansion, imports of U.S. products in categories that had been subject to negotiations during the 1980s rose at an even higher pace. A recent Con-gressional Research Service study found that the average annual growth rate of U.S. products in these particular categories was 30 percent in the 1985 to 1990 period, compared to a 21 percent average annual growth rate for U.S. exports to Japan as a whole.[28] Rapid import growth brought the ratio of manufactured imports to GDP up from 2.6 percent in 1985 to 3.8 percent by 1990.[29] This change represents a substantial rapid improve-ment, but still leaves manufactured import penetration as a share of GDP in Japan at less than half the level of the United States—8.1 percent in 1988—and by far the lowest in the Organization for Economic Coopera-tion and Development. A more rapid increase in this ratio than what actu-ally prevailed in this five-year period might not have been possible, but for Japanese behavior to converge more closely to that of other industrial nations will require a continuation of these trends of the past several years.

An argument can be made that the nominal figures understate the real change in imports. Because the yen appreciated against the dollar, the same physical volume of foreign manufactured goods could be purchased with fewer yen. The yen's strengthened purchasing power actually caused the ratio of manufactured imports to GDP to drop from 1985 through 1987 even though the dollar value of manufactured imports was expanding. Nevertheless, the nominal ratio is more important for evaluating Japanese import behavior because it indicates how the society is allocating its in-come between domestic products and imports; a yen appreciation that pro-duced a rise in the volume of imports while the Japanese actually spent fewer yen buying them (causing the ratio of manufactured imports to GDP to fall) would imply that behavior had not changed in any fundamental sense. Only a choice to allocate a larger share of nominal GDP to the pur-chase of manufactured imports demonstrates a shift in behavior in a more open direction that is consistent with the patterns of other nations.

Intra-industry trade has also experienced some change since 1985. One factor complicating this measurement, though, is the 1988 shift of all major nations to a new standardized industrial classification for international trade, making a direct comparison back to 1985 difficult. Detailed Japanese data denominated in yen, however, are now available through 1990. Calculations based on these data, using a four-digit Harmonized Commodity Description and Coding System (HS) industry classification, show that the index number measuring intra-industry trade increased from 24.8 in 1988 to 29.0 in 1990, a 17 percent increase in the two years.[30] These numbers are not directly comparable to those cited above because of both the different classification scheme and the denomination of trade in yen instead of dollars. Nevertheless, they certainly sustain a conclusion that the degree to which Japan engages in intra-industry trade has increased.

The increases are fairly broadly distributed. Of the 973 industries in the four-digit HS classification, 551 show an increase in the degree of intra-industry trade. An additional unusual feature of Japan's trade patterns has been that in those industries that generate large exports, the level of intra-industry has been exceptionally low (that is, imports have been very low), in contrast to much higher levels of intra-industry trade characterizing the successful export industries of other countries. But from 1988 to 1990, intra-industry trade increased in eight of the ten largest four-digit export industries, suggesting that even here some progressive change has taken place (in at least modest contrast to the results obtained by John Ravenhill reported above).

In addition, the United Nations continued to compile trade data for 1989 on the older Standard International Trade Classification (SITC). Those data (using three-digit industry categories) show Japan's intra-industry trade index number to have increased to 34 (a 30 percent increase from 1985) and an increase for the United States to 67, leaving Japan still at roughly half the level of the United States.[31] Possibly a broad international comparison based on 1990 data would show some further modest improvement in Japan's relative position.

The data on both manufactured imports and intra-industry trade for Japan are moderately encouraging. The ratio of manufactured imports to GDP and the level of intra-industry trade have increased, and these changes are substantial enough to suggest an alteration of real behavior in a direction that makes markets more open in Japan to foreign products. The critical question for the 1990s is whether these changes will continue. Because the changes through 1990 leave Japan still far behind other major industrial nations, further change will be necessary to demonstrate that Japan is not an unusual outlier in the international system.

The evidence on continuation of changes leading to import expansion remains mixed. For consumer luxury goods, the rapid increase in imports was related to the unusual financial developments of the late 1980s, in which conspicuous consumption was enhanced by the bubbles in the stock market and in real estate. Expensive German-made cars were a particular beneficiary in this period, but now automobile imports in Japan are actually declining because of the collapse of the financial bubbles. The trade data cited above suggest that the increase in manufactured imports and intra-industry trade goes well beyond luxury consumer goods, and, for these other product areas, the trends that began in the late 1980s might be sustained into the 1990s.

Foreign direct investment also has a bearing on these trends. The rapid rise in Japanese direct investment in manufacturing abroad is bringing with it an increase in Japanese imports from overseas manufacturing subsidiaries. One of the factors involved in Japan's extremely low levels of manufactured imports in the past has been the paucity of this sort of intra-firm imports from overseas operations. Because the factors causing foreign direct investment will intensify during the 1990s, it is reasonable to assume that imports from those operations will also continue to increase, a trend that ought to cause a rise in intra-industry trade as well.

On the other hand, a worrisome development is now occurring. From 1987 to 1989, the Japanese government appeared to be receptive and progressive toward the rapid increase in manufactured imports, an attitude that represents a sharp contrast to those prevailing throughout most of the postwar period. Government surveys concluding that retail prices were considerably higher in Japan than in other countries, white papers arguing that imports were beneficial to the nation, and a variety of programs promoting imports were part of the new attitudes.[32] More recently, however, attitudes again appear to be changing. Japanese government officials again are repeating the refrain that all of the adjustment has been made and that Japanese trade behavior is no longer different from that of other nations. This argument has been a familiar part of the arsenal of excuses and rebuttals made in the past thirty to forty years. As is usually the case when such arguments are put forth, they are untrue. Japan has made considerable adjustment, but trade behavior remains substantially different from other major industrial nations.

Representative of these hardening attitudes is an article by an official of the Ministry of International Trade and Industry in the MITI English-language publication, *Journal of Japanese Trade and Industry*, which argues that foreign research pointing out the low level of manufactured imports or low intra-industry trade is based on misunderstandings or misuse of the statistics.[33] As is usual in such defensive pieces, this one deals largely with the ratio of manufactured imports to total imports rather than to the GNP, a ratio that does not have any particular meaning. Its discussion of intra-industry trade also displays a complete lack of understanding of the issue, arguing that intra-industry trade is low because Japanese firms are successful at exporting.[34] Coming after several years of relatively progressive statements about the desirability of increasing manufactured imports and acknowledgment of some of the differences between Japan and the rest of the world, this type of misguided, feisty defensive posture is rather disturbing.

It is worthwhile to repeat that further Japanese progress on these issues is likely to be a prerequisite to healthier economic ties between Japan and its economic partners. Less conflictual economic links, in turn, will facilitate a broader Japanese international leadership role.

Conclusion

For Japan to play a larger role in world economic and political policy affairs, two elements are necessary: (1) an ability to become actively involved in international policy formation, and (2) an ability to behave in a manner that creates a willingness on the part of other nations to accept Japan's policy role. Several chapters in this volume address the first of these elements; the second concern is addressed in this chapter.

Framed in this manner, the academic debate over whether the Japanese market is distinctively less open to trade and investment than are other countries takes on a meaning that is quite different than that usually assumed. Those who believe that the market is open feel that pressure on Japan to open its markets is misdirected. But this debate misses a far more important point. From the standpoint of Japanese leadership or participation in international policymaking, it is critical that other nations perceive Japan as a nation whose behavior and policies are desirable or acceptable.

Even if the asymmetry in investment behavior, the relatively low ratio of manufactured imports to GNP, or the low intra-industry trade level could be explained by a set of unique historical and current economic factors, negative reactions to Japan would not be erased. All three of these features of trade and investment behavior are consistent with the general pattern of Japanese insularity, and that pattern does not inspire confidence on the part of other nations. If one really believed that such features of trade and investment were due to rational economic factors, the dilemma facing Japan would be even more difficult. In order to gain the confidence of its trading partners, Japan would have to adopt unusual nonmarket-driven behavior at home—that is, unusually high levels of imports, intra-industry trade, and inward investment.

The changes that occurred in the 1985–1990 period are real and encouraging. Manufactured import penetration of the economy increased, intra-industry trade increased (even in most of the leading export industries in Japan), and inward direct investment grew more rapidly. But at the present time these changes remain insufficient; in fact, the asymmetry on investment has increased because of the enormous burst of outward investment. If these changes represent a one-time shift in Japanese behavior, they leave all the measures at a level still too low to inspire the confidence abroad that will be critical to a larger and more productive Japanese role in world affairs. Whether these measures of foreign penetration of Japan will continue to increase, and thereby produce that confidence, remains in considerable doubt at the present time.

Notes

1. Economic Planning Agency, *Annual Report on National Income Statistics* (Tokyo: Ministry of Finance Printing Office, various years).

2. The relationship between a current-account surplus and a net capital outflow is a straightforward accounting result. Put in the simplest terms, if a nation has a current-account surplus, it has chosen not to buy as many goods and services from the rest of the world as it has sold. The difference represents the purchase of the assets of these countries instead. Even if one thinks of an extreme case, in which the surplus is held in the form of foreign currency (e.g., the Japanese simply decide to hold the dollars they receive for their exports and buy nothing with them at all), a capital transaction has taken place because currency represents non–interest-bearing debt instruments of governments. In reality, most of the surplus dollars or other foreign currencies resulting from the trade transactions are invested in real and financial assets that yield a positive return.

3. Bank of Japan, International Department, *Balance of Payments Monthly* (Tokyo: Bank of Japan, April 1991), p. 83.

4. Ibid. It is not possible to make strong comparisons among countries because on a balance-of-payments basis investments are counted at their original value, not their current market value. A U.S. investment of $100 in the Japanese stock market in 1960, for example, would still be listed in the U.S. statistics as $100. The United States reported U.S. ownership of $1.3 trillion in foreign assets as of the end of 1988, and a cumulative foreign direct investment of $329 billion. U.S. Department of Commerce, Bureau of the Census, *Statistical Abstract of the United States 1990* (Washington, D.C.: U.S. Government Printing Office, 1990), pp. 793–794.

5. *Balance of Payments Monthly.* Keep in mind that these statistics differ somewhat from the Ministry of Finance series on foreign direct investment. Those figures showed a larger cumaluative direct investment value of $254 billion as of 1989. The source for this information is *Okurasho Kokusai Kin'yukyoku Nenpo* (Annual Report of the Ministry of Finance International Finance Bureau) (Tokyo: Kin'yu Zaisei Jijo Kenkyukai, 1990), p. 447. The balance-of-payments figures were used here for the sake of comparison to total investment. The Ministry of Finance data yield a somewhat lower 24 percent average annual growth rate over the course of the decade.

6. *Okurasho Kokusai Kin'yukyoku Nenpo,* 1982, pp. 351, 355; 1990, pp. 443–447. Note that the definition of Europe in these statistics includes Eastern Europe and the Soviet Union.

7. Ibid., 1982, p. 357; 1990, p. 449.

8. Ministry of International Trade and Industry, *Kaigai Toshi Tokei Soran* (Overview of overseas investment statistics) (Tokyo: Ministry of Finance Printing Office, 1991), p. 19. This ratio was actually down slightly from a peak of 16.7 percent in 1987.

9. *Balance of Payments Monthly*, December 1991, p. 65. Foreign purchases of Japanese corporate equity went from an actual negative $13 billion in 1990 (where negative means net liquidation of holdings), to a positive $46 billion in 1991—a $59 billion shift in one year. This accounts for a large part of the jump in foreign long-term investment in Japan in 1991. Bonds (with purchases up $4 billion over the 1990 level) and increased issues of foreign bond issues by Japanese firms (up $17 billion) accounted for the rest of the increase.

10. Data are from Bank of Japan, "Recent Changes in Japan's Labor Market and Their Impact—Synopsis," Special Paper no. 202, May 1991, p. 30. These developments are unaffected by the population forecast issued later that summer because all members of these age segment had already been born. The new population estimates do, however, imply a steeper decline than anticipated in earlier forecasts in the working-age population pool after the year 2006.

11. See Shoji Yoneda, *Nihon ga Abunai: Bokai no Kiki ni Do Taisho Suru* (Japan in danger: How to deal with the crisis of collapse) (Tokyo: Daiyamondo, 1989), pp. 19–21, 24–25; see also Shoji Yoneda, *Nihon Jinko Hokai: Shusseiritsu Ijo Teika no Gen'in to Taisaku* (Japan's population collapse: The causes of and policies toward the abnormal decline of the birth rate) (Tokyo: Koseido Shuppan, 1991), p. 25, in which Yoneda argues that the purchase of Japanese companies by foreigners must be avoided at all costs.

12. Bill Emmott, *The Sun Also Sets: Why Japan Will Not Be Number One* (New York: Simon and Schuster, 1989), esp. pp. 221–241. Emmott also assumes that the trend of rising manufactured imports will continue (driven by changing tastes in society), as will expansion of foreign travel by Japanese.

13. *Balance of Payments Monthly*, April 1991, pp. 59, 65, 83. These balance-of-payments figures actually show a contraction of cumulative foreign investments in Japan in 1989. The Ministry of Finance data show a higher 18 percent growth rate for inward direct investment for 1980 to 1989 (*Okurasho Kokusai Kin'yukyoku Nenpo*, 1982, p. 364; 1990, p. 467). But an essentially similar asymmetry characterizes the new flow of investment in this data series; the inflow for 1989 was $2.9 billion, compared to a $57 billion outflow.

14. Dennis J. Encarnation, *Beyond Trade: Foreign Investment in the US-Japan Rivalry* (Ithaca, N.Y.: Cornell University Press, forthcoming).

15. Ibid.

16. A. T. Kearny, Inc., *Trade and Investment in Japan: The Current Environment* (Tokyo: The American Chamber of Commerce in Japan, June 1991), p. 19.

17. Masayuki Hara, "U.S. Direct Investment in Japan," *Journal of Japanese Trade and Industry* (November/December 1990): 17.

18. Jon Choy, "Japan and Mergers: Oil and Water?" *JEI Report*, no. 14A (April 6, 1990): 3, 9. Note that the statistics on the number of foreign acquisitions in both the United States and Japan do not measure the size of the corporations acquired. The asset value of firms would probably make the disparity even larger. For mergers and acquisitions as a whole, 2,032 transactions took place in the United States in 1987, compared to an even larger 2,364 in Japan, although the value of assets involved was $164 billion in the United States and only $24 billion in Japan.

19. In the recent past the government was also part of the problem as well. The Ministry of Finance was seeking a bank to acquire the failing Heiwa Sogo Bank in 1985, and quickly pushed Sumitomo Bank into the role of suitor when Citicorp expressed a strong interest in the acquisition.

20. Edward J. Lincoln, *Japan's Unequal Trade* (Washington, D.C.: Brookings Institution, 1990).

21. Ibid., p. 47. Intra-industry trade is usually measured statistically by the following formula:

$$IIT_i = [1 - \frac{|x_i - m_i|}{(x_i + m_i)}] \, 100$$

where IIT_i is the index of intra-industry trade for industry i, and x_i and m_i are exports and imports, respectively, in industry i. This formula produces a statistic that ranges from 0 to 100, with the intuitive outcome that 0 represents no intra-industry trade (either exports or imports are zero) and 100 represents perfect intra-industry trade (exports exactly equal imports). To calculate the extent of intra-industry trade for the nation as a whole (IIT), the statistic for individual industries is normally summed using the weights of each in total trade:

$$IIT = \sum_{i=1}^{n} IIT_i \, \frac{x_i + m_i}{X + M}$$

where X and M are total exports and total imports, respectively, of manufactures for the nation:

$$X = \sum_{i=1}^{n} X_i \; ; \; M = \sum_{i=1}^{n} m_i$$

22. Philip William Lowe, "Resource Convergence and Intra-Industry Trade," unpublished paper from the Reserve Bank of Australia, July 1991, esp. p. 27. In Lowe's model, a dummy variable for Japan tests as significantly different from zero, after inclusion of variables for economic size, resource endowment, and factor endowment.

23. John Ravenhill, "Managing Pacific Trade Relations: Economic Dynamism and Political Immobilism," unpublished paper prepared for the First Australian Fulbright Symposium, Australian National University, December 16–17, 1991.

24. Masaharu Yoshitomi, "Keiretsu: An Insider's Guide to Japan's Conglomerates," *International Economic Insights* (September/October 1990).

25. For a recent introduction to both the horizontal and vertical *keiretsu*, see Michael L. Gerlach, *The Keiretsu: A Primer* (New York: The Japan Society, 1992).

26. Robert Z. Lawrence, "Efficient or Exclusionist? The Import Behavior of Japanese Corporate Groups," *The Brookings Papers on Economic Activity*, no. 1 (1991): 311–341. Lawrence does find, however, some weak evidence that vertical *keiretsu* also have a positive impact on exports, suggesting that their trade behavior might be associated with efficiency gains.

27. Marcus Noland, "Public Policy, Private Preferences, and the Japanese Trade Pattern," unpublished paper, January 1991.

28. Peter L. Gold and Dick K. Nanto, "Japan-U.S. Trade: U.S. Exports of Negotiated Products, 1985–1990," Congressional Research Service Report, Washington, D.C., November 26, 1991, p. 10. This report measures export growth and not market share; whether these products grew faster because barriers were reduced or because the markets for these products were growing unusually rapidly during this period is a question outside the scope of the study.

29. See Lincoln, *Japan's Unequal Trade*, p. 19 for 1985 data; 1990 data are calculated from Bank of Japan, *Economic Statistics Annual 1990* (Tokyo: Bank of Japan, 1991). The 1990 ratio uses GNP rather than GDP.

30. Customs Bureau, Ministry of Finance, *Japan's Exports and Imports: Commodity by Country* (Tokyo: Japan Tariff Association, December 1988, December 1989, and December 1990).

31. John Ravenhill, "Managing Pacific Trade Relations," table 3.

32. See Lincoln, *Japan's Unequal Trade*, pp. 114–120.

33. Satoshi Kuwahara, "The Fallacy of Trade Ratios," *Journal of Japanese Trade and Industry* (January/February 1992).

34. Ibid., pp. 44–46.

10

Japan's Capital Exports: Molding East Asia

Danny Unger

Japan's potential to act as a global leader rests on its desire and ability to use its enormous economic power. Potentially the most important basis of Japan's influence lies in its dominant role in global financial markets. Japan is now a major purveyor of credit to a world in need of funds for investment.

This chapter addresses ways in which Japanese capital exports, private and public, have been and are likely to be used to serve Japanese global interests. The principal substantive foci are on Japanese Official Development Assistance policies and Japanese interest in, and encouragement of, closer economic integration in East Asia. These two issues are combined here because of Asia's predominant role as a recipient of official Japanese capital outflows and of private outflows used to facilitate industrial restructuring in Japan.

Japan emerged in the late 1980s as the world's principal source of capital. During the 1970s and into the 1980s, the Japanese government's deficit spending offset the high rate of savings among Japanese households. Because public sector deficits abated while household savings remained high, Japanese savings moved offshore, particularly to the United States, to meet foreign demand. The United States became the world's largest debtor, and Japan grew to become the principal capital surplus country. Financial activity in Japan picked up; the Nikkei Stock Exchange temporarily surpassed the New York exchange in terms of volume of transactions and Japanese banks rapidly increased their share of international bank lending. Private Japanese businesses moved offshore, establishing foreign subsidiaries, buying foreign operations, and investing in overseas equity markets and various financial instruments. Japanese government ODA expanded, as Japan, along with the United States, became the world's major source of development assistance.

The United States consumed by far the greatest share of Japan's capital surpluses, and the industrializing capitalist economies of East Asia were the principal beneficiaries among developing countries. Japanese Ministry of Finance figures indicate that during fiscal year 1989, East Asian countries received more than $8 billion in Japanese direct investment, some 12 percent of Japan's total for the year and far more than other developing regions. In 1991, Japanese firms made direct investments in East Asia of nearly $6 billion, more than 14 percent of total investments for that year.[1] Whereas the developing world as a whole began to experience net outflows of capital in the early 1980s, largely a result of massive debt repayments, East Asian industrializing countries received large inflows of Japanese public assistance. Real foreign direct investment in developing countries declined through the 1980s, but Japanese firms in East Asia made major new investments, in part to establish new offshore manufacturing facilities.

Different actors operating according to disparate logics control Japan's public and private offshore capital flows. Nonetheless, the two processes sometimes work in tandem and complement each other. Nowhere is this more evident than in developing East Asia. In the 1970s, this region attracted a major share of both public and private Japanese capital moving abroad. Today, the East Asian share of vastly increased private capital flows is much smaller, even as the absolute amount of Japanese investment in the region has increased dramatically. And although the region's share of Japanese ODA also is diminishing, here, too, the absolute level of assistance has grown dramatically, and East Asia continues to receive some 60 percent of all Japanese bilateral aid.

The level of Japanese private capital flows to the East Asian region pales beside that going to the European Community or the United States, but nonetheless these investments play a crucial role in the Japanese and East Asian economies. A large part of private investment in the other industrialized countries is driven by a concern to outflank protectionist movements; most Japanese firms, however, look to East Asia to exploit various cost advantages, particularly lower wages. Japanese private investment flows, including direct investment aimed at securing management control of offshore productive activities, stimulate processes of industrial restructuring both in Japan and in the recipient economies. As part of these processes, Japanese manufacturers are establishing new plants in East Asian developing countries and increasing their shipments of goods from overseas subsidiaries back to Japan.[2] Meanwhile, Japanese public development assistance facilitates this process of mutual adaptation.

More broadly, capital exports represent the first critical postwar test of Japanese foreign policy goals and operational style. Both ODA and direct investment flows involve closer commitments than generally are involved in trading relations. (Chapter 9 by Edward Lincoln makes this point in greater depth.) Generally, capital exports afford greater influence than can be derived from trade relations.

Japan's share of global trade has never approached its dominant role as a purveyor of capital: Japan's cumulative current-account surplus is more than half a trillion dollars, several times the peak registered by the United States in 1981. Because U.S. and West European contributions to the global capital stock are limited by balance-of-payments deficits, former communist countries initiating structural economic reforms, Arab countries rebuilding from the Gulf War, U.S. residents wanting to borrow against the future, and would-be developing countries now turn to Japan to meet their needs for capital.[3]

Japanese leaders long have been interested in fostering closer economic links with the other economies of East Asia. Even in the late nineteenth century, some Japanese believed that the region was "bound to emerge in the coming century as a great theater of world politics and trade."[4] At the time, it was natural to believe that Japan "is destined to create an East Asian economic empire."[5] Indeed, with the rapid expansion of aid, investment, and trade links in the late 1980s, many analyses have focused on Japan's role in creating an integrated regional economy under Japan's leadership. The nature and extent of these developments will be decided, in large part, by forces outside of Japan (as discussed more fully in Chapter 2 by Robert Gilpin).

Official Development Assistance Policies

One estimate suggests that Japan now provides a quarter of net resource flows to developing countries.[6] In 1989 the funds included more than $8.9 billion in ODA, $13.5 billion in direct investment, and $36 billion in commercial lending.[7] Japan and the United States are the world's leading donors of ODA. Japan is the largest source of assistance in more than a score of developing countries and now plays an important role in providing aid to African states. As Japan has increased its development lending, it has also changed the nature of that assistance (see Table 10.1). A greater share of Japanese aid is now available in the form of grants than in the past (although Japan still ranks at the bottom among donor countries in terms of the grant element of its ODA); more aid provided on softer terms is going to countries in which Japan's commercial interests are limited; technical assistance is increasing while the emphasis on infrastructure is declining (from 49 percent of total bilateral aid in 1988 to 32 percent in 1990); and Japan is now more prone to exercise its potential influence to shape politics and development strategies in recipient countries.[8] Japan is providing aid to countries in Eastern Europe and the Commonwealth of Independent States. Poland ($150 million) and Turkey ($324 million) were among the top ten recipients of Japanese aid in 1990.[9] Japan is also a key player in efforts to alleviate the debt burdens afflicting many developing

countries, including much of Central America.[10] Aid to Latin America increased from $118 million in 1980 to $563 million in 1989.[11] In pursuing
diverse goals through ODA, Japan tries to coordinate its efforts with other
donor countries.[12]

Table 10.1 Japan's 1990 ODA (in $ millions)

Bilateral grant assistance	1,374
Bilateral technical assistance	1,645
Bilateral loans	3,920
Contributions to multilateral organizations	2,282
Total	9,221

Source: Ministry of Foreign Affairs, *Official Development Assistance, 1991* (Tokyo:
Association for Promotion of International Cooperation, 1992).

Japan also has increased its lending in support of environmental goals,
an area in which Japanese ODA policies have been deficient in the past. At
the 1992 Rio conference, Japan committed $7 billion over five years to as-
sist developing countries in addressing environmental problems.[13] Japan
also has introduced more small-scale grant aid, assistance for structural adjustment, and aid to nongovernmental organizations. Further changes in
Japan's ODA may follow publication of the report on ODA programs by
the Provisional Council for the Promotion of Administrative Reform.

In addition, Japan has moved to reformulate the rationales underlying
its aid program. In part in response to foreign criticism, some Japanese
want to use Japan's ODA to serve such political goals as supporting the
development of democracy. This new political emphasis was evident in the
"Kuranari Doctrine" outlining Japanese aid programs in the Western
Pacific.[14] The Foreign Ministry signaled a shift in Japanese approaches in
its 1990 white paper on ODA, in which it suggested that ODA could be
conditioned on recipient countries' adoption of appropriate development
strategies, limit of military spending, and progress toward democratization.[15] In a speech before the Diet in 1990, Prime Minister Kaifu outlined
a plan to use ODA in support of a new international order:

> The new international order that we are seeking must first of all guaran-
> tee peace and security. Second, there must be respect for freedom and
> democracy. Third, we must work to achieve world prosperity under an
> open, market-oriented economy. Fourth, we must create an environment
> in which people can enjoy humane living conditions. Fifth, we must es-
> tablish stable international relations based on dialogue and harmony.[16]

The 1991 edition of the white paper codified the so-called Kaifu Doctrine.
Japan suspended (and later restored) its ODA to China and Myanmar
(Burma) in response to human rights concerns; it also cut off aid to Haiti

following the military coup in 1991.[17] Also that year, Prime Minister Kiichi Miyazawa suggested that Japanese aid to Indonesia (nearly $2 billion in 1991) and Myanmar might be linked to progress on human rights. The Japanese government also has adopted an ODA charter that lays out the underlying philosophy and principles of its aid.

In recent years, Japan has moved rapidly to reduce the level of its tied aid. Formally, very little Japanese aid is tied relative to that of other donor countries. Of Japanese loans, 90 percent is "general untied" aid.[18] Looking at the awarding of contracts based on Japanese ODA, the share going to (undisguised) Japanese firms dropped from 75 percent in 1984 to 27 percent in 1990.[19] These figures, provided by official Japanese sources, should not be taken too seriously. There is, however, considerable evidence of a trend away from tied aid.

Nonetheless, Japanese government-business cooperation in foreign economic relations continues in the areas of investment, aid, and trade. Japan initiated establishment of the $2 billion ASEAN-Japan Development Fund in 1987 to provide financing for joint ventures in the ASEAN region. The Japanese government also launched the Japan-ASEAN Investment Corporation in 1981. Ministry of International Trade and Industry officials in Southeast Asia have attempted to reproduce some of the instruments of industrial policy as practiced in Japan. It is consistent with the general Japanese perception regarding its economic assistance that in Japanese usage the term "economic cooperation" encompasses not only grant aid and concessionary loans, but private loans and investment flows as well. Both MITI and the Japanese Economic Planning Agency have economic cooperation bureaus, reflecting a basic assumption about the potential for, and desirability of, "harmonizing" Japan's economic cooperation with the needs of Japan as well as developing countries to adjust their industrial structures.

Japan has been strikingly successful in achieving this harmony between its interests and those of developing Asian economies. Japanese manufacturing firms moved offshore into Asia in the late 1960s and early 1970s, and again in the mid-1980s, responding in both cases to the appreciation of the yen. In each instance, Japanese firms going offshore found hospitable production sites in Asian countries, accelerating shifts from import-substituting to export-oriented industrialization strategies.[20]

Japanese officials, particularly in MITI, are trying to create economic complementarities among the smaller East Asian economies and Japan. Not all officials assume that this will result naturally from the play of market forces. In fact, MITI hopes to target particular industries in specific ASEAN countries.[21]

The Japanese government recognizes the role that its ODA can play in stimulating private investment in developing countries. As the Foreign Ministry notes,

The development of vigorous business activity by the private sector is vital to the advancement of the developing countries, and it is important to recognize that aid can contribute to the creation of environments for such activity through the improvement of industrial and social infrastructure.[22]

In 1989, private Japanese capital flows to developing countries far exceeded public ones—$13.5 billion versus $9 billion—although the latter figure exceeded the former in 1990—$9.2 billion versus $6.3 billion.[23]

A look at some Japanese economic assistance institutions will help to illustrate the ways in which the Japanese government and private business firms are able to cooperate in providing economic assistance to developing countries.[24] The Japan Overseas Development Corporation (JODC) is funded by the Japanese government as well as by private sources. It supports a range of services including sending Japanese technicians abroad to train local workers (the Japan Expert Service Abroad program). It also provides finance for smaller-sized Japanese firms investing abroad and finances the import of primary and processed goods that are produced by Japanese joint ventures supported by the Japanese government.[25] More than two-thirds of the cases of JODC concessional financing through the 1980s were for projects in East Asia, and more than half of those were in the ASEAN countries. JODC also dispatches most of its experts to East Asia. For example, of 880 cases as of the late 1980s, 260 were for the textile industry and 222 of those went to East Asia, including 88 to Indonesia, 45 to the Philippines, 32 to Thailand, and 27 to Taiwan.[26]

The Association for Overseas Technical Scholarship (AOTS) was founded in 1959 with MITI backing. By 1989 it had trained more than 40,000 workers, the vast majority Asians. The program is funded by the Japanese government (three-fourths) and private industry. The largest numbers of workers trained have been Indonesian, South Korean, Thai, and Chinese. AOTS training is most common in the transport machinery, electrical and electronics, chemicals, metallurgical, and textile industries.[27] Japanese firms in these industries have been important investors in East Asia.

The Japan International Cooperation Agency (JICA) also is active in bringing Asian trainees to Japan and sending Japanese technicians to Asian developing countries. For the ASEAN countries alone, the flow of people in each direction between 1954 and 1986 was about 25,000.[28]

Economic Structural Adjustment
for International Harmony

Along with the other members of the Group of Five leading capitalist economies (later expanded, with the inclusion of Canada and Italy, to become the Group of Seven), Japan and the United States agreed in September 1985 to seek the yen's appreciation against the dollar as a means of stemming Japan's growing trade surpluses and ever-larger U.S. deficits. In response to the yen's rapid rise, MITI devised a regional industrialization plan that responded to foreign pressures while promising relief for Japan's smaller export-oriented industries that were hard hit by the yen's takeoff.

The MITI draft report called for increasing the use of indirect loans to private firms in recipient countries.[29] The MITI plan proposed a rapid increase in Japanese foreign assistance, efforts to increase imports of manufactured goods from developing countries, and assistance for smaller Japanese manufacturers hurt by the yen's steep rise.[30] The scheme would facilitate adaptive restructuring of Japanese industry, but would cope with balance-of-payments surpluses through capital exports rather than simply increasing domestic consumption.[31] It envisioned greater assistance for infrastructure for export-oriented industries, technical cooperation for exporting industries (largely through JICA), investment and financial support for exporting industries, and "cooperation" in liberalizing recipient country tax systems and investment policies.[32] An MITI official described the plan as reflecting "the need for pursuing comprehensive cooperation involving aid, investment, and trade" and argued that Japan "must assist each country in determining which industries will best meet its needs."[33] Japanese aid would be serving, in part, as a subsidy to Japanese firms setting up shop abroad. Japanese firms' direct foreign investment in Asia, much of it in manufacturing, was taking off. In fiscal year 1989 it soared above $8 billion before receding the following year to just above $7 billion and then to less than $6 billion in 1991.[34]

The Japanese were prepared to lobby for policies that would stimulate inflows of foreign capital. The MITI proposal called for efforts to "expand economic cooperation to improve the environment for investment in the developing countries."[35] An MITI report on the plan suggested that it is "vital for Japan . . . to pave the way to enable Japanese enterprises to make direct investments smoothly in developing countries." The plan is explicit in its call "for support in cultivating industries that will attract foreign investment from mainly private-sector sources."[36] To do so, however, requires laying the appropriate groundwork:

> As Japan seeks to expand the flow of capital to developing countries with a view toward improving each recipient country's foreign-currency earning power, it is important that this flow of capital be accompanied by a full complement of service and information-oriented cooperation, ranging from consultation regarding economic policy and development project planning to transfers of technologies and expertise for specific industrial levels. Such cooperation is essential from the perspective of cultivating an attractive investment environment which, as mentioned earlier, is a prerequisite for expanding the flow of private-sector capital.[37]

The MITI plan was never formally endorsed. The plan faced bureaucratic infighting as well as suspicious reactions abroad. The plan's outlines suggest levels of overall direction of Japanese ODA programs that have yet to be achieved. Instead, Japanese ODA planning and implementation continue to be plagued by problems associated with shared responsibility among several competing agencies, not one of which is able to provide overall direction. Indeed, the problems may be becoming more severe; the growth of the ODA program is attracting more interest in its potential utility to a variety of Japanese interests. Late in 1991, a consultative committee on administrative reform sent to Prime Minister Miyazawa a report calling for a clearer general outline of Japan's ODA program along with a statement of guiding principles. Opposition political parties have made similar calls in addition to urging that ODA programs be submitted to the Diet for approval. Until it became entangled in a series of political scandals (Sagawa Kyubin, involving payments from a trucking firm; and high-level cooperation with rightist gangsters), the Liberal Democratic Party itself was considering tax increases to fund further ODA expansion.[38]

The MITI plan is significant, however, for the insight it provides into a possible approach to dealing comprehensively with a variety of goals in the region. Furthermore, despite the lack of any official endorsement, MITI has continued to implement elements of the plan, building on traditional Japanese approaches to economic cooperation.

Terutomo Ozawa suggests that the Japanese approach to development assistance represents

> [a] new, hybrid form of economic co-operation, a combination of official aid alongside private-sector transfers of production capacities . . . which the Japanese government has dubbed "a comprehensive development strategy," [and which] is designed to recycle not only surplus capital but also "surplus" industrial capacities to those host economies that are capable of absorbing these economic resources productively.[39]

Industrial Policy

Japanese are not merely strengthening the international extension of their own industrial policy; they are also advocating that other countries learn from Japan's successful application of industrial policies. In a 1988 report on economic cooperation, MITI spelled out the role of industrial policy, noting that development does not necessarily result from simply removing government-imposed obstacles. When risks stem from an "immature market structure," weakness of financial institutions, or market failures, an industrial policy is appropriate, the report suggests. Industrial policy should involve consensus between industry and government, enabling the financial system to undertake industrial finance and helping to upgrade industrial structure. A Ministry of Foreign Affairs official put the issue more boldly: "Laissez-faire can't be recommended. Careful utilization of market forces is always ideal."[40] An official government report, noting the shift of developing countries from state-led to private-led development strategies, suggests that "it is debatable whether, without any government intervention at all, sufficient catch-up oriented economic development can be achieved."[41]

When the Japanese attempt to exercise their potential influence, they sometimes are unsure what they have to offer. As expressed by one business executive, "We have come to the point where we are not the student any longer. We have something to teach. The problem is we don't know where to start."[42] In fact, however, by example the Japanese have been teaching developing East Asian countries a great deal about industrial policy. The Overseas Economic Cooperation Fund (OECF) has been collaborating with the World Bank in structural adjustment lending since the mid-1980s and is beginning to critique certain World Bank policies. One OECF report notes that successful structural adjustment depends on factors other than efficiency and may neglect the importance of investment promotion, industrial policy, tariff protection, and particular development institutions.[43] The World Bank seeks to work more closely with Japan and wants Japan "to produce a development manual explaining the country's remarkable post-war transition."[44]

Regionalism

Given the global reach of its economic interests, it is unlikely that Japan will push for an exclusive East Asian economic zone. Although it is impressive to realize the degree to which the rapid increase of intraregional economic activity makes it possible to even conceive of an East Asian economic bloc surviving some degree of isolation from other markets, that option is clearly not the optimal one. Nonetheless, just as President Woodrow Wilson resisted calls for the creation of an economic bloc in the Western Hemisphere early this century and was opposed by his secretary of state, Robert Lansing ("the best way to fight combination is by combination"),[45] Japanese leaders are sensitive to the potential utility of an East Asian economic organization. Furthermore, increasing protectionism in the European Community and the Western Hemisphere could lead Japanese leaders to conclude that a regionally based global economy is inevitable. Such a conclusion would represent a reprise of the experience of Japan's late nineteenth century "expansionists," in which "the unfortunate experiences [with emigration] in North America had turned them to greater willingness to espouse the idea of Asian empire."[46]

In 1989, Japanese investment in Asia totaled about 16 percent of total Japanese overseas investment.[47] That same year, 43 percent of foreign direct investment by smaller firms went to Asia, down from 73 percent in 1987.[48] Official Japanese aid is helping to facilitate the movement offshore of Japanese manufacturing firms, which, in turn, stimulates Japanese trade with other Asian economies. Intra-industry trade (primarily intrafirm) is increasing rapidly and is producing tighter regional economic integration. Japanese aid, investment, and trade are helping to integrate the economies of East Asia.

In Korea, Manchuria, and Taiwan earlier this century, Japan laid the groundwork for the later economic development of those areas. Without direct control or coercion, Japan is now helping to lay a similar foundation in Southeast Asia. A comparison of Japan's current policies with those of the prewar period is instructive. In the 1930s, many Japanese hoped to create an integrated East Asian economy. It was believed that a Japan-led regional economic bloc would be a means of driving the Western powers from Asia, of enhancing Japan's economic security, and of enabling Japan to lead Asians in developing their productive capacities. Realizing these goals would require self-conscious adjustment of Japan's industrial structure—in other words, an industrial policy.[49] Before implementing such a policy, Japan would have to prepare thoroughly:

> A distinctive feature of Japanese colonialism was that its colonial governments, in addition to providing essential services such as law and order, health, education, modern transportation and communication, also actively promoted selected industries, introduced new technology, and funded economic undertakings. The Japanese planned their development programs with considerable care, paying unusual attention to research. They systematically surveyed and investigated economic resources and local customs and planned their economic programs on the basis of these studies.[50]

With Japan's rapidly growing capital exports, including overseas economic assistance, a variety of Japanese institutions is exploring ways in which Japan can use its aid and investment, as well as its trade, to further its foreign policy goals. This is a tentative and difficult process, given the limited consensus within Japan concerning its appropriate international role. In the past, most Japanese were content to leave the Ministry of Foreign Affairs in charge of maintaining good relations with the United States while MITI helped Japanese firms secure access to resources and markets. Today, an increasing number of actors seek to exert or enlarge their influence over Japan's foreign economic policy. It is not so much the case that Japanese officials and business elites are now pursuing new goals as that the continuing pursuit of fundamental national interests dictates a more externally oriented posture.

Increasing attention to Japan's place in the broader order of things flows from the internationalization of Japanese firms' production strategies and the role that the economies of East Asia will play as Japan continues to upgrade its industrial structure. Japanese trade with other

Asian economies is growing faster than total Japanese trade. With rising trade and capital flows, Japanese firms are integrating the region's economies. For Japan to realize the goal of becoming "a culturally oriented industrial state" (the status of a major power without inordinate military power), Japan's Choices Study Group suggests that Japan will have to work to create new economic relations with its Asian neighbors "based on a well-coordinated horizontal division of labor."[51]

Most recent private initiatives and study groups concerned with reshaping Japan's international role are focused on enlarging Japan's role in Asia. Japanese have had greater exposure to Asian countries than to other developing countries, and Japan already has well-developed economic and political ties with the countries of Asia.

Many Asians predictably harbor uneasiness with Japan's increasingly dominant regional role. At the same time, however, Japan's image in the region is much better than it was two decades ago. This shift in Asian views of Japan reflects the attraction of power, an increasingly sensitive Japanese diplomacy, Japan's promise as a source of needed capital and technology, and growing annoyance with U.S. foreign economic policies. Furthermore, the nature of Japan's economic links with East Asian developing countries, including rapid increases in Japanese imports of manufactured goods, has been changing quickly. The prime ministers of Malaysia and Thailand have been particularly vocal in expressing their support for an increasingly large Japanese role in the region.

Nonetheless, there is concern in Japan about pushing too energetically for the creation of an Asian economic grouping. Japanese officials worry that doing so could accelerate tendencies afoot in North America and Western Europe to emphasize regional economic associations at the expense of multilateralism. The Bush administration has been direct in voicing its opposition to any East Asian economic grouping that does not include the United States. Japanese are also nervous about being seen by other Asian countries as overly aggressive in promoting any schemes over which Japan will inevitably loom as the dominant actor. Some of these neighbors recall Japan's earlier empire when, in the interests of being self-sufficient within its East Asian sphere of influence, Japan worked "to develop the industrial resources in her colonies and to rearrange the division of labor between her industries at home and those in the colonies."[52]

Given this concern, Japanese officials were pleased in 1989 at the generally favorable response in Asia to a proposed Asia Pacific political and economic grouping, to include the ASEAN countries, the Asian NICs, Australia, Canada, China, Japan, New Zealand, and the United States.[53] Australian initiative helped to calm disquiet stemming from the perception that such an organization would serve as a Trojan horse for still greater Japanese economic dominance in the region.[54] Ding Xinghao of the

Shanghai Institute of International Studies expressed such anxieties: "Japan's view is always a flying goose formation with Japan as the head goose. Our memories are long, so we aren't about to fly in Japan's forma- tion."[55] By and large, however, political and economic elites across Asia find they gain more by joining the flock than they lose. For example, in December 1990, Malaysian Prime Minister Mahathir Mohamad proposed the creation of an East Asian Economic Group, and Singapore Prime Min- ister Goh Chok Tong subsequently endorsed the idea.

Proposals for an Asian economic organization have been booted about for quite some time. Japanese politicians have expressed interest in such an idea since the 1950s. Economists Saburo Okita and Kiyoshi Kojima championed the cause of an Asian economic grouping in the early 1960s. The notion is gaining salience recently because of nervousness about pos- sible further limitations on East Asian access to European and North American markets. The 1992 Charter for American-Russian Partnership and Friendship declared that the two countries would create a "strategic partnership" aimed at strengthening a "Euro-Atlantic Community," which some observers may interpret as excluding Asia.[56] Such concerns may stimulate Japanese efforts to forge an East Asian economic organization.

A similar stimulus-response dynamic was evident in the late 1950s, when the signing of the Treaty of Rome aggravated Japanese fears of iso- lation and prompted initial research into the feasibility of an Asian eco- nomic community. Such a response also was evident in prewar Japan. Even in 1941, former Japanese Foreign Minister Hachiro Arita wrote:

> When the doctrines of freedom of communications and trade prevailed
> the world over . . . it was possible even for small nations . . . to maintain
> a respectable existence side by side with the great Powers. . . . Now,
> however . . . with the great Powers' closing or threatening to close their
> doors to others, small countries have no other choice left but to strive as
> best they can to form their own economic blocs.[57]

The current Japanese position is similar to that of the United States early in this century. With the European powers moving away from free trade, the United States then was concerned about the impact on its own economy. Particularly disconcerting was Great Britain's clear rejection of liberalism in favor of a mercantilist foreign economic policy. Senator Henry Cabot Lodge suggested that for the United States "the essential thing is so to organize our industries that they will be strong, independent, and ready for the conflict when and if it comes."[58] At the time, many British leaders were increasingly doubtful of their industries' capacity to compete with those of Germany and the United States. Today, Japanese see ample evidence that many in the United States are reaching similar conclusions.

Leader Without a Cause?

Leaders in other Asian countries are concerned that the United States and West European nations will be increasingly preoccupied with events in Eastern Europe, the former Soviet Union, the Middle East, and Latin America. Japan will be left to dominate the region. On the one hand, these Asians fear that the result will be the absence of any challenge to Japan's economic supremacy in East Asia. On the other hand, they want to be sure that their future fortunes are tied to those of the Japanese economy. Japanese officials, for their part, recognize that the importance of Japanese links with East Asia is rising rapidly.

The Japanese search for security is best served by an open international economy guided by multilateral institutions supporting liberal economic norms. Recent trends in the global political economy, however, cannot reassure Japanese leaders that its preferred outcomes will be realized. Hence, the Japanese economy must be prepared to adjust to undesirable trends. Leon Hollerman suggests that Japan is doing precisely that, having established itself inside the European Community and the North American market: "In its headquarters strategy Japan is prepared to play the global game either in a regionalized or in a wholly multilateral world economy."[59]

This outlook, however, betrays a continuing tendency to accept the world as given while underestimating Japan's capacity to shape global trends to suit its interests. The latter task will depend on the exercise of leadership and clear definition and articulation of Japanese interests and strategies. Such qualities, however, continue in short supply, as was evident when a Foreign Ministry official noted of Japan's policy following Peruvian President Alberto Fujimori's declaration of martial law: "We have not decided not to stop assistance [to Peru], nor have we decided to stop it."[60]

Notes

1. Hong Kong, Singapore, and Thailand each received more than $1 billion; and China, Indonesia, Malaysia, South Korea, and Taiwan all received more than $430 million. The only other developing countries to receive comparable levels were offshore banking centers such as the Caymans, Liberia, and Panama. Figures are from Japan Economic Institute Report 23B, June 19, 1992, pp. 10–11.

2. Fujio Uryu, Yuichi Koishi, and Tetsuro Shinohara, "Too Ajia Chiiki ni okeru Ware ga Koku Kigyo no Kaigai Chokusetsu to Boeki" (Japanese firms' foreign direct investment and trade in East Asia), Discussion Paper Series no. 91-DOJ-27, Research Institute of International Trade and Industry, Tokyo, 1991.

3. Eric Helleiner provides a useful discussion of Japanese influence, distinguishing between the relational power afforded by Japan's creditor status and the

structural power resulting from the dominance of Japanese institutions in global financial markets. He also suggests the conditions under which creditor status is likely to afford significant international influence. Eric Helleiner, "Money and Influence: Japanese Power in the International and Financial System," in Kathleen Newland, ed., *The International Relations of Japan* (New York: St. Martin's Press, 1990), pp. 23–44.

4. Inagaki Manjiro, quoted in Akira Iriye, *Pacific Estrangement: Japanese and American Expansionism, 1897–1911* (Cambridge, Mass.: Harvard University Press, 1972), p. 35.

5. Kazan Kayahara, in Iriye, *Pacific Estrangement*, p. 97.

6. Japan Institute of International Affairs, *White Papers of Japan, 1988–1989* (Tokyo: Japan Institute of International Affairs, 1990), pp. 24–27.

7. *Far Eastern Economic Review*, June 20, 1991, p. 62.

8. For example, in May 1990, Prime Minister Toshiki Kaifu was in South Asia and Southeast Asia urging those countries to address problems of environmental degradation, terrorism, population growth, and development policy reform.

9. Ministry of Foreign Affairs, *Official Development Assistance, 1991* (Tokyo: Association for Promotion of International Cooperation, 1992), p. 65.

10. Thomas L. Friedman, *New York Times Magazine*, June 28, 1992.

11. Ministry of Foreign Affairs, *Official Development Assistance*, p. 63.

12. Takashi Inoguchi, "Japan's Global Role in a Multipolar World," in Shafiqul Islam, ed., *Yen for Development* (New York: Council on Foreign Relations Press, 1991), p. 22; Julia Chang Bloch, "A U.S.-Japan Aid Alliance," in Islam, *Yen for Development*, p. 81.

13. Karl Schoenberger, *San Francisco Chronicle*, June 15, 1992.

14. Alan Rix, "Japan's Foreign Aid Policy: A Capacity for Leadership?" *Pacific Affairs* 62, no. 4 (1989–1990): 461–475.

15. *The Economist*, October 18, 1990, p. 76.

16. Ministry of Foreign Affairs, *Official Development Assistance*, p. 3.

17. *Japan Times*, October 14–20, 1991.

18. Masamichi Hanabusa, *San Jose Mercury News*, June 1, 1992.

19. *Tokyo Business Today*, September 1991. These figures probably overstate the changes because Japanese firms increasingly disguise their interests in local firms winning bidding contracts. For a more detailed discussion of this issue, see Toru Yanagihara and Anne Emig, "An Overview of Japan's Foreign Aid," in Islam, *Yen for Development*.

20. Takao Taniura, *Ajia no kogyoka to chokusetsutoshi* (Asia's direct foreign investment and industrialization) (Tokyo: Institute for Developing Economies, 1989).

21. Interviews with MITI officials in Tokyo and Bangkok, December 1989 and January 1990.

22. Ministry of Foreign Affairs, *Official Development Assistance*, p. 11.

23. Ibid., p. 69.

24. The Overseas Economic Cooperation Fund and the Japan International Cooperation Agency distribute the great bulk of official development assistance.

25. *Japan Overseas Development Corporation*, English edition (Tokyo: Japan Overseas Development Corporation, 1990).

26. Ibid.

27. *Guide to AOTS, 1989* (Tokyo: Association for Overseas Technical Scholarships, 1989).

28. Anny Wong, "Japan's National Security and Cultivation of ASEAN Elites," *Contemporary Southeast Asia* 12, no. 4 (March 1991): 306–330.

29. Interview with official at Keizai Doyukai (Organization for Economic Co-operation), 1987.

30. Interviews with officials at Keidanren, MITI, and Ministry of Foreign Affairs, 1986–1987.

31. Saburo Okita has called for Japan to maintain its current-account surplus at about 1 percent of gross national product so that Japan can continue to meet global demands for capital.

32. MITI, "New Aid Plan," press release mimeo, June 1987.

33. Masaaki Nangaku, "Japan's Economic Cooperation to Support the Industrialization of Asian Nations," paper presented at the Tokyo Conference on Global Adjustment and the Future of Asia-Pacific Economies, hosted by the Institute for Developing Economies and the Pacific Development Centre, Tokyo, May 11–13, 1988.

34. Richard Cronin, *Japan, the United States and Prospects for the Asia-Pacific Century: Three Scenarios for the Future* (Singapore: Institute for Southeast Asian Studies, March 1992); Japan Economic Institute (JEI) Report 23B, June 19, 1992, pp. 10–11.

35. MITI, "The Present State and Problems of Economic Cooperation," Foreign Press Center, Japan, 1986.

36. Ibid.

37. Ibid.

38. *Japan Times*, January 1, 1992.

39. Terutomo Ozawa, *Recycling Japan's Surplus for Developing Countries* (Paris: Development Centre of the Organization for Economic Cooperation and Development, 1989), p. 11.

40. Quoted in *Asian Wall Street Journal*, August 20, 1990, p. 1.

41. Japan Institute of International Affairs, *White Papers of Japan, 1988–1989*, pp. 126–127.

42. David E. Sanger, *New York Times*, March 5, 1992.

43. Overseas Economic Cooperation Fund, "Issues Related to the World Bank's Approach to Structural Adjustment," Occasional Paper no. 1, October 1991.

44. *Far Eastern Economic Review*, June 13, 1991, p. 70.

45. Carl P. Parrini, *Heir to Empire: U.S. Economic Diplomacy, 1916–1923* (Pittsburgh: University of Pittsburgh Press, 1969), p. 21.

46. Iriye, *Pacific Estrangement*, p. 230.

47. Ministry of Finance figures.

48. MITI mimeo on Japanese direct foreign investment, Small and Medium Enterprise Agency figures.

49. Samuel Pao-San Ho, "Colonialism and Development: Korea, Taiwan, and Kwangtung," in Ramon H. Myers and Mark R. Peattie, eds., *The Japanese Colonial Empire, 1895–1945* (Princeton, N.J.: Princeton University Press, 1984), p. 351.

50. Ibid., p. 355.

51. Ibid., p. 41.

52. Ho, "Colonialism and Development," p. 351.

53. At the meeting in Canberra in late 1989, China, Hong Kong, and Taiwan were excluded. The grouping subsequently settled on a formula for their inclusion.

54. Australian Prime Minister Robert Hawke proposed consultations with Japan on creation of an Asia Pacific grouping during Prime Minister Takeshita's visit to Australia in July 1988. In 1980, Prime Minister Ohira made a similar proposal to his counterpart, Australian Prime Minister Malcolm Fraser, resulting in

the creation of a Pacific Basin study group and the first meeting of the Pacific Economic Cooperation Council in Canberra that year. The group held its seventh meeting in November 1989.

55. Quoted in Chalmers Johnson, "The Problem of Japan in an Era of Structural Change," Graduate School of International Relations and Pacific Studies, University of California at San Diego, Research Report 89-04, June 1989.

56. Henry Kissinger, *Washington Post*, July 5, 1992.

57. Joyce Chapman-Lebra, *Japan's Greater East Asia Co-prosperity Sphere in World War II* (New York: Oxford University Press, 1975), pp. 74–75.

58. Parrini, *Heir to Empire*, p. 32.

59. Leon Hollerman, "The Headquarters Nation," *The National Interest* (Fall 1991): 16–25.

60. JEI Report 17B, May 1, 1992, pp. 6–7.

11

Japanese Technology and Global Influence

David C. Mowery

The perception has grown since the 1970s that economic interdependence, at least among the developed capitalist democracies, is changing the underlying bases of national power. This view has been particularly important when considering Japan, a country with limited military power and great economic resources. In Chapters 9 and 10, Edward Lincoln and Danny Unger argue that Japanese capital exports provide Japan with new and important sources of international influence. This chapter examines the technological bases of Japan's rising economic strength. Given the U.S. penchant for charging that Japan "free rides" on U.S.-supplied public goods —goods for which others cannot be excluded from their consumption and whose supply does not diminish as a result of others' consumption (for example, clean air)—this chapter also considers the degree to which Japanese research and development (R&D) is concentrated in producing private, as opposed to public, goods. A related issue concerns charges from the United States that U.S. firms enjoy only limited access to Japanese scientific and technological advances. Finally, this chapter reviews the weak record of Japan-U.S. research and development cooperation, looking in particular at the superconducting supercollider and space station projects.

Japan's domestic R&D expenditure patterns do not themselves support the free-rider characterization. Nonetheless, because of the contrasting structure of U.S. and Japanese domestic R&D systems, concerns over "symmetrical access" have some basis in reality. But the interdependent relationship between a scientifically strong U.S. research system and a technologically strong Japanese research system also creates some potential for the development of new avenues for bilateral cooperation.

Rethinking the Economics of Basic and Applied Research Investment

The critical assessment of Japanese R&D as free-riding asserts that the quality and quantity of Japanese investments in scientific research are low.[1] Low levels of domestic investment in basic research may not impede Japanese economic performance, however, if the returns from these investments are impossible for any single firm or nation to capture—that is, if basic research is a strict public good. Rather than basic research, Japanese firms and government agencies may choose to invest in technological development, with economic returns that can be captured by their creators. In this view, Japanese investments in technology development rely on the results of U.S.-financed basic research and exploit international public goods for improved national competitiveness. The public-good nature of U.S. research investments is further heightened by the fact that foreign students, managers, and public officials can readily gain access to most U.S.-based university and federal laboratories, whereas comparable access to the most important institutions of Japanese research, many of which are industrial laboratories, often is more restricted.

This view of the relationship between U.S. and Japanese R&D activities has influenced a number of other U.S. and Japanese science policy initiatives. Concern over the "leakage" of basic research results from U.S. laboratories contributed to the decision to restrict foreign access to the 1987 White House–National Science Foundation symposium on high-temperature superconductivity, as well as other proposals to restrict foreign access to federal and university laboratories.[2] More recent U.S. requests for Japanese government participation in such "big science" projects as the space station and the superconducting supercollider also are based in part on the belief that Japan must expand its contribution to the global pool of scientific knowledge.

Despite its influence on policy, the classification of basic research as a strict public good needs elaboration and qualification. Important firm-specific and national benefits flow to the investors in basic research. In many instances, however, these benefits influence national innovative performance in an indirect and lagged fashion and often require extensive complementary investments and skills. Moreover, applied research and technology development themselves generate important "generic" or public goods, with returns that cannot always be fully captured by their creator.

How Public a Good Is Basic Research?

Basic research blends public- and private-good attributes. Some portion of the expanding basic research investments of Japanese firms is motivated by the perceived need to develop in-house scientific knowledge and capabilities that can support the intrafirm absorption and application of the results of basic research performed externally. This concern also underpins the investment of many Japanese firms in research facilities in the United States and Western Europe in biotechnology and computer science.[3] Publicly funded basic research also generates domestic economic spillovers that may not be easily captured by foreign economies. In other words, some forms of publicly financed basic research yield "national public goods" rather than always producing "international public goods." These domestic economic spillovers are affected by the structure of the institutions in which a nation's basic research is performed. University-based basic research, for example, plays an important role in training a nation's scientists and engineers. National research systems in which universities are less important performers of basic research may reap fewer of these domestic economic spillovers from publicly funded basic research. The universities' production of scientists and engineers trained in advanced research also facilitates the transfer to industry of advances in research techniques, instrumentation, and measurement.

The distinction between national and international public goods in basic research now is less important than in earlier decades.[4] Nevertheless, the limited international mobility of much scientific and engineering talent among the industrial economies and the continued importance of domestic capabilities for monitoring and absorbing foreign research mean that significant national benefits still flow from basic research investments.

Despite the long-established view that product innovation and technological change depend on a well-stocked "reservoir" of basic scientific knowledge,[5] the competitive performance of the United States and other nations during the postwar period suggests, at least in the short run, that investment in basic research alone will not improve national economic or innovative performance. The results of basic research can improve the effectiveness of the empirical and search activities that underpin applied research and technology development, but, with some important exceptions, basic research discoveries rarely are translated directly into new commercial products.

Basic research produces a blend of international and national public goods and firm-specific private goods. Efforts to restrict dissemination of the results of basic research in order to increase the national returns to such investments are therefore misguided and impractical. Such a focus on basic research alone also overlooks the need for complementary investments in technology development, manufacturing, and other activities to realize the economic returns to basic research. The ability of a given firm or nation to realize the economic returns to its basic research investments is thus crucially affected by investments in the public and private goods— publicly supported investments in production worker skills or private firms' investments in manufacturing, marketing, and engineering, for example—necessary to commercialize the technological fruits of basic research. The faith of some officials in the U.S. executive branch and Congress, as well as the U.S. scientific community,[6] that increased basic research spending alone will improve U.S. economic competitiveness lacks strong empirical support.

How Private a Good Is Technology?

Appropriating the returns from technological innovation often is difficult. This nonexcludability characteristic of much technological R&D gives it some "public-good" features. Protection of intellectual property is rarely complete, for example, meaning that some "leakage" of the information underlying an innovation is likely. Even in the face of strong protection of intellectual property, however, markets for technology are imperfect because they involve relatively small numbers of buyers and sellers and are often plagued by opportunism and uncertainty concerning the characteristics of the goods being sold.

Technology also contains a great deal of so-called generic knowledge, a term that describes familiarity with the physical properties of materials; regularities in the behavior of certain chemicals; and techniques for testing, modeling, and evaluating experimental data.[7] This kind of knowledge often has limited scientific underpinnings. The advancement and dissemination of these technology public goods have been central goals of the public technology policies of Japan and other industrial economies, such as Sweden and Germany.[8] In contrast to U.S. postwar technology policy (outside of agriculture), these nations devote substantial resources to supporting domestic technology adoption, a critical factor in reaping the economic benefits from innovation. The "market failure" argument—which states that the unaided market will fail to produce the socially optimal level of investment in research and development that has justified the postwar concentration of U.S. nondefense public research funds on basic research—thus may also justify public investments in technology development. Indeed, in industries such as commercial aircraft and agriculture, federal funds have been employed for precisely these purposes.[9]

Funding and Performance in Basic Research and Technology Development: Comparing Japan and Other Industrial Economies

A comparison of Japanese R&D spending and innovative performance with those of other industrial economies leads to two conclusions. First, Japan's basic research spending, measured as a share of national R&D spending, is not significantly smaller than that of other industrial economies. And second, the limited data on the output of Japanese basic research suggest that Japanese scientific research performance has improved considerably during the past two decades. An even more substantial improvement, however, has occurred during this period in Japan's development of new technologies. In many respects, the status of Japan currently resembles that of the United States during the interwar period[10] —much stronger in the development and application of industrial technologies than in scientific research, even as its scientific performance improves.

Basic Research in the United States, Japan, and other Industrial Economies

Table 11.1 shows that reported expenditures on basic research within Japan account for a share of overall national R&D investment that is roughly equal to that in the United States. Indeed, these data suggest that both Japan and the United States allocate a smaller share of their national R&D investment to basic research than do France, Germany, or Sweden.[11] Japan remains an outlier with respect to the share of national R&D financed by government as opposed to industry. Table 11.2 displays the shares of national R&D expenditures (including applied research and development, in addition to basic research) accounted for by industry, government, and other sources. The share of national R&D financed by the Japanese government (20 percent) in 1988 was significantly lower than that in other industrial economies, and was less than one-half the share observed in the United States (46 percent).

Industry in Japan accounts for a much larger share of total national R&D spending than does industry in most other industrial economies, including France, Great Britain, and the United States. Japanese patterns of R&D financing by source resemble those of the former West Germany, and for both nations reflect the lack of a large military establishment. Nevertheless, the share of Japanese national nondefense R&D financed by industry exceeds the share of U.S. nondefense R&D supported by industry.[12]

Basic research spending accounts for more than 6.5 percent of Japanese industrially financed R&D, higher than the share observed in the United States (roughly 4.2 percent) or France (3 percent).[13] The share of basic research in Japanese industrially financed R&D spending has grown since the mid-1970s—in 1977, this share stood at 4.7 percent—in the face of rapid growth in total industrially financed R&D. In itself, the size and growth of industrially financed Japanese basic research investment raises questions about the validity of the strict public good characterization of basic research investment.

How does the output of Japanese basic research compare with that of other industrial nations? Tables 11.3 and 11.4 present data on the contributions of Japan and other industrial nations to a large sample of

Table 11.1 Basic Research as a Percentage of Total R&D Expenditures: 1975–1988

	France	West Germany	Japan	United Kingdom	Italy	Sweden	United States
1975	NA	26	12	14	20	NA	13
1976	NA	25	15	13	20	NA	13
1977	21	25	15	13	20	18	13
1978	NA	22	16	13	19	NA	13
1979	21	21	15	13	16	18	13
1980	21	21	14	13	15	NA	13
1981	21	22	13	13	15	23	13
1982	21	21	13	NA	15	NA	13
1983	21	21	13	NA	16	NA	13
1984	20	NA	13	NA	16	NA	12
1985	20	18	12	NA	16	20	12
1986	20	NA	13	NA	17	NA	12
1987	23	19	13	NA	NA	23	12
1988	NA	NA	13	NA	NA	NA	13

Notes: The data for basic research are somewhat less reliable than those for total R&D expenditures. Each percentage generally relates to the total current R&D expenditures, which for some countries other than the United States may include some general university funds. Data for France and the United Kingdom are estimated for some years. NA indicates that data were not available.

Source: National Science Foundation, *International Science and Technology Update: 1991* (Washington, D.C.: National Science Foundation, 1991), p. 27.

Table 11.2 Percentage Distribution of R&D Expenditures by Source of Funds: 1975 and 1988

Year and Source	France	West Germany	Japan	United Kingdom	Sweden	Italy	United States
1975							
Government	54	47	29	52	39	43	51
Industry	39	50	55	41	57	51	45
Higher education	1	—	15	1	1	1	2
Other[a]	6	2	1	7	3	5	2
Total	100	100	100	100	100	100	100
1988[b]							
Government	51	36	20	39	38	54	46
Industry	43	63	70	50	60	42	50
Higher education	—	—	9	[c]	[c]	—	3
Other[a]	6	1	1	11	1	4	1
Total	100	100	100	100	100	100	100
Percentage change							
Government	-3	-11	-9	-13	-1	+11	-5
Industry	+4	+13	+15	+9	+3	-9	+5
Higher education	-1	—	-6	-1	-1	-1	+1
Other[a]	0	-1	0	+4	-2	-1	-1

[a] Private nonprofit institutions and funds from abroad.
[b] French and Japanese figures for 1988 are NSF estimates; United Kingdom, Swedish, and Italian data are for 1987.
[c] Less than 0.5 percent.

Note: Because of rounding, figures may not add up to 100 percent.

Source: National Science Foundation, *International Science and Technology Update: 1991* (Washington, D.C.: National Science Foundation, 1991), p. 17.

scientific journals. Table 11.3 compares these contributions by field for 1986 and reveals several interesting contrasts between Japan and other industrial nations. Japanese contributors account for a larger share of "engineering and technology" journal articles than those of any other nation except the United States. This profile is consistent with other evidence, discussed below, on Japan's growing technological capabilities.[14]

The data in Table 11.4 compare national shares of world scientific publications for 1973–1986, revealing growth in Japanese scientific contributions. Japan and Italy were the only two nations in this tabulation to expand their shares of scientific publications between 1973 and 1986.

Japan's Technological Performance

Japanese firms have progressed during the postwar period from borrowing, modifying, and successfully commercializing foreign technologies to operating at the technological frontier. No individual indicator of this shift is definitive, but together they are suggestive.[15] Data from the surveys of Japanese technology imports and exports conducted by the Management and Coordination Agency show that the ratio of Japan's technology exports to technology imports (actually, the ratio of value of licensing fees and royalties associated with technology exports and imports) has increased from 39.4 percent in fiscal 1975 to 99.8 percent in fiscal 1989—a state of virtual equality between imports and exports of technology.[16]

Alone among industrial nations, Japan registered an increase, rather than a decrease, in the number of patents received per scientist and engineer during 1967–1984, as well as an increase in the number of patents received in foreign countries. The U.S. National Science Foundation (NSF) reported in 1988 that Japanese firms accounted for the largest single share of foreign-origin U.S. patents.[17] Moreover, according to the NSF report, Japanese-origin U.S. patents were cited more than proportionately in other patent applications, an indicator of their high quality.[18]

Other indicators of technological performance also suggest considerable Japanese strength. The rate of adoption and intensity of utilization of advanced manufacturing technologies (including robotics, computer-integrated-manufacturing workcells, and flexible manufacturing systems) in Japanese manufacturing both exceed the corresponding levels in U.S. manufacturing.[19] Kim Clark, Takahiro Fujimoto, and others have documented the ability of Japanese automotive firms to bring new models to market more rapidly than U.S. auto firms,[20] and Edwin Mansfield's research indicates that Japanese firms develop and commercialize technologies based on sources of knowledge outside of the firm significantly faster than do U.S. firms.[21]

The structure of both Japanese and U.S. R&D systems is changing,[22] but in the near future the U.S. system seems likely to remain strong as a performer of basic research, even as the Japanese R&D system strengthens its considerable capabilities in the creation, modification, and adoption of technology. Structural contrasts between the U.S. and Japanese research systems, however, remain significant and are not likely to fade rapidly. Many of these structural differences are rooted in these nations' different systems of industrial finance and governance, which means that changes in public policy will work slowly and incompletely to remove structural impediments to access.

Policy Issues and Challenges

The data discussed in the previous section provide little support for criticism of Japanese science and technology policy as free-riding on U.S. financial and intellectual contributions to global science. Moreover, the characteristics of the economic returns to basic research investments are such that Japanese firms and government agencies have substantial incentives to sustain and (as in university basic research) expand their investment in basic research. Nevertheless, burden sharing in large science projects and "reciprocal access" will remain important issues in U.S.-Japan discussions on science policy. Significant progress in these areas will be difficult, however, without improvements in each government's domestic science and technology policy planning and resource allocation systems.

U.S.-Japan collaboration might also benefit from a greater U.S. commitment to public support of domestic technology development projects in selected areas, based on the public goods arguments above. Cooperative research in these areas would match growing Japanese strengths with increasing U.S. needs in the adoption and commercialization of new manufacturing and industrial technologies. By strengthening the commercialization capabilities of U.S. firms, such collaborative research activity might also increase the national and private U.S. returns to investments in basic research. Government-sponsored cooperation in this area, however, will require a recognition that in many areas of industrial technology Japan leads U.S. industrial practice.

Burden-sharing

Improved cooperation between the U.S. and Japanese governments in large-scale science projects requires change in each government's science policy apparatus. In contrast to the relatively clear lines of authority governing the establishment of priorities and (modest) public funding for technology development projects,[23] Japanese public science policy suffers from divided authority and intense interagency rivalries. In the case of the Human Frontier Science Project, announced at the Venice economic summit in 1987, rivalries among the Ministry of Education, the Ministry of International Trade and Industry, and the Science and Technology Agency (part of the Office of the Prime Minister) contributed to erosion in the proposed program budget from several billion dollars to less than $30 million, a funding level that failed to attract much international participation.

The science policy apparatus of the U.S. government is also unable to control interagency rivalries or to establish stable research funding priorities.[24] Moreover, the prominent role of Congress, endowed with a decisionmaking process even more fragmented than that of the executive branch, makes it difficult to establish credible priorities and commitments to research programs in which international cost-sharing is sought. The resulting instability in U.S. scientific research and funding priorities makes it difficult to attract or retain cooperation and financial contributions from foreign governments, including that of Japan. The space station and superconducting supercollider projects illustrate these problems.

The U.S. executive branch has had limited success in justifying the enormous costs of either the space station or the supercollider projects. Neither the U.S. Congress nor Japan have been convinced that the potential benefits in terms of scientific knowledge or technological advances are sufficient to justify the necessary investments. As a result, Congress has threatened to cut funding for the space station despite significant financial contributions from Japan and other participants.[25] Japan also has been reluctant to contribute the $1 billion requested by the U.S. government for the collider project, a program that has been portrayed within the executive branch and Congress as a high-technology public works undertaking.

The recent history of U.S.-Japanese cooperation in "big science" projects suggests several impediments to such cooperation. The fundamental problem appears to flow from a perception that burden sharing in scientific research, much more than burden-sharing in such areas as North Atlantic defense, thus far has meant that one government's financial contribution becomes hostage to another's complex (and often unstable) science policy process. Improved cost-sharing requires that both the United States and Japan involve the other nation's science policymakers in project design at an earlier point in the process. But improved cooperation also depends on stronger decisionmaking processes within each government for the establishment of spending priorities and project choices.

Another avenue for international burden-sharing is joint technology development projects. U.S.-Japan cooperation in this area may require more significant adjustments by U.S. policymakers than their Japanese counterparts for two reasons. First, Japan's domestic decisionmaking apparatus for identifying and supporting (with rather modest public investments) new technologies is far better developed than any similar process in the United States. Second, many U.S. policymakers have been slow to recognize the change in Japan's technological capabilities.

Table 11.3　Country Shares of World Scientific Literature by Field of Science: 1986 (in percentage)

Field	France	West Germany	Japan	United Kingdom	United States	Soviet Union	Italy	All Others
All fields	4.9	5.8	7.7	8.2	35.6	7.6	2.3	27.9
Clinical medicine	4.6	5.6	6.4	10.4	40.0	2.9	2.9	27.2
Biomedical research	5.0	5.2	7.1	8.0	38.4	8.3	2.0	26.0
Biology	3.1	4.3	6.5	9.5	38.1	2.4	1.0	35.1
Chemistry	5.6	6.9	10.7	5.7	22.2	15.1	2.7	31.1
Physics	6.5	6.9	8.6	5.6	30.3	14.7	2.5	24.9
Earth and space sciences	4.3	4.0	3.7	7.9	42.6	7.0	1.9	28.6
Engineering and technology	3.6	7.0	12.7	7.5	37.3	5.6	1.4	24.9
Mathematics	4.7	7.9	3.4	7.5	40.3	4.9	2.7	28.6

Notes: Data are based on the articles, notes, and reviews in the journals carried on the Science Citation Index corporate tapes of the Institute of Scientific Information. Prior to 1981, data are based on a fixed set of about 2,300 journals. After 1981, data are based on a fixed journal set of about 3,500 journals. A new modification of the journal set occurred in 1985. Articles are assigned by country of authorship. When an article is written by researchers from more than one country, it is prorated across the countries involved rather than the number of institutions represented by the authors. For example, if a given article has several authors from France and the United States, it is counted as one-half an article for the United States and one-half an article for France.

Source: National Science Foundation, *International Science and Technology Update: 1991* (Washington, D.C.: National Science Foundation, 1991), p. 89.

Table 11.4 Country Shares of World Scientific Literature by Field of Science: 1973–1986 (in percentage)

Country and Field	Publication Year of Articles													
	1973	1974	1975	1976	1977	1978	1979	1980	1981	1982	1983	1984	1985	1986
France														
All fields	5.6	5.6	5.8	5.5	5.6	5.1	5.3	5.4	5.0	4.9	4.8	4.8	4.7	4.9
Clinical medicine	5.7	5.5	5.7	5.5	5.9	5.1	5.5	5.6	5.2	5.0	4.7	4.8	4.3	4.6
Biomedical research	7.0	7.0	7.1	6.4	6.6	5.7	5.8	6.0	5.2	5.0	4.9	5.0	5.0	5.0
Biology	3.9	4.2	4.1	3.7	3.9	3.9	3.9	3.4	3.5	3.3	3.4	3.3	3.3	3.1
Chemistry	6.7	6.9	7.0	6.7	6.2	5.8	5.6	5.5	5.9	5.6	5.2	5.3	5.9	5.6
Physics	5.3	5.6	5.7	5.8	6.2	5.3	5.6	6.3	5.9	5.9	6.3	6.5	6.0	6.5
Earth and space sciences	4.9	4.8	4.6	4.6	4.1	3.5	4.2	4.6	4.6	4.5	4.5	4.3	3.8	4.4
Engineering and technology	2.8	2.7	3.0	2.9	3.0	3.1	3.7	3.5	3.3	3.6	3.0	3.1	3.0	3.6
Mathematics	6.9	7.2	8.0	7.4	8.6	8.1	7.9	7.8	5.6	5.9	6.2	6.7	6.9	4.7
West Germany														
All fields	6.0	6.5	6.4	6.4	6.3	6.7	6.3	6.2	5.3	6.2	6.0	6.0	6.1	5.8
Clinical medicine	6.9	7.5	7.1	6.7	6.4	6.8	6.1	6.1	6.4	6.3	6.2	5.9	5.9	5.6
Biomedical research	5.8	6.3	5.7	6.3	5.7	6.2	6.1	6.0	6.1	6.3	6.1	5.7	5.3	5.2
Biology	3.9	3.4	3.8	3.9	4.2	3.8	4.2	4.2	4.7	4.6	4.3	4.7	4.5	4.3
Chemistry	6.1	6.7	6.6	6.7	6.7	7.8	6.7	6.9	6.6	6.3	6.2	6.1	7.6	6.9
Physics	5.4	6.1	5.6	6.8	6.9	6.8	6.7	6.6	6.7	7.0	7.1	7.3	7.1	6.9
Earth and space sciences	3.1	3.8	3.9	3.5	3.8	4.3	3.9	4.1	4.4	4.4	4.4	4.1	4.5	4.0
Engineering and technology	7.6	7.5	7.9	7.6	7.8	7.8	8.2	7.5	7.0	6.9	6.3	7.0	6.8	7.0
Mathematics	6.6	7.6	7.0	8.6	9.5	10.0	9.9	9.1	9.0	6.8	6.3	6.4	6.9	7.9

Table 11.4 (continued)

Country and Field	Publication Year of Articles													
	1973	1974	1975	1976	1977	1978	1979	1980	1981	1982	1983	1984	1985	1986
Japan														
All fields	5.3	5.2	5.4	5.8	6.0	6.2	6.4	6.8	6.8	7.0	7.1	7.3	7.6	7.7
Clinical medicine	3.5	3.8	4.1	4.3	4.3	4.7	4.8	5.0	5.1	5.3	5.6	5.9	6.3	6.4
Biomedical research	4.0	4.2	4.3	4.8	5.3	5.4	5.3	5.9	6.2	6.4	6.6	6.7	6.7	7.1
Biology	5.3	4.9	5.3	5.5	5.7	6.3	6.0	6.5	6.1	6.3	6.3	6.7	7.0	6.5
Chemistry	9.4	8.9	8.8	9.5	10.0	9.6	10.9	10.9	10.9	10.7	10.3	10.6	10.7	10.7
Physics	6.5	6.5	6.7	7.1	7.3	7.9	8.0	8.6	8.2	8.3	8.0	8.1	8.8	8.6
Earth and space sciences	2.0	2.4	2.1	2.0	2.2	2.1	2.4	2.4	2.3	2.2	2.3	2.5	3.3	3.7
Engineering and technology	5.4	4.7	5.7	6.4	6.7	6.9	6.0	7.2	9.2	9.6	10.3	10.9	11.5	12.7
Mathematics	3.9	4.3	3.6	4.0	3.9	4.4	5.0	4.8	4.3	5.0	5.3	6.3	5.2	3.4
United Kingdom														
All fields	9.2	9.3	9.5	9.2	8.9	8.6	8.3	8.3	8.3	8.3	8.4	8.2	8.3	8.2
Clinical medicine	10.4	10.6	10.4	10.1	9.7	9.5	9.3	9.3	9.8	9.6	9.9	9.8	10.6	10.4
Biomedical research	9.4	9.8	9.6	9.2	9.3	8.8	8.4	8.4	8.5	8.7	8.8	8.3	8.2	8.0
Biology	9.5	9.5	10.7	10.5	10.3	10.8	10.3	10.2	9.0	8.8	9.1	9.1	8.9	9.5
Chemistry	7.8	7.8	8.3	8.2	7.4	7.0	7.0	6.8	6.6	6.7	6.3	6.1	6.0	5.7
Physics	7.7	7.4	7.4	6.9	7.0	6.3	6.1	5.9	6.4	6.1	6.1	5.8	5.6	5.6
Earth and space sciences	8.1	8.0	9.5	8.7	9.1	8.9	8.8	9.5	8.5	8.7	8.7	8.7	8.3	7.9
Engineering and technology	10.7	10.5	11.0	10.9	10.6	9.4	8.8	9.5	8.5	8.3	8.0	7.7	7.9	7.5
Mathematics	7.4	7.1	8.1	6.9	6.8	7.0	6.6	7.0	6.1	6.5	6.7	6.4	6.9	7.5

David C. Mowery

Table 11.4 (continued)

Country and Field	Publication Year of Articles													
	1973	1974	1975	1976	1977	1978	1979	1980	1981	1982	1983	1984	1985	1986
United States														
All fields	38.2	37.7	37.3	37.4	37.1	36.7	37.1	36.5	35.9	35.9	35.4	35.4	35.3	35.6
Clinical medicine	42.8	42.5	42.6	43.0	43.2	43.1	43.1	43.0	41.1	41.1	40.3	40.9	40.3	40.0
Biomedical research	39.2	38.4	38.6	38.8	39.1	38.7	40.5	39.7	39.5	39.7	39.3	39.5	37.8	38.4
Biology	46.4	45.7	44.7	44.2	41.7	41.7	42.7	42.0	37.6	38.4	37.6	37.2	37.5	38.1
Chemistry	23.3	22.2	21.7	21.8	21.7	21.1	21.2	20.8	20.0	21.2	20.3	20.6	21.0	22.2
Physics	32.7	33.5	32.4	31.2	30.5	30.8	30.0	30.1	28.7	28.1	27.8	27.3	29.4	30.3
Earth and space sciences	46.7	46.8	43.8	48.1	45.1	44.9	44.6	42.4	42.7	42.4	41.6	41.3	43.0	42.6
Engineering and technology	41.8	41.7	40.6	41.1	40.2	39.4	40.7	39.4	40.7	40.6	40.9	39.5	38.6	37.3
Mathematics	47.9	45.0	44.0	42.9	41.1	40.4	40.5	39.7	38.2	39.0	38.5	37.2	38.3	40.3
Soviet Union														
All fields	9.0	8.2	7.9	7.9	7.9	8.2	8.0	7.8	8.0	8.2	8.3	7.9	7.8	7.6
Clinical medicine	3.2	2.7	2.3	2.7	2.5	2.9	2.7	2.6	3.3	3.3	3.3	3.1	2.9	2.9
Biomedical research	6.7	5.9	5.7	6.0	5.9	6.6	5.8	6.2	5.7	6.3	6.0	6.0	8.7	8.3
Biology	1.6	1.7	1.4	1.5	1.5	1.6	1.3	1.5	2.8	2.8	2.8	2.9	2.7	2.4
Chemistry	16.4	15.7	15.3	15.1	15.7	15.8	15.7	15.2	16.7	16.7	18.6	17.3	15.3	15.1
Physics	18.5	16.4	16.2	16.6	16.4	16.3	16.8	15.7	16.8	16.8	16.3	16.5	15.6	14.7
Earth and space sciences	11.2	9.4	11.3	9.4	9.9	9.6	9.6	9.7	10.0	10.6	10.6	9.5	7.1	7.0
Engineering and technology	11.4	10.8	10.0	8.8	9.4	10.1	9.4	8.8	7.6	7.3	7.2	7.0	5.9	5.6
Mathematics	2.7	2.7	2.8	2.7	3.4	4.2	4.1	4.6	7.6	6.7	6.3	5.9	2.9	4.5

Table 11.4 (continued)

Country and Field	Publication Year of Articles													
	1973	1974	1975	1976	1977	1978	1979	1980	1981	1982	1983	1984	1985	1986
Italy														
All fields	1.7	1.9	2.0	1.9	1.8	1.8	2.0	2.0	2.1	2.2	2.4	2.4	2.4	2.3
Clinical medicine	1.5	1.5	1.7	1.7	1.8	1.8	2.2	2.0	2.3	2.4	2.6	2.6	2.9	2.9
Biomedical research	2.4	2.5	2.6	2.4	1.6	1.6	1.8	1.6	2.0	2.0	2.3	2.3	2.1	2.0
Biology	0.5	0.7	0.7	0.6	0.6	0.7	1.0	0.8	1.2	1.4	1.1	1.2	1.0	1.0
Chemistry	2.3	2.8	2.8	2.8	2.7	2.5	2.8	2.9	2.7	2.8	3.1	3.3	2.8	2.7
Physics	2.1	2.3	2.3	2.1	2.2	2.2	2.4	2.6	2.5	2.8	3.0	2.9	2.8	2.5
Earth and space sciences	1.7	2.0	1.7	2.0	1.9	1.5	1.6	1.9	2.1	2.0	2.0	1.9	1.8	1.9
Engineering and technology	1.5	1.4	1.5	1.5	1.2	1.3	1.3	1.3	1.4	1.5	1.5	1.6	1.7	1.4
Mathematics	0.6	0.9	0.9	0.7	0.8	1.2	1.2	1.5	1.3	1.7	1.7	2.3	2.3	2.7

Notes: Data are based on the articles, notes, and reviews in the journals carried on the Science Citation Index corporate tapes of the Institute for Scientific Information. Prior to 1981, data are based on a fixed set of 2,300 journals. After 1981, data are based on a fixed journal set of about 3,500 journals. A new modification of the journal set occurred in 1985. Articles are assigned by country of authorship. When an article is written by researchers from more than one country, it is prorated across the countries involved rather than the number of institutions represented by the authors. For example, if a given article has several authors from France and the United States, it is counted as one-half an article for the United States and one-half an article for France.

Source: National Science Foundation, *International Science and Technology Update: 1991* (Washington, D.C.: National Science Foundation, 1991), pp. 91, 93.

The proposed Intelligent Manufacturing Systems (IMS) project illustrates some of the promises and problems of U.S.-Japan collaboration in a technological, as opposed to a scientific, research program. The IMS project focused on an area (advanced manufacturing process technologies) in which Japanese firms are in a leadership position and to which they could make significant contributions.[26] Partly because U.S. government policymakers felt they were not sufficiently consulted by the IMS project's Japanese sponsors, the U.S. government was initially reluctant to support the IMS proposal. In addition to perceiving a lack of advance consultation, some U.S. policymakers expressed concern that U.S. firms would contribute more to the undertaking than they would receive, and thereby transfer U.S. technology to Japanese firms.

This latter concern appears to be misplaced. It is based on an outdated assessment of U.S. and Japanese technological strengths in manufacturing. In fact, the IMS appears to contain considerable potential benefits for U.S. corporate participants. The recent history of the IMS project suggests that increased intergovernmental cooperation in technology programs will require more careful advance consultation among U.S. and Japanese government agencies. At this time, however, these tasks are hampered by the lack of a clear "lead agency" within the U.S. government for the organization, oversight, and coordination of domestic or international programs in technology development.

Reciprocal Access

The growth of Japan's technological strength has raised to high levels of the U.S. and Japanese governments the issue of access by foreign firms to the Japanese research system. The Japanese R&D system is difficult for foreign firms to penetrate for reasons that reflect the historical legacy of government policies, as well as differences in industry structure and in the structure of capital markets, rather than being solely a result of current policy. The complex origins of these structural differences in the organization of national R&D systems and in the ease with which foreigners can gain access to national R&D systems mean that government-to-government negotiations and agreements are not likely to address all of the causes and consequences of "asymmetrical access."

U.S.-Japanese contrasts in the role of government R&D funding are linked to other important differences in the structure of the U.S. and Japanese national research systems—a term meant to include both public and private research organizations. Along with a relatively open market for imports and foreign investment, the United States maintains a relatively open research system.

The importance within the Japanese R&D system of "open" universities and "closed" private firms contrasts with that of the United States. The contribution of Japanese universities to basic knowledge historically has been modest. The Japanese economy's system of industrial finance and governance also makes it difficult for U.S. and other foreign firms to gain access to industrial technologies through acquisitions of firms or intellectual property.

The structural differences between the U.S. and foreign research systems are such that a strict requirement of reciprocity in access to research facilities is either worthless or infeasible. Assurances by the Japanese government of complete access to Japanese universities, for example, may be of limited interest to U.S. firms, in view of the modest amount of world-class research performed by Japanese university researchers. Foreign acquisitions of U.S. firms, especially small, high-technology firms, are frequently cited as another important source of asymmetry in technology access because such firms have few analogues in the Japanese or West European economies. This concern, however, fails to recognize the degree to which the critical knowledge is often "tacit" (for example, not codified in blueprints or other documents), consisting of know-how and other less easily transferred forms, and is embodied in the firm's employees.

In the vast majority of acquisitions by foreign enterprises of U.S. firms, these human assets do not leave the United States following the acquisition—indeed, they often leave the firm, transferring their skills and know-how to other U.S. firms. As such, the putative "drain" of U.S. technology through foreign acquisitions of high-technology firms may be exaggerated.[27] Rather than to restrict foreign investment in the United States, policies are needed to reduce the obstacles faced by many start-up firms in raising capital from domestic sources[28] and to increase the willingness by U.S. managers in established firms to seek out U.S. start-up firms for joint development projects.

A second important issue in reciprocal access to research concerns the role of universities.[29] By developing links with U.S. universities, foreign firms may gain access to research that has been funded largely or partially by U.S. public funds through research grants or overhead payments to the academic institution. To the extent that the establishment of cooperative research agreements between U.S. universities and foreign firms allows these firms to gain access to research results without repaying these subsidies, they may be able to free-ride. Just as state universities charge higher tuition to nonresident students, however, U.S. universities may be well advised to consider assessing higher overhead charges on foreign firms with whom they negotiate research agreements, in recognition of the substantial contribution of public funds to their research prominence.[30]

As and if the quality and amount of world-class research performed in Japanese universities and quasi-public "hybrid" institutions improve, access to these facilities may be more attractive and important for informed U.S. and European firms. The processes of institutional change that will reduce the structural differences between these two national innovation systems, however, will operate so slowly that the issue of reciprocal access will remain difficult for the foreseeable future.

Conclusion

Recent debates about Japan's contribution to global scientific research have suffered from a portrayal of Japanese R&D investment patterns that is not supported by the available data. The significant differences between U.S. and Japanese R&D investment patterns reflect the contrasting roles of the Japanese and U.S. governments in supporting R&D spending and the contrasting importance of universities and industry as performers of basic research. Although most indicators of the quality or quantity of the output of the large Japanese basic research investment suggest that Japan lags behind some other industrial economies, this situation is changing. U.S.-Japanese differences in R&D funding and performance—along with other differences in capital markets, firm structure, and corporate governance—affect the "accessibility" of each nation's overall R&D system to foreign firms.

Japan's newfound strength in generic or quasi–public-good industrial technologies provides an array of possibilities for U.S.-Japan cooperation in technology development. Many of the private collaborative ventures between U.S. and Japanese firms that have been formed during the past decade reflect a recognition by U.S. managers of the possibilities for gainful collaboration in this area.[31] These private collaborative relationships could be strengthened and complemented by government-sponsored collaboration in generic technology development ventures.

Improving U.S.-Japan relations in science and technology requires more than a change in the conceptual framework utilized by U.S. officials (the public good/private good distinction between basic research, on the one hand, and technology development, on the other hand) in formulating domestic and international science and technology policy initiatives. Japanese government science policy requires reform and rationalization, reducing the current fragmentation in funding and in the establishment of priorities. A stronger "science agency" might also accelerate the pace of change in the structure of Japanese basic research. Current efforts to improve the environment and funding of Japanese university research and to increase public financing for nonuniversity institutions should improve the openness and quality of Japanese basic research. Stronger enforcement of competition policy and continued liberalization of Japanese capital markets also will reduce some of the obstacles to foreign acquisition of

Japanese industrial assets that now impede foreign access to the Japanese industrial technology base.

Both the U.S. and Japanese governments have been inconsistent and uncertain in their advance consultation with one another concerning science and technology burden-sharing. Joint consultation and joint participation in the selection and design of programs for international collaboration are essential to the development of a more productive relationship in science and technology programs. But genuine cooperation requires that each government establish a clearer, more credible voice in science and technology policy. A more fruitful cooperative relationship also cannot flourish in an atmosphere of U.S.-Japan economic tensions. In the long run, smoother U.S.-Japan collaboration in science and technology programs is unlikely without a reduction in tensions in the overall economic relationship between the United States and Japan.

Japan is likely to continue to be an international leader in technology development. Japan's technological prowess will play a central role in sustaining Japan's economic expansion and international influence. The extent to which Japanese technological leadership will expand Japanese contributions to international public goods in research, however, will be constrained by the unique structure of Japanese private and public institutions of research funding and performance. Although some of these are changing, any process of change will operate slowly. As this chapter has suggested, however, the degree to which Japan is able to contribute to international public goods also depends on the ability of institutions in other countries, notably the United States, to adapt to Japanese institutions in order to exploit the available opportunities.

Notes

Research for this chapter was supported by the Alfred P. Sloan Foundation and the Consortium on Competitiveness and Cooperation.

1. These issues are covered in more detail in an earlier draft of this chapter presented at the Georgetown University–Japan Economic Institute conference, Japan's Future Global Role, Washington, D.C., March 11–14, 1992.

2. See David C. Mowery and Nathan Rosenberg, *Technology and the Pursuit of Economic Growth* (New York: Cambridge University Press, 1989), for additional discussion.

3. David C. Mowery and David J. Teece, "The Changing Place of Japan in the Global Scientific and Technological Enterprise," presented at the National Research Council conference, Japan's Growing Technological Capabilities: Implications for the United States, October 18–19, 1991. See also Phyllis A. Genther and Donald H. Dalton, *Japanese Direct Investment in U.S. Manufacturing*, U.S. Department of Commerce (Washington, D.C.: U.S. Government Printing Office, 1990).

4. This is true because of the increased speed and quality of international communication of research results and the enhanced "receptor" capabilities of foreign

firms and researchers. See Richard R. Nelson, *High-Technology Policies: A Five Nation Comparison* (Washington, D.C.: American Enterprise Institute, 1984), for a related discussion of "leading" and "strategic" industries and technologies.

5. *"More and better scientific research is essential to the achievement of our goal of full employment.*

Basic research leads to new knowledge. It provides scientific capital. It creates the fund from which the practical applications of knowledge must be drawn. They are founded on new principles and new conceptions which in turn are painstakingly developed by research in the purest realms of science." Vannevar Bush, *Science: The Endless Frontier* (Washington, D.C.: U.S. Government Printing Office, 1945), pp. 18–19. (Emphasis in the original.)

6. Leon Lederman, "The Value of Fundamental Science," *Scientific American* 251, no. 5 (November 1984): 40–47.

7. According to Nelson, "in almost all technologies a considerable portion of generic understanding about how things work, key variables affecting performance, the currently binding constraints and promising approaches to pushing these back, stems from operating and design experience with products and machines and their components, and analytic generalizations reflecting on these. These understandings may have only limited grounding in any fundamental science, standing, as it were, largely on their own bottom." Richard R. Nelson, "What is 'Commercial' and What is 'Public' About Technology, and What Should Be?" in Nathan Rosenberg, Ralph Landau, and David C. Mowery, eds., *Technology and the Wealth of Nations* (Stanford, Calif.: Stanford University Press, 1992), p. 60.

8. Henry Ergas, "Does Technology Policy Matter?" in Harvey Brooks and Bruce R. Guile, eds., *Technology in Global Industry* (Washington, D.C.: National Academy Press, 1987).

9. Richard R. Nelson, *Government and Technical Progress: A Cross-Industry Comparison* (New York: Pergamon Press, 1982), especially the chapter by David C. Mowery and Nathan Rosenberg, "The Commercial Aircraft Industry." See also David C. Mowery and Nathan Rosenberg, *Technology and the Pursuit of Economic Growth* (New York: Cambridge University Press, 1989).

10. See David C. Mowery and Nathan Rosenberg, "The U.S. National Innovation System," in Richard R. Nelson, ed., *National Innovation Systems: A Comparative Study* (New York: Oxford University Press, 1993), for a discussion of the interwar United States.

11. All data on basic research spending must be treated with care because flaws in the economic theory of basic research contribute to problems in the definition of basic research used by statistical agencies. A strict definition of basic research as "research conducted without attention to application," after all, describes an investment that the managers of many U.S. firms engaged in self-financed basic research would reject. The definition of basic research employed by different national statistical agencies also varies somewhat, despite the efforts of the OECD to standardize these data.

12. Nondefense R&D expenditures amounted to 1.9 percent of Japanese GNP in 1971, and rose to 2.8 by 1988. This ratio stood at 1.6 percent in the United States in 1971 and 1.9 percent by 1988. National Science Foundation, *International Science and Technology Update: 1991* (Washington, D.C.: National Science Foundation, 1991), p. 9.

13. The source for the Japanese and French basic research data is the Organization for Economic Cooperation and Development, *Science and Technolo*

Indicators, 1990 (Paris: OECD, 1990), which reports Japanese basic research spending for 1988 and French basic research spending for 1982; the U.S. data are taken from the National Science Foundation, *Research and Development in Industry: 1985–86* (Washington, D.C.: National Science Foundation, 1989), and report basic research spending for 1985.

14. Table 11.3 also reveals the large contribution by U.S. researchers to the world's scientific literature in the life sciences and medicine (nearly 40 percent of total publications in the fields of biology, biomedical research, and clinical medicine), which reflects the enormous postwar research effort in this area funded by the U.S. National Institutes of Health.

15. See Mowery and Teece, "The Changing Place of Japan," for a more detailed discussion, on which this statement draws.

16. These data incorporate many older licenses and say little about the balance of trade in new technology licensing agreements. Data on new technology agreements indicate that the value of Japanese technology exports has exceeded that of imports for all but two years of the fiscal 1975–1989 period, and in fiscal 1989 amounted to 137 percent of the value of imports. Japan Economic Institute, "Research and Development in Japan: 1991 Update," JEI Report 36A, September 27, 1991.

17. National Science Foundation, "The Science and Technology Resources of Japan: A Comparison with the United States," NSF Report 88–318, Washington, D.C., 1988, p. 33.

18. "Given their total representation in the U.S. patent system, Japanese patents account for 45 percent more of the top 1 percent most highly cited U.S. patents than expected. The highest citation rates for Japanese patents are in the automotive, semiconductor electronics, photocopying and photography, and pharmaceuticals patent classes." (Ibid., p. xii)

The relatively high quality of Japanese firms' U.S. patents, however, may reflect some tendency for these firms to seek U.S. patents only for their most important technological advances. Sully Taylor and Kozo Yamamura, "Japan's Technological Capabilities and Its Future: Overview and Assessments," in Gunter Heiduk and Kozo Yamamura, eds., *Technological Competition and Interdependence: The Search for Policy in the United States, West Germany, and Japan* (Seattle: University of Washington Press, 1990), argue that Japanese firms are far more likely to seek domestic patent protection for minor technical advances than are U.S. firms.

19. Kenneth Flamm, "The Changing Pattern of Industrial Robot Use," in R. M. Cyert and David C. Mowery, eds., *The Impact of Technological Change on Employment and Economic Growth* (Cambridge, Mass.: Ballinger Publishers, 1988); E. Mansfield, "The Diffusion of Industrial Robots in Japan and the United States," *Research Policy* 18 (1989): 183–192; C. Edquist, and S. Jacobsson, *Flexible Automation* (Oxford: Blackwell, 1988).

20. Kim B. Clark et al., "Product Development in the World Automobile Industry," *Brookings Papers on Economic Activity* (Washington, D.C.: The Brookings Institution, 1987), pp. 729–771; Kim B. Clark and Takahiro Fujimoto, *Product Development Performances: Strategy, Organization, and Management in the World Auto Industry* (Boston: Harvard Business School Press, 1991).

21. Edwin Mansfield, "Industrial Innovation in Japan and the United States," *Science* (September 30, 1988): 1769–1974.

22. Lennart Stenberg, "Molecular Beam Epitaxy—A Mesoview of Japanese Research Organization," unpublished manuscript, Research Policy Institute, University of Lund, Sweden, 1990, for example, notes that Japanese university

research has played an important role in the development of molecular beam epitaxy (MBE), a semiconductor component manufacturing process: "While universities played a minor role in MBE research in the early 1980's in Japan, they are ten years later contributing very actively, especially in research related to quantum materials and quantum-effect devices. The pattern is similar in other countries and partly a consequence of changes in MBE technology and related research topics. The development of MBE technology has, for example, become increasingly dependent on an understanding of the basic mechanisms of the MBE growth process and as the sophistication of MBE technology has grown it has become possible to grow materials and structures which can be used to study scientifically increasingly more interesting physical effects, changes which both have served to attract academic scientists to MBE research. Although Japanese universities have responded vigorously to the new challenges opening up, their response has been weaker, in quantitative terms, than that of the American universities but comparable to that of European universities." (P. 56)

23. This contrast between Japanese science policy and technology policy should not be understated because intense interagency rivalries are present in many areas of technology policy. For example, MITI has long jousted with the Ministry of Posts and Telecommunications for primacy in the information technology field. See Chalmers Johnson, "MITI, MPT, and the Telecom Wars: How Japan Makes Policy for High Technology," in Chalmers Johnson et al., eds., *Politics and Productivity: How Japan's Development Strategy Works* (Cambridge, Mass.: Ballinger Publishers, 1988).

24. Office of Technology Assessment, U.S. Congress, *Federally Funded Research: Decisions for a Decade* (Washington, D.C.: U.S. Government Printing Office, 1991).

25. Describing the international politics surrounding the congressional votes to restore funding for the space station project, *Nature* noted that "the Japanese have been the most vocal protesters [against the threat of congressional appropriators to eliminate funding], both because they have the most to lose and because they seem likely to have the most leverage on US science policy. Japan's Science and Technology Agency (STA) has already invested ¥40,000 million (about $300 million) in developing the Japanese Experimental Module for the station—the module is expected to cost about $2,000 million when complete—and the station's share of STA's space budget has been growing rapidly year by year. . . . A cancellation of the space station would be disastrous for Japan's space programme." "Japan, Europe Lobby US Over Space Station," *Nature* 351 (June 6, 1990): 428.

26. George R. Heaton, "International R&D Cooperation: Lessons from the Intelligent Manufacturing Systems Proposal," Manufacturing Forum Discussion Paper no. 2, National Academy of Engineering, Washington, D.C., 1991.

27. There are other potential problems created by foreign acquisition of U.S. firms if these acquisitions enable a foreign enterprise to acquire a position of significant market power. These possibilities can be controlled, however, through U.S. Justice Department review of the competitive consequences of such acquisitions.

28. David J. Teece, "Foreign Investment and Technological Development in Silicon Valley," in Donald McFetridge, ed., *Foreign Investment, Technology and Economic Growth* (Calgary, Alberta: University of Calgary Press, 1991).

29. See the 1989 reports of the National Research Council, Office of Japan Affairs, "The Working Environment for Research in U.S. and Japanese Universities" and "Learning the R&D System," both published by the National Academy Press, Washington, D.C.

30. The recent internal study of foreign corporate sponsorship of research at the Massachusetts Institute of Technology notes that foreign participants in the university's Industrial Liaison Program pay higher membership fees. See Massachusetts Institute of Technology, "The International Relations of MIT in a Technologically Competitive World," MIT, Cambridge, Mass., 1991.

31. Mowery and Teece, "The Changing Place of Japan."

Part 4

Conclusion

12

What Next?

Danny Unger

Japan has been playing industrial catch-up for more than a century. In the postwar period alone, Japan vastly increased its wealth and its share of global investment, production, and trade. Japanese economic growth rates tended to decline as the gap between Japan and the wealthiest countries steadily diminished. Nonetheless, even during that period, Japan's annual rates of economic expansion generally outstripped those of the European Community or the United States. Caught up with the West, Japan now asks itself, what next? Even in the best of times, Japan's postwar economic miracle would be a tough act to follow.

The 1990s, however, pose crucial challenges for Japan. With its financial institutions weakened, asset prices collapsing, trade frictions persisting, and its foreign policies in flux, Japan faces a difficult period. In addition, sharp and sudden changes in the international political economy have transformed the environment within which Japanese policymakers have framed their foreign policy decisions for the last forty years. This disjuncture in postwar global politics throws into sharper relief the choices that now face Japan as pressures at home and abroad combine to push it toward assuming a more active international role. This concluding chapter asks two questions: First, can Japan sustain relatively robust economic growth—the basis of increasing Japanese global influence? And second, through what channels will Japan attempt to exercise what influence it has?

Doubts about Japan's economic staying power are hardly new. Throughout most of the last 120 years Japanese and foreigners alike have believed in the fragility of Japan's economic accomplishments. This was only natural, given Japan's paucity of natural resources and, hence, its dependence on foreign trade. When scholars put greater weight on technological change in explaining Japan's economic successes, they assumed that Japan's growth would slow as it closed the gap separating it from the world's leading economies. Japan would lose the advantages of backwardness.

And, in fact, this is exactly what happened. Very suddenly, Japanese rates of economic growth collapsed in the 1970s. Japan, nevertheless, continued to grow faster than all other industrialized countries in the Organization for Economic Cooperation and Development. The extraordinary growth rates of the 1960s were over, but Japan continued to outshine all other countries in terms of economic expansion.

Policymakers and scholars have generated an interesting debate in their efforts to understand why Japan consistently outperforms other economies. Two perspectives dominate this debate. (In fact, of course, the two are not completely exclusive of one another. Neither do they exhaust all the many factors called upon to explain the Japanese phenomenon.)

One school sees Japan as essentially similar to other countries. The Japanese miracle, suggests this view, can be explained by high Japanese investment and savings rates, the limited size of the public sector, widespread education, and new management and production methods, among other factors. Advocates of this view are prone to see the collapse of Japan's asset prices in the late 1980s and early 1990s as the long-postponed but inevitable return to normalcy of an economy caught in a speculative fever that sustained a high rate of economic growth for five years beginning in 1987.[1] Deregulation and internationalization of the Japanese economy, particularly its financial system, ensured that the Japanese economy could not continue long in its upward spiral.

The market-based explanation of the Japanese economy is perhaps more convincing in its explanation of the collapse of Japanese asset prices than in its view of why Japan has been able for so long to outpace other nations. Will Japan, in fact, continue to enjoy the kind of strong economic growth that will allow it to continue to play a major global role as a supplier of capital? Economic changes in Japan beginning in the late 1980s suggest that Japan's economic growth will slow from the rapid rates achieved following adjustment to the yen's sharp appreciation beginning in 1985.[2]

Economist Arthur Alexander argues that a variety of demographic, economic, and regulatory factors are working together to induce a fall in Japan's national savings rate, increases in the cost of capital, and rising labor costs that, together with the end of Japan's catch-up phase of industrial expansion, will result in slower rates of economic growth in Japan.[3] These factors lead some observers to question Japan's ability over the long term to exploit its current role as the world's major source of capital. Japanese trade surpluses, however, continue to expand, helping to fuel growing current account surpluses.

A second school puts less emphasis on market mechanisms in explaining Japan's remarkable economic record. By and large, advocates of this second view appreciate that Japan's growth could have been produced only within a market economy. Markets alone, however, argue adherents of this school, are not sufficient to understand Japan's accomplishments.

As important as an appreciation of the efficiency of markets are insights into the ways in which Japanese institutions mediate between market forces and market players—individuals and firms. Innovations in industrial organization (Japan's *keiretsu*), in labor-management relations, and, in particular, in institutions fostering cooperation between government and business have made it possible for Japan to sustain rapid economic growth. On key economic issues, the view contends, policymakers are relatively insulated from pressures for policies that would serve consumers at the expense of producers. Adherents of this perspective, then, hold that the strength of Japanese corporations, the skills of the Japanese work force, and continuing cooperation between public and private sectors will enable Japan to continue to outdo other rich industrialized countries.

Even if demographic changes result in Japan's current account surpluses turning to deficits, the very size of the Japanese economy and the strength of its corporations, including its financial institutions, ensure a continuing Japanese capacity to exercise influence globally. All other things being equal, this conclusion suggests, in turn, that Japanese economic and technological leadership will continue to afford Japan the means of fashioning a foreign policy based on these strengths.

Are all other things, in fact, equal? Even if Japan emerges as the world's largest economy with the most powerful finance, manufacturing, and service industries, will Japan develop commensurate global influence? As the first chapter argued, different answers to this question stem from alternative understandings of how the international political economy operates. For some, an economically preponderant Japan will necessarily mean a politically dominant Japan. For others, however, Japan will emerge as a global leader only when its economic assets are backed either by military power or ideological appeal or both. Among this latter group are those who hold that Japan's overseas assets will lead ineluctably to Japan's adoption of a more strategic foreign policy. As early as the 1970s, political scientist Donald Hellmann predicted, "Politics and economics are no longer separable, and Japan's extensive overseas economic involvement, especially in Asia, will force the development of a foreign policy in which strategic considerations have a greatly expanded role."[4]

Clearly, Japan's foreign policies face major challenges. As the chapters in this book attest, Japan is, in fact, moving to address emerging issues. In 1992 alone, Japan made the decision enabling it to send forces overseas and within months sent a detachment to Cambodia, and Japan attended the Rio conference on global environmental issues and pledged $7 billion in environmental assistance to developing countries.

That same year, however, Japan's Ministry of Foreign Affairs received fresh evidence of the difficult tasks it must tackle. Accompanying U.S. President George Bush on his January 1992 trip to Japan were top executives of U.S. automobile companies demanding a diminution in Japan's large automobile trade surplus with the United States. Plans for

Emperor Akihito's travel to China encountered problems both within
Japan and between China and Japan as a result of continuing differences
stemming from Japan's aggression against China during World War II.
Russian President Boris Yeltsin's scheduled visit to Japan was canceled
abruptly as a result of an inability to narrow the differences between Japan
and Russia over the issue of the contested islands north of Hokkaido (part
of the Kuril Islands, known in Japan as the Northern Territories).

Faced with new and lingering international tensions, through what
means will Japan attempt to secure its national interests? Japan would like
to gain a seat as a permanent member on the UN Security Council.
Japanese leaders feel that with Japan's large contributions to the United Nations (larger than all the permanent members except the United States) and
its enormous resources, Japan should be allowed to join the current five
permanent members. Although the United States has long supported the
Japanese stance on this issue, the official U.S. position remains that such a
change in the UN Charter must be taken with great care and deliberation.

One reason for past U.S. reluctance actively to support Japan's becoming a permanent member of the UN Security Council concerned the restrictions that the Japanese government accepted on its ability to deploy
forces overseas. If Japan could not fulfill its commitments under the UN
Charter to enforce collective action, how could it serve on the Security
Council? In response, Japanese officials typically pointed out that Japan
was able to contribute to the maintenance of international peace and security in a variety of ways that did not depend on the exercise of military
power.[5] Now, of course, Japan has greater leeway (although still sharply
circumscribed) to dispatch forces abroad in support of UN deployments.

Japanese aspirations to a permanent seat on the Security Council are
linked to the broader issue of Japan's capacity to carve out a global role
that serves Japan's national interests and stems from Japan's particular capabilities. Such a role must be one that enjoys support within Japan and
that elicits acceptance abroad. Japanese leadership will have to be based
on Japan's unique strengths, in particular its status as a great economic
power and dominant purveyor of capital.

Ultimately, the goals that Japan pursues and the means adopted to
achieve those goals will be influenced by developments within Japan as
well as by the structure of the global political economy. The authors in this
volume have attempted to focus their analyses on developments immediately affecting Japan. Nevertheless, all the chapters make clear that future
Japanese foreign policy will be shaped in considerable degree by developments in Japan-U.S. relations. The United States retains great capacity to
shape the future directions in which Japan moves, both through its policies
toward Japan specifically as well as through broader U.S. initiatives shaping the global political economy. Japan also now has the capacity to shape

its context (to exercise structural power) as well as to adjust to the environment in which it finds itself. This capacity will have a major influence on the nature of the twenty-first century international political economy.

Notes

1. See Arthur Alexander, "Japan's Economy: A Transformation?" Japan Economic Institute Report no. 11A, March 20, 1992.

2. See Keikichi Honda, "The Japanese Economy: The 1980s in Retrospect and the Prospect for 1992," paper presented at Georgetown University conference, Japan's Global Role, Washington, D.C., March 1992.

3. Ibid.

4. Donald Hellmann, "Japanese Security and Postwar Japanese Foreign Policy," in Robert A. Scalapino, ed., *The Foreign Policy of Modern Japan* (Berkeley: University of California Press, 1977), p. 340.

5. U.S. failure to support actively Japanese desires to gain membership to the Permanent Five stems from the feeling that amending the UN Charter will lead to changes that could spin out of control. By "opening Pandora's box," Japan risks undermining UN effectiveness at a time when the end of the Cold War is allowing the United States to serve better its global interests.

For their part, Japanese leaders note that other members of the Permanent Five (China, for example) resist sending forces overseas as part of UN peacekeeping operations and that, in any case, as of June 1992 Japan is no longer proscribed from sending its own forces overseas on such missions.

About the Contributors

Paul Blackburn is minister-counselor for public affairs in the U.S. embassy in Tokyo. During the course of this study, he was a diplomatic associate at Georgetown University's Institute for the Study of Diplomacy.

Kent E. Calder is director of the Program on U.S.-Japan Relations at Princeton University and a professor at its Woodrow Wilson School of Public and International Affairs.

Robert Gilpin is Eisenhower Professor of International Affairs at Princeton University.

Norman D. Levin is senior staff member of RAND's International Policy Department.

Edward J. Lincoln is senior fellow in the Foreign Policy Studies Program at the Brookings Institution, specializing on the Japanese economy and U.S. economic policy toward Asia.

David C. Mowery is associate professor of business and public policy in the Walter A. Haas School of Business at the University of California, Berkeley.

Masashi Nishihara is professor of international relations at the National Defense Academy of Japan.

Yoshio Okawara retired after a distinguished career in Japan's Ministry of Foreign Affairs; he continues to serve as a senior adviser to the foreign minister. He is also an executive adviser to Keidanren and Kobe Steel Ltd.

Kenneth B. Pyle is professor of history and Asian studies at the University of Washington, where from 1978 to 1988 he was the director of the Henry M. Jackson School of International Studies.

Masaru Tamamoto is assistant professor and director of the Center for Asian Studies at the School of International Service, The American University, Washington, D.C.

Danny Unger is assistant professor of government at Georgetown University.

Index

Aid, foreign: bureaucracy in, 127; and promotion of commercial interests, 33; role of business in, 32; tied, 158
Akihito, Emperor, 3, 200
Alexander, Arthur, 198
Arita, Hachiro, 166
ASEAN. *See* Association of Southeast Asian Nations
ASEAN-Japan Development Fund, 159
Asia: economic growth, 32, 61; economic integration, 5, 6, 13, 155; economic regionalism in, 157; Japanese influence in, 5, 32, 61, 107–108, 110–116, 155–167; leadership in, 31–32; reduction of U.S. military presence in, 7; regionalism in, 31–33; trade with Japan, 6
Asian Development Bank, 33, 59
Asia Pacific Economic Cooperation conference, 32, 87
Association for Overseas Technical Scholarship, 160
Association of Southeast Asian Nations, 7, 31, 32, 112

Baerwald, Hans, 5
Balance of payments, 6, 137–138*tab*, 140, 151*n4*, 161
Bergsten, C. Fred, 33
Bureaucracy: foreign aid, 127; structure, 17; weakened prime minister position, 15, 48–49, 127, 128
Bush, George, 7–8, 17, 21, 27, 39, 40, 42–43, 50, 58, 75, 78, 90, 105, 165, 199

Calder, Kent, 17, 121–130
Cambodia, 58, 59, 199
Capital: costs of, 198; exports, 155–167; flow internationalization, 78; inflow, 140, 142, 161; outflow, 134, 135, 136, 139, 140, 142, 151*n2*, 156; private, 160; shortage, 60
Capitalism, 15; competition between systems, 24; cooperative relations in, 16; differing systems of, 43
Change vs. continuity, 3–4, 7
Charter for American-Russian Partnership and Friendship, 166
China: arms exports, 59, 88, 91; assistance from Japan, 167*n1*; defense budget, 88; international isolation, 87, 88, 91; recognition by United States, 6; relations with Japan, 6, 7, 19*n8*, 85–88, 92, 158; role in Asia, 17; trade with Japan, 6, 19*n8*
Chinese Territorial Waters law, 95, 96
Clark, Kim, 178
Commonwealth of Independent States. *See* Soviet Union
Competition: capitalistic, 24; corporate, 38; defense technology, 77; economic, 18, 24, 25, 34; with European Community, 18; foreign, 31; ideological, 24; international, 27, 77, 81; and leadership, 47–49; military, 24; price, 139
Conflict: economic, 34; ethnic, 58; international, 23; interstate, 12; political, 34; in post-Cold War era,

About the Book

Grappling with the implications of Japan's emergence as a key global player, the contributors to this book isolate the opportunities and obstacles—both at home and abroad—that are shaping the ways in which the Japanese define and pursue their global interests.

The authors give serious attention to issues of political economy as they consider Japan's capability, as well as its willingness, to take on a stronger international role. Their new insights into the sources of constraints on Japanese foreign policy will attract Japan scholars, and the clarity and comprehensiveness of their contributions make this book ideal for use in courses on Japan's foreign policy and political economy.